MANAGING TO CHANGE THE WORLD

The Nonprofit Manager's Guide to Getting Results

ALISON GREEN AND JERRY HAUSER

THE
MANAGEMENT
CENTER

JOSSEY-BASS
A Wiley Imprint
www.josseybass.com

Published by Jossey-Bass
A Wiley Imprint
One Montgomery Street, Suite 1200, San Francisco, CA 94104-4594—www.josseybass.com

Jossey-Bass books and products are available through most bookstores. To contact Jossey-Bass directly call our Customer Care Department within the U.S. at 800-956-7739, outside the U.S. at 317-572-3986, or fax 317-572-4002.

Wiley publishes in a variety of print and electronic formats and by print-on-demand. Some material included with standard print versions of this book may not be included in e-books or in print-on-demand. If this book refers to media such as a CD or DVD that is not included in the version you purchased, you may download this material at http://booksupport.wiley.com. For more information about Wiley products, visit www.wiley.com.

Library of Congress Cataloging-in-Publication Data

Green, Alison.
  Managing to change the world: the nonprofit manager's guide to getting results / Alison Green and Jerry Hauser, The Management Center. —First edition.
    pages cm
  Summary Includes bibliographical references.
    ISBN 978-1-118-13761-1 (pbk.); ISBN 978-1-118-20590-7 (ebk)
      1. Nonprofit organizations—Management. I. Hauser, Jerry. II. Title.
  HD62.6.G74 2012
  658'.048—dc23

                                                          2011052644

Printed in the United States of America
FIRST EDITION

PB Printing   10 9 8 7 6 5 4 3 2

CONTENTS

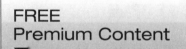

FREE
Premium Content

JOSSEY-BASS™
An Imprint of
WILEY

This book includes premium content that can be accessed from our Web site when you register at **www.josseybass.com/go/managingtochangetheworld** using the password *professional*.

LIST OF TOOLS

CHAPTER

THE JOB
OF A MANAGER

We bet you had trouble finding the time to read this book. If so, it's probably because you're feeling serious stress, like many of the nonprofit leaders with whom we work. You're under pressure from funders, your staff, constituents, perhaps your boss, and ultimately yourself, to be getting more done. Too much of the burden of making things happen is falling on you.

Effective management—how you get things done through other people—could help you accomplish more with less stress, but you may not know where to start. And if that's the case, you're not alone. Nonprofit leaders often end up in their roles not because they're great managers, but because they are experts on a particular issue or excel at a specific function like communications or program design. If you're one of these talented, committed people, you may have been highly effective at getting results on your own, but you may now have hit the point in your career where your impact will be more a function of what you get done through others than what you do directly yourself.

Fortunately, good management is pretty straightforward. Our goal in writing this book was to create an easy-to-use manual with hands-on, practical advice and tools that will help nonprofit managers get better results in their work. We'll cover a range of skills, representing what we think are the most important areas for managers to master—from delegating tasks, to setting and holding people accountable to clear goals, to hiring and firing, to staying organized and using your own time effectively. Exercised properly, these practices will make your life much easier.

Most important, though, not only does good management make your life easier, but it also makes it easier for you to get great results.

Although this probably sounds obvious, as managers ourselves we didn't automatically grasp it from the start. Jerry's first real management experience came at Teach For America, a large, national nonprofit where, as the second in command, he was responsible for managing the day-to-day work of the organization. A former teacher, he had been drawn to management partly because he liked seeing people learn and develop to their full potential. He wanted staff members to be happy and fulfilled in their work, and he viewed it as his job to mentor them so that they grew and developed.

That was fine as far as it went, but Teach For America had ambitious aspirations: it was trying to triple in size, raise the quality of its teachers, strengthen its alumni network, raise more money, and build a stronger organization to make it all happen. Early in Jerry's tenure, when he was more focused on mentoring and viewing his staff members' satisfaction as an end goal, he wasn't always producing the kind of progress that was needed. Most of his staff members worked extremely hard, but not everyone did. And many excelled at their jobs, but in several critical cases, the organization's needs had outgrown his staff members' skills.

And that brings us to the fundamental premise of this book: your job as a manager is to get results.

One day Jerry was complaining to a friend about how much pressure he was under and how difficult it was to get things done without making people hate him. She looked at him and said, "Well, if you're doing your job, you might just be the least popular person there." With those not-so-reassuring words, Jerry's friend helped him realize that he was thinking about his job in the wrong way. The organization was never going to achieve its aims if he didn't make some people unhappy. He needed to hold people to more ambitious goals, be clearer with people when they weren't meeting expectations, and, ultimately, tell some of his staff members that they weren't the right people for the job.

Through this stage in his work, Jerry came to appreciate more fully what his true job was as a manager. Yes, it was good to develop people, empower them, help them be fulfilled at work, and mentor them. Those things helped make his job enjoyable, and in some cases they helped make his people better at what they did, but ultimately, they were means to an end. Fundamentally his job was to make sure the organization got the results it aspired to. That's why it existed as an organization, and that's what Jerry was getting paid to do. Teach For America's donors funded it to help expand opportunities for students in low-income communities, the students whom Teach For America served needed it to deliver, and that's what his job was about, not to make the staff happy. If Jerry wasn't doing what it took to make Teach For America as effective as possible in pursuing its mission, then he wasn't doing his job.

As it happens, we believe you can get things done *and* be well liked, at least most of the time. In fact, by being clear about what you expect, helping people meet your expectations, ensuring people are in roles in which they excel, and getting everyone aligned around a common purpose, you'll build your staff's morale in the long run. Treating people well also happens to be the best way to sustain your results over the long haul, because you'll never get good people to work for you otherwise. Time and time again, though, we've found that managers confuse being "supportive" bosses who "empower" their people with being effective managers who actually get things done. And in the short term, getting things done sometimes requires you to make others unhappy with you.

Two examples from clients of ours might help illustrate what happens when managers do, or don't, fully feel the weight of responsibility for getting results in their realms. In the first case, the manager oversaw the field operations for her organization. When the organization realized that it needed to shift resources from one part of the field program to another in order to improve its results, this manager made only incremental changes in staffing levels to meet that need—changes that would certainly not suffice to generate the results needed. At a meeting with the head of the organization, the field manager explained her plan, saying, "Imagine the uproar if I had proposed really shifting people around." Her explanation made it clear that she was weighing the potential staff reaction to changes (or, perhaps more accurately, her own discomfort with that reaction) more heavily than the important results that the organization needed her to generate. Fortunately, the field director's own manager caught the issue before it was too late and insisted on more dramatic changes.

In contrast with this approach, our client in the second case did what it took to get results. This client is the executive director of an organization whose work gets carried out through multiple state offices, with those offices overseen directly by a regional director. The executive director and the regional director had agreed on ambitious, critically important goals for what each state office would produce over the coming four months, before the organization's next fundraising cycle began. But after only a couple of weeks, it was painfully clear that the regional director was proceeding under business as usual and that the state offices were nowhere near on track to producing the results they needed.

In this kind of situation, many managers would continue to work through the regional director, checking in periodically, hoping the regional director would deliver in the end, and perhaps blaming him if he didn't come through. In this case, though, the executive director understood that if the hoped-for results did not materialize, he himself was ultimately responsible. He was not simply a passive overseer of the results the team generated, but was ultimately responsible for those results himself. He also understood that in this case, the results had to happen: the organization would not fulfill its mission without them, and it would not be able to raise funds to keep supporting itself. Given that, the executive director took a much more hands-on approach, one that many management books might suggest was micromanaging. Among other things, he insisted that he and the regional director conduct daily calls with each of the state offices to discuss what steps the states were taking to produce the results. After just a few days, the energy at the state level changed, and within a couple of weeks, dramatically different results began to appear. The regional director, who was initially not thrilled with what he viewed as the executive director's heavy-handed approach, learned a valuable lesson about how to generate results. And once the new plans were on track, the executive director was able to step back and take a more normal approach to managing by working through his regional director.

When we highlight examples like these and stress the importance of being results oriented, people sometimes ask us whether that means we think nonprofits should be run like hard-nosed businesses. Our answer is that because the work nonprofits do is so important, we need to be *more* hard-nosed about management than for-profit enterprises are. Given what nonprofits do, we have a moral imperative to commit to strong, effective management practices because what's at stake is much more important than a business's bottom line.

And that's the main reason we wrote this book. We want to see more strong, effective nonprofits that are changing the world.

This book contains the tools you need to make it easier for you to get results. We intend for this book to be helpful to new managers as well as to those who have experience and need a refresher, and to managers of individual teams or departments as well as to executive directors of entire organizations. You won't find information on fundraising or working with the media or other topics on specific functions already covered by myriad other books. Instead, you'll find step-by-step guidance on how to manage any single area or an organization as a whole.

As we noted earlier, management is how you get things done through other people. (When you're doing it yourself, it's called "work"!) There are three components to that definition of management: getting things done, the other people, and you. We've divided the book along the lines of those three pieces, covering in each part the practices in which the best managers we've seen excel:

- *Managing the work.* We begin with the things you're getting done because this is what most people think of when they think of management, and it's the most immediate challenge that most new managers face. We'll start with the most specific level of things you might want to get done, which is looking at how you delegate a discrete task or project. We'll then look at how you can assign bigger pieces of work and broader responsibilities by using meaningful roles and clear goals with concrete measures of success. Then knowing that beyond the things you discuss explicitly with your staff, there are thousands of tiny actions that people take every day within your organization, we'll examine how you can use culture to guide your staff members on those items. Finally, we'll bring it all together by looking at a couple of easy-to-implement management systems that help you stay on top of it all.

- *Managing the people.* Using practices to make sure you have the right "other people" to get things done for you may be the single most important lever you have, and yet it's the area most neglected by managers. We'll discuss how to build a staff of superstars: hiring them, developing them, and making sure you hold on to the best and let go those who fall short.

- *Managing yourself.* The final part of this book explains how to apply to yourself the same rigor that you apply to your management of others, including using your time effectively, staying organized, working with your boss, and exercising authority. As a manager, what you do in this area sets the limits on or, we hope, removes the limits from, the results you can get.

We believe that the practices in this book will help you build and lead a high-performing organization that achieves outstanding results over the long haul. And for nonprofits working to change the world, and the people who run them, that's what it should be all about.

PART

MANAGING
THE WORK

Whether you're managing a single team or an entire organization, there's going to be more work than you can handle on your own. And if you accept the fundamental premise of this book—that managing effectively is about getting results in your realm—then you're going to be feeling a lot of pressure to get things done, and to get them done well.

In Part One, we'll talk about how to manage the work—ideally, how to transfer some of the weight on your shoulders to your staff members. If you do this right, your staff members will feel energized because they will have responsibility, your team will get dramatically more done than you would have been able to on your own, and you'll be freed up to focus on areas where you'll have the biggest impact.

So how do you do it? Whether the work you're trying to get someone to do is as straightforward as handling logistics for a meeting or as complex as raising your organization's visibility in the mass media, the same basic principles apply: you have to be clear from the start about what you expect, stay engaged enough along the way to increase the likelihood of success, and hold people accountable for whether they deliver.

In Part One, we'll look at how you can apply these principles of expectations, engagement, and accountability to manage different types of work:

- The most common thing most managers do is *hand off specific tasks or projects.* In Chapter Two, we look at how you can do this through strong delegation. Once you've mastered basic delegation, all the other ways in which you'll manage work follow easily, because the same principles apply.

- Ultimately, you'll *maximize your impact when you can hand over not just specific tasks, but broader responsibilities.* In Chapter Three, we look at how you do this by creating meaningful roles on your team and setting and reinforcing clear, measurable goals for what your team members should accomplish. Doing these pieces in tandem will enable you to fully share the pressure (and joys!) not just of day-to-day tasks but also of driving your organization forward.

- Whether in pursuit of specific projects or broad responsibilities, your staff members are going to perform thousands of tiny activities that you never discuss explicitly, but which will be key to the quality of the results you attain. In Chapter Four, we look at how you can create a powerful culture that will guide how your staff members approach and execute every aspect of their work.

- Finally, in Chapter Five, we'll look at two systems that will help you bring all of this together—how in the real world with multiple staff members each handling a range of projects and responsibilities, you can stay on top of it all to ensure great results.

As you'll see, the details vary depending on the context, but the basic principles of making sure people know what you expect of them, engaging with them to maximize their chances of success, and holding them accountable are the same.

CHAPTER

MANAGING SPECIFIC TASKS

Basic Delegation

Does either of these scenarios sound familiar to you?

- You ask your staff member to write a fundraising appeal for your new campaign. When you review the draft, the emphasis is on the wrong points and key pieces are missing, so you start editing it—and soon find that you've rewritten the entire piece. Your staffer is frustrated because it's not her letter anymore; it's yours. "Why didn't you just do it yourself to begin with?" she wants to know.

- The next time you assign your staff member a piece of writing, you try to give her more leeway so she doesn't feel micromanaged. But when you look at what she's written on the day it's scheduled to be mailed out, the tone is off, the pitch for funding isn't strong enough, and it doesn't feel compelling to you. You're frustrated and unhappy with it, and when you tell her, you can tell she's frustrated too.

If you're like most managers we work with, one, if not both, of these will ring true. In fact, many managers we know go back and forth between being too hands-on and too hands-off. Frequently a manager will start off at one extreme, discover that it doesn't get the desired results, and react by moving to the opposite extreme, only to find that doesn't work either. For instance, after giving staffers a great deal of leeway to run with a project and not having it go according to plan, a manager may vow to be involved in every step of the next project. And managers who get feedback that they've been too intensively involved will often start suppressing their natural desire to sit in on crucial project meetings and get interim project reports, inevitably to find out at the end of the project that they should have listened to their gut. At that point, it can be tempting to throw up your hands in exasperation and feel that you're damned if you do and damned if you don't.

It's no wonder managers get exasperated, because neither extreme works. In this chapter, we discuss how to get the balance right and will walk you through each step of good delegation.

EXACTLY HOW HANDS-ON SHOULD YOU BE?

Wouldn't it be nice if there were an easy answer to the question of how hands-on to be? ("Finally! Now I know that I should be 58 percent hands-on!") Although there's no one-size-fits-all formula, we've come to a paradoxical-sounding belief from our work with managers that most managers need to be more hands-on than they are—but also more hands-off.

Huh?

Contrary to the popular belief that managers just need to empower their people and let them go, we believe managers need to be significantly more hands-on in key respects. They need to be more hands-on in clearly communicating their expectations for the outcomes of the work, making sure they and their staff are on the same page about how the work will proceed, checking in on ongoing work, and creating accountability and learning at the end.

Guide more so your staff is more likely to succeed, and you'll be able to do less yourself.

At the same time, managers need to be more hands-off in actually doing the work. For every manager we see who's too hands-off in making expectations clear on the front end and in monitoring ongoing work, we see another (or often the same) who's too hands-on in pushing the day-to-day of the work forward and often doing much of it herself. The point of managing other people is to get more done than you would on your own, but too often we see managers fail to gain the benefit of having other people make the work happen.

We can sum up our advice in this way: guide more, do less.

You might be wondering whether following our advice won't actually take more of your time. In the long run, definitely not. *Guiding more* means that you may spend more time than you otherwise would in explaining a project at the start. You also might spend five minutes more than you did in the past reviewing data on progress along the way. But you'll radically increase the chances that whatever you're delegating will be a success. Everyone will be happier, and you'll ultimately get to *do* less because you won't end up redoing the work (and dealing with an unhappy staff member). Over time you'll be able to delegate bigger and bigger pieces of work and know that they'll come out successfully. When that happens, you can focus your energies on the work that only you can do.

THE COMPONENTS OF GOOD DELEGATION

What does guiding more and doing less look like in practice? As we mentioned in the introduction to this part of the book, there are three key steps to managing work generally and in the delegation process more specifically:

1. *Agree on expectations.* Ensure that your staff member understands what you want achieved.

2. *Stay engaged.* Make sure the work is on track to succeed before it's too late.

3. *Create accountability and learning.* Reinforce responsibility for good or bad results, and draw lessons for the future.

How exactly these principles apply depends on the context, so we'll discuss a fourth principle, which most people do intuitively: adapt your approach to fit the person and project. Figure 2.1 summarizes the basic process.

Ultimately this process is about setting your staff members up for success in their work. We've seen a lot of managers who think of delegation as consisting only of the first part of this cycle, that is, asking someone to complete a piece of work. But if you skip the next steps in the cycle, you're likely to find yourself in the situations we described in the opening of this chapter: frustrated that the work doesn't look like you'd envisioned it or doing too much of it yourself.

When you're assigning work, look for opportunities to make the assignment truly a conversation, as opposed to simply dictating every element. For instance, if there's flexibility in what the finished project should look like, ask the staff member what she thinks the outcome should be. You can also ask questions around the other pieces of delegation, such as, "So who else do you think needs to be involved?" and "Do we have samples that might be useful here?" and "What timeline makes sense?"

Now we'll walk through each of the four steps of the cycle.

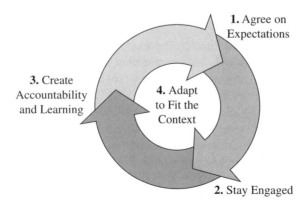

FIGURE 2.1. *The Delegation Cycle*

THE FIVE W'S AND AN H

Teach your staff to ask about the five W's if you haven't already communicated them:

Who: Who should be involved?

What: What does success look like on this?

When: When is the project due?

Where: Where might the staff member go for resources?

Why: Why does this work matter?

And a little bit of . . . *How* you should approach the work.

Step 1: Agree on Expectations

The first step in launching the work is for you and your staffer to come to a clear, shared understanding about what results you expect. It may sound straightforward, but it can be harder than you might think to get to the point where you and your staff would give the same answers to questions like, "What are you trying to accomplish?" and "What does success look like?" Just giving a quick rundown of the project usually won't get you there.

One way to do a better job of communicating your expectations is to remember the five W's from your high school English teacher, who probably taught you that every good news story begins by laying out the who, what, when, where, and why. When you're delegating, think about each of those W's, as well as a little bit of the How. We'll look closely at each piece, although we're taking a bit of creative license and covering the what before the who. And Tool 2.1 at the end of the chapter provides a worksheet to use when you are delegating work to your staff.

What Does Success Look Like for This Assignment?

Most managers we know hate being labeled micromanagers, and with good reason: micromanagers tell staff exactly how to do a project or, worse, do (or redo) the work for them. What will let you delegate effectively while not micromanaging is setting clear expectations for success. By being extremely clear about what you want achieved, you free your staff up to figure out how to get there, so you'll start by agreeing on what success will look like.

Sometimes identifying what success will look like is easy. For instance, when you are putting a staff member in charge of organizing a gala event, you might have a predetermined aim, such as raising net revenue of $250,000. But in other cases, the definition of success might not be as clear. In those cases, you might ask your staff to take the lead in proposing what a successful outcome would be, saying something like this: "You're in charge of logistics for this event. What do you think doing that successfully should look like?"

In either case, the outcomes that you and your staff agree to should be as specific as possible. Quantitative targets are often ideal, since they leave little room for misunderstanding. But quantifying outcomes isn't always feasible, so you can also agree on qualitative aims. In these cases, you should be as specific as you can about the qualitative target, that is, how you will know it when you see it. For the staff member you put in charge of logistics, the qualitative aim of having an event run smoothly might more specifically be, "Everything is set up and ready to go on time; if we run out of supplies, we have extras at the ready; we anticipate basic needs and provide for them; and we have someone ready to deal with extraordinary requests."

But sometimes even qualitative outcomes are hard to pin down. In these cases, making sure that your staff member understands the full context of what you're trying to accomplish can go a long way toward defining the outcome. For instance, in delegating a funding proposal, you could explain what the funder cares about and what will turn her off (the context), and you could explain that the finished document needs to resonate emotionally with the donor and convince her that the project is in line with her interests and goals (the outcome).

Finally, don't define the task too narrowly. For instance, let's say you're preparing for an upcoming meeting and you'd like your assistant to help make it go smoothly. Many managers in this situation will give the assistant specific tasks to do, such as, "Please check that there are enough pads and pens in the conference room, and make sure people are offered water and coffee." But a broader, and often much more effective, approach is to tell the assistant that she's in charge of all logistics preparations for the meeting. The first time you do this, you'd agree on what that should look like, but from there, she'd take on the broad responsibility of ensuring smooth logistics. That way, she'd presumably take the initiative to clear the unrelated papers from the conference table that you didn't even realize were there, ensure the speakerphone is set up and ready to go, and do all kinds of other tasks that you might not have thought to assign. This broader approach will make the assistant's job more challenging and your life easier, and it will get the job done better than if you'd assigned it more narrowly.

So when you're addressing success, go broad, not narrow.

USE SAMPLES AND TEMPLATES TO CLARIFY   When possible, offering samples can be an incredibly useful way to give your staff a clearer idea of what you're looking for. For example, if you and your head of communications agree that the Web site she is developing should look "clean and crisp," you might send her links to sites that you feel look that way. Similarly, you could give your new development director a successful grant proposal from a previous year to show her the tone and style she should be striving for in this year's report.

If the assignment is a new type of work, providing a template can help structure the work in the way you're envisioning. For example, rather than simply asking a staff member to give you research about other organizations working on a particular issue, you might create a chart with the specific headings you are looking for (for instance, organization name, mission, budget, and so forth) and have her fill it in.

"Make sure your staff members can answer the question,
'What do I have to do to delight my boss?'"

PETER B. LEWIS, CHAIRMAN, PROGRESSIVE CORPORATION

Who Should Be Involved?

However broadly you define the task, be unambiguous with your staff member that she is ultimately responsible for it. Too often we hear managers say, "Can you help me with logistics for the meeting?" when what they really mean to say is, "You're in charge of making sure logistics for the meeting go smoothly." The key here is to make sure your staff member understands that she is the owner—a word we love—of the task. She might call on you or others for ideas or even help with the task, but she is the one making sure that all of the helpers do their jobs and that the task is done well.

One way to instill the idea of ownership is to use a simple tool we call MOCHA, an acronym for the different roles for a piece of work. We developed it because we had a lot of clients who rightly placed a high value on inclusion, and therefore had projects that ended up involving lots of people. Too often, though, those projects devolved into confusion when people were not clear on their roles and the project lacked a clear driver or decision maker.

In projects where a number of people are playing roles, then, being clear about the who is key. MOCHA helps solve the who issue by providing a standard vocabulary within the organization for describing how people might be involved. (You can remember "MOCHA" because if you get this right, your job becomes easier and you can sit at a café all day sipping mochas.) Here's what the different pieces of MOCHA stand for:[1]

Manager	Assigns responsibility and holds owner accountable. Makes suggestions, asks hard questions, reviews progress, serves as a resource, and intervenes if the work is off track.
Owner	Has overall responsibility for the success or failure of the project. Ensures that all the work gets done (directly or with helpers) and that others are involved appropriately. There should be only one owner.
Consulted	Should be asked for input or needs to be bought in to the project.
Helper	Available to help do part of the work.
Approver	Signs off on decisions before they're final. May be the manager, though might also be the executive director, external partner, or board chair.

---

[1] We adapted this model from the DARCI decision-making model taught in some programs: Decider, Accountable, Responsible, Consulted, Informed.

GIVE WORK TO THE RIGHT PERSON We sometimes see managers fail at delegation because they assign a project to the wrong person in the first place, trying to fit a round peg into a square hole—for example, assigning the artistic director, who is a creative genius but a disaster with numbers, to prepare a detailed project budget. When delegating work, consider who has the talent and skills to get the job done rather than who should be able to do the task at hand given her background or position. Of course, if you regularly find yourself reluctant to delegate a responsibility that the staff member in that position should be able to handle, you need to assess whether that person is a good fit for the role and determine an appropriate course of action. We discuss this and other performance issues in Chapter Nine.

Let's say that you're a development director and your development associate is in charge of the upcoming gala. You might be the M (manager) on this project, and the associate would be the O (owner). The communications director and program director should be consulted (C), the development assistant is an H (helper), and the executive director might be both an H (helper by making calls to the largest donors to ask them to buy tables) and the A (approver on the final program and the table assignments).

If you do nothing else when you're delegating, make sure that there's a clear owner for making the project succeed. The owner might then figure out the rest of the MOCHA, but you need to know who is responsible for making the project successful. In fact, one way to think about your challenge as you take on more and more management responsibility is to recognize that your job is to go from being an owner to being a manager. That means that as you find yourself the owner of specific responsibilities, you might be asking yourself, "Should I really be the owner on this, or should I be handing that over to someone else?"

When Is the Project Due?

We realize it sounds obvious to be clear about the when, but we'll say it anyway: make sure your staff member knows when the project is due and where it falls relative to her other priorities. Over and over again, we see managers who delegate a project without being explicit about the due date, expecting it to be finished or at least well under way a week later, and then check back in and discover that the staffer hasn't started it yet. Again, it comes down to being clear about your expectations: state the timeline you expect and how the work fits with other priorities.

It's okay to leave the timing up to the staffer, but be specific about any qualifiers attached to that. You might say something like, "There's no rush for this, so it's fine to do it as time allows, but it should be wrapped up by August. This isn't as important as the memo for the board, so you can turn to it after that." You can also make this part very much a conversation by asking your staff member when she thinks it would be reasonable to have the work done and how she sees it fitting in with her other priorities.

Where Might the Staff Member Go for Resources?

What money, people, supplies, and other tools can your staff member use? Is there a rough budget for the project? Are there other people with expertise on this issue to whom she might turn (you might capture these people within the MOCHA as those who are consulted or helpers).

Within that list, one of the most valuable resources you can offer your staff is your own time. Make it clear that staffers can approach you to clarify expectations, answer questions, review progress, and help brainstorm solutions. In doing this, make sure that they maintain ownership of the project, so a staffer can say, "I'm wrestling with X. The best solution I can come up with is ABC, but I worry that it's not the most cost-effective approach. Do you have any suggestions about other options I might consider?" Staffers shouldn't say, "I'm stuck on X. What should I do?"

Why Does This Work Matter?

Finally, both of us have been guilty of giving assignments in a hurry without explaining where the project is coming from and why it matters, and even why we've chosen to give it to the person we're asking to handle it. We've both also gotten reasonably good outcomes at times when we have skipped this step, but each time we do it well, we've been struck by how much more excitement and buy-in we've seen when we communicate the why of a project as staff members go from compliance to commitment. For instance, if you're asking your assistant to handle the logistics for an upcoming funder visit to your office, you might remind her that the funder has shown interest in the organization but hasn't yet committed, that the funder in the past has been skeptical of grassroots organizations like yours so you want to make sure you look extra "on the ball," and that your assistant did such a good job organizing the community dinner that you know she can make this visit a smashing success.

. . . And a Little Bit of How You Should Approach the Work

The standard line in management textbooks is that if you have good people, you shouldn't need to tell them how to do everything. This is largely true, and by being clear with your staff about what success looks like, you're freeing them up to think about how to get there.

That said, if you have input about the project, you should give it to your staff member on the front end. There are few things more frustrating for staff members than putting the effort in figuring out something you already knew. If you know from experience that having a Web site vendor in a different city has been a nightmare in the past, don't hesitate to tell your head of communications that.

Similarly, make sure you mention any constraints that the staff member should be aware of. These might be constraints around the process (such as who needs to sign off on an item before it goes out the door) or the substance (such as items to include in the budget). For instance, in the Web design example, you might ask your staff member to submit draft design options to the head of development before she makes a final recommendation (a process constraint). You might also indicate that the organization's logo must appear on every page (a substantive constraint).

Agreeing on How to Move Forward

Once you've shared your expectations for the project, the final step in the expectations stage is to make sure your staff member understands the assignment and, where relevant, creates a plan of attack.

The repeat-back.   As we mentioned earlier, time and time again we see managers who think they have been crystal clear about their expectations and then are shocked to discover that their staff members heard something very different. We're often reminded of the children's game of telephone, where a whispered message gets passed from person to person and comes out humorously different at the end than it was at the beginning.

The best way to prevent this telephone syndrome and to be sure your staff member understands the project the way you do is simple: ask. That is, find a way to get your staff member to repeat back to you what she has taken the assignment to be. In simple cases, the repeat-back might be verbal. Before ending a discussion about an assignment, you might simply say, "So, just to make sure we're on the same page, can you tell me what you're taking away from this?" When an assignment is more complicated or will take more than a day or two to complete, you might ask the staff member to send you a brief e-mail summarizing the assignment, including expected outcomes and next steps—for example:

> Hi Jenny,
>
> Here's what I took from our discussion about the memo for the field volunteers:
>
> - Should include targets (and rationale)
> - Should be short (fewer than 3 pages)
> - Could be like the health care memo from last month
> - Deadline: out the door next Friday; I'll send you an outline this Friday
>
> Let me know if I'm missing anything here. Thanks—
>
> Alice

This might feel awkward at first, but you can even blame your own fallibility by saying something like, "I know I'm not always as clear as I think I am, so just to make sure there's nothing lost in translation, can you take five minutes to capture what we've agreed to here and e-mail it back to me, so we both have down what we've agreed to?" Almost invariably, in looking back over the e-mail, you'll find one or two details where you and the staff member weren't aligned.

The plan.   The quick verbal summary and the five-minute e-mail are less formal versions of what can become a more extensive plan on more complicated projects. The level of

AVOID THE GAME OF TELEPHONE WITH THE REPEAT-BACK A simple, "Can you tell me what you're taking away?" can help to ensure that you and the staff member are in agreement on what needs to be done before she spends hours on something that doesn't line up with what you have in mind.

detail will vary from situation to situation, but the basic ingredients of any plan include the key activities needed to reach the desired outcomes, a timeline for when those activities will occur, and who is responsible for each step. In other words, plans should spell out who will do what by when.

For complex projects, ask your staff member to create a written plan that will be the staff member's tool for juggling the work's many pieces; it should include information about each step, interim deadlines, and notes on MOCHA-type stakeholders. For instance, if your staff member is organizing a conference, the plan would cover steps associated with choosing the venue, designing and printing invitations, developing the agenda, and confirming speakers. The plan should be in a format that is easy to update, since your staff member will likely be making small adjustments to those interim deadlines as the work progresses. Because this sort of planning requires your staff member to think through each step and plan backward, she may spot early steps (like securing a venue) that could otherwise have slipped until too late.

While your staff members should take the lead in proposing the plan, as the manager you should ensure that it's realistic and as comprehensive as it needs to be. This might mean asking questions about the plan ("Is it really possible for you to go from mock-ups of the Web pages to having the pages coded within two weeks as you've proposed?") and making recommendations based on your expertise and experience ("I worked with vendors on a Web site remotely once, and it was a disaster. You might think about finding someone you could easily meet with in person"). Don't be shy about playing the role of skeptic, pushing against the plan and the results to date to help the staff member refine the plan. The ideal outcome is a plan that is better than either you or your staff member might have developed on your own. Tool 2.2 provides a sample project plan.

Step 2: Stay Engaged

Now that you and your staff member have gotten crystal clear about what you expect, you're done, right? Not if you care about results. Time after time, we see managers who think they have been totally clear about what they expect end up surprised by the implementation gap, where what happens in practice looks very different from what they expected. That's because the most common way managers fail at delegating is by not staying involved to check on progress.

You can avoid the implementation gap by continuing to engage with your staff during the course of the work, getting a sense of how the work is proceeding, and making sure that tasks are either completed according to plan or that the plan is adapted as needed. Managers sometimes feel awkward about doing this, but you can be direct with your staff. Tell them that you're hoping to check in on things along the way, both to see how things are going so you can help them avoid any implementation gap and so that you can serve as a better resource to them.

There are a lot of ways to ensure your staff is making progress, but four of the most powerful are checking in with staff directly, reviewing interim work, reviewing data, and seeing the work for yourself firsthand.

Checking In with Staff Directly

Checking in can be done by e-mail, phone calls, or in-person conversations, including regular weekly meetings, meetings on specific topics, and quick stop-bys to see how things are going.

Regardless of the exact forum, in addition to being helpful on whatever issues your staff member might raise, your job is to ask probing questions that get beneath the surface to make sure that work is on track. For instance, in preparing for an upcoming conference, rather than simply asking, "So, is everything going okay?" and receiving a yes answer, you might ask your staff to review progress against the plan, discuss steps around a particularly tough issue ("How are you approaching the issue of diversity on the panels?"), and report on the number of confirmed attendees and speakers.

In formulating these questions, think about what could go wrong, and probe around those areas in particular. Don't let yourself assume things are proceeding smoothly; assume your job is to look for trouble, not to assume things are proceeding smoothly. You can do this in a tone that won't make your staffer think that you lack confidence in her, and you might even quickly agree with her that you're going to do it. For instance, you might say, "So I know we really want this to go smoothly.

PROJECT PLANNING: THE FOUR S'S

In creating a project plan, your staff members might think through the Four S's:

1. *Success:* What are the desired outcomes of the project?
2. *Streams:* What are the main categories of work?
3. *Steps:* What are the specific, detailed steps that need to happen within each stream of the project?
4. *Stakeholders:* Who else needs to be involved, and how? Use MOCHA as a tool to think through who needs to be involved in what.

Can I ask you about some of the areas where I've seen events like this go wrong in the past?" Then you might ask questions like, "Do we know how the hotel will deal with malfunctioning equipment?" and "Is there anything we can do to be prepared to accommodate attendees with disabilities?" You could even ask, "What could go wrong? What's your worst-case scenario?" and brainstorm about ways to address those possibilities.

Reviewing a Slice of the Work

One pattern happens over and over: you assign a piece of writing, your staff member spends two weeks on it, and when it comes back to you, it's not at all what you were picturing. Many managers think to ask for a draft in advance, but even at that stage, your staff member has put significant time into the project. A less common but very helpful technique here can be to ask to see a small sample of the whole before the person has put substantial energy into getting all the way through it. For instance, you might ask for a short segment of a document, an outline of an argument, or one page from the new Web design before the whole site is created. Or if you have an intern preparing references for a report, you might ask to see the first three citations to make sure the format she is using is correct. The basic idea is that just as you don't need to eat a whole pie to know how it tastes, you can sample a small piece of the work to know whether it's on track, and thereby save tremendous frustration down the road after your staff member has put significant energy into a more finished product.

Reviewing Data

Also ask to see regular reports with data indicating progress toward the desired outcome—for instance, a weekly report on progress toward a fundraising goal, a monthly chart showing Web site traffic compared to prior months, or a weekly list of targeted lawmakers and their positions on a pending piece of legislation. As part of delegating the work originally, you might think about what data will be meaningful to monitor along the way and how often, or even better, ask your staff member, "What data can we look at along the way to make sure this is on track?" so she can propose the best approach.

Seeing the Work Firsthand

A less common but extremely powerful way to see how things are going is to directly observe the work in action. Staff members might be completely forthright in reporting on progress, but managers often find that getting a feel for the actual work leads them to a much greater understanding of what is going on. For instance, joining your staff on a lobby visit, sitting in on a media training, attending a meeting with a prospective funder to hear your staff's pitch, or observing a phone bank to see how volunteers deliver an agreed-on appeal can all offer valuable insights into how what is happening in reality compares to what was outlined in the plan.

When you're managing work that's executed outside the office (as opposed to, say, overseeing a team that is producing reports that you will see directly), seeing the work firsthand is particularly important. If your organization runs training programs, sit in on some of them. If you're running a ballot initiative campaign in another state, make site visits to observe how the work is being run on the ground. One executive director we know started sitting in (with permission) on randomly selected calls between his head of regional operations and the organization's regional staff. He was shocked to discover how different what was happening in the field was from what he had been assuming.

To explain to your staff member why you're doing this, you might say something like, "I want to stay in touch with how all our grand plans are really playing out, so I'm going to be getting out into the field or on to your calls every once in a while to see how things are going in practice," or "I want to stay in touch with how things are playing out in the field so I can be a better resource to you."

Firsthand observation also helps you serve as a resource to your staff members as they consider changing the plan to reflect how things are playing out in the real world. Ideally, you would conduct observations like these with your staff member at your side, so that both of you have the same facts about how things are unfolding. Following these observations, you should debrief with your staff to share your impressions and make sure that there is agreement about any changes going forward. In the ballot initiative campaign, the executive director sat down with his head of regional operations so they could debrief the calls, acknowledge what wasn't working as expected, and generate solutions.

KEEP THE MONKEY ON YOUR STAFFER'S BACK

Once you've delegated a responsibility, make sure you keep the ownership for the project squarely with the staff member. Authors William Oncken Jr. and Donald Wass suggest thinking of each project or task as a monkey someone is carrying around on her back. When you assign a project to a staffer, you're handing over the monkey. But often that staffer will find ways to return the monkey to your back. For instance, if you see that a phone bank script isn't working well, don't "take the monkey back" by rewriting the script. Rather, after you talk with your staffer about the elements that need changing, she should do the rewrite so that the monkey stays on your staffer's back and doesn't hop back to yours.

Commonly, taking back the monkey happens in response to a seemingly legitimate question. Rather than suggesting solutions yourself, try to get the staff member to propose solutions herself. "What do you think?" is a great question to use in ensuring you don't inadvertently take on monkeys you have delegated.

For a more complete explanation of how to ensure that staff members do not pass the buck back to their managers, see William Oncken Jr. and Donald Wass, "Management Time: Who's Got the Monkey?" *Harvard Business Review,* November–December 1999.

Step 3: Create Accountability and Learning

We recently met with a frustrated manager who had delegated the task of writing an important memo to one of his staff members. He had set expectations appropriately, made sure the staff member understood them, and reviewed a draft along the way to make sure it was on track. The end product, though, was missing a crucial ingredient, and the manager's reaction was typical: "This just shows that you can't delegate anything and expect it to get done right!"

Although we shared his frustration, we reminded him that there was one more piece to the delegation process he needed to pursue: creating accountability. He needed to go back to the author of the letter and in a direct and assertive but not hostile way, share his reaction to it (see Chapter Ten). By doing this, the manager would get the product he wanted; perhaps more important, he would set himself up for better results the next time by sending a clear message that slipshod work was not acceptable.

Creating accountability at the end of a process is the first step in setting expectations for the next iteration of the delegation cycle. Fundamentally the message is, "I mean what I say." Of course, this goes for rewarding positive outcomes as well. When staff members have done a good job and produced the desired results, managers should recognize their effort and celebrate their success, so staff members know that doing things well matters.

In addition to reinforcing responsibilities, the accountability stage can produce lessons for the future. Even when a project has gone well, both you and your staffer have likely learned from the experience and seen parts of it that could be done differently next time to get even better results. A write-up of these lessons, even as a quick bulleted list, can be an invaluable resource the next time you conduct a similar project. One small step that can make a large difference in producing lessons and accountability is to schedule or, better yet, have your staff member schedule a brief reflection meeting for the end of a project and to get it on the calendar right from the start so it doesn't feel punitive when you suggest it at the end.

DON'T PUNISH THE WHOLE CLASS   We occasionally see managers who are trying to hold a group accountable for the actions of individuals. When you're trying to make clear that you mean what you say, you'll be much more effective if you deliver that message to one person at a time. For instance, if three of your staffers miss a deadline you've set, you'll create a culture of accountability more quickly by going to each of the three individually (even if it's sending each an identical e-mail, customized just with their name) than by talking to the whole group to stress the importance of deadlines.

THE VALUE OF DEBRIEFING

Harvard Business School researchers found that among a group of surgeons learning a new operating technique, those who discussed each case in detail and debriefed with team members after procedures managed to halve their operating time. Those who didn't discuss and debrief hardly improved their time at all. (Atul Gawande, "The Learning Curve," *The New Yorker,* January 28, 2002.)

Step 4: Adapt to Fit the Context

When assigning work to staffers, you should apply the three steps in the delegation cycle above, but how you apply them will vary depending on the person to whom you're delegating (the who) and the nature of the project (the what).

When it comes to the who, consider your staff members' skill and will.

Skill

You will likely learn from experience who is best at turning around a high-quality written assignment and who is a superstar at building connections with an external constituent (these are rarely the same person). Yet when you assess skill level, don't automatically assume that stellar employees need little guidance, since even the best employees have areas where they need closer management. You might have an otherwise outstanding worker who has trouble meeting deadlines, so you might ensure she creates a timeline with built-in room on the front end for unexpected delays. Or you might have someone who hates putting plans in writing but always delivers high-quality work on time. With that person, you might waive your normal expectation of a written plan and instead agree verbally on a path forward.

A subset of skill is the person's experience in your organization. You may have just hired a master fundraiser, but because the person is new to your organization, you want to work with her more closely on early projects than you would on the same projects three months from now.

Will

Considering will means assessing what people like and dislike. Your program manager's well-known hatred for doing budgets should lead you to take a more hands-on approach, because it's reasonable to think she might be inclined to put the work off or put less energy into it than into work she loves. (Of course, if she does an otherwise excellent job as a program manager, it might be reasonable to find someone else to handle those budgets, since you'll likely get better results by assigning that work to someone with more enthusiasm for numbers.)

Beyond the who, you need to consider the what—the nature of the task and how difficult and important it is.

Difficulty

Obviously the more difficult the assignment is, the more time you'll want to spend discussing it on the front end and checking in as the work progresses. And conversely, relatively easy, straightforward tasks will require less of your oversight. For instance, if you are asking your experienced advocacy coordinator to create letter-to-the-editor templates for activists to use, you might simply talk about the topics you want to cover and show her templates that have been used in the past. But if the same person has been assigned to devise and implement a plan for a new initiative to establish local chapters, you'll want to talk in depth at the outset about the goals, process, and potential pitfalls; check in regularly to give advice as the plan develops; and stay in very close contact as the implementation begins.

Importance

How important is the assignment? What are the potential ramifications of success or failure? For instance, if your organization's most important ally in the Senate is speaking at your conference, you would want to be more actively engaged in ensuring that everything goes smoothly than you would be in supervising the setup for your management team's monthly meeting. (See Figure 2.2.)

After weighing all of these factors, decide on a general approach. Should you take a highly hands-on approach, be moderately hands-on, or be fairly hands-off? If your consideration of these factors leads you to determine that a hands-on approach is called for, it can be helpful to let your employee know this. You might tell her, "I'm going to be checking in pretty closely since this is the first time you've done this and we really can't afford to have any delays in getting these out to our funders."

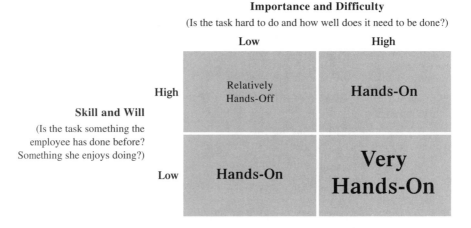

FIGURE 2.2. *Hands-On or Hands-Off? Determining Your Approach*

MANAGING SIDEWAYS What about overseeing a project or delegating work when you don't have authority over the people involved? Actually, the same principles still apply:

- Determine how hands-on you need to be based on the nature of the project and what you know about the people involved.
- Agree on clear outcomes, constraints, resources, and prioritization.
- Check in during the course of the work.
- Structure learning and even an opportunity for group accountability at the end.

If you feel awkward about managing a peer on a project, remember that the key is to be transparent about why you're taking this approach. For instance, you might explain, "There's potential for us to end up on different pages once we go off and start working on this, so why don't we check in next week and make sure our heads are still in the same place?"

We've thrown a lot at you, but after going through a couple of rounds of the delegation cycle to get the hang of it, including debriefing how the process went, much of what we have addressed here will become second nature. And once the principles of agreeing on expectations, staying engaged, and creating accountability are in place, your team will produce stronger work products with a lot more efficiency, helping you get the results you need.

KEY POINTS

- Remember the basic rule: guide more and do less.

- Guiding well means setting clear expectations, staying engaged enough to ensure that corrections are made along the way, and creating accountability and learning on the back end.

- In setting expectations, remember the five W's and an H:

  - Who should be involved?

  - What does success look like?

  - When is the project due?

  - Where might the staff member go for resources?

  - Why does this work matter?

  - And a little bit of how you should approach the work.

- A simple repeat-back of expectations from your staff member can do wonders to avoid miscommunication.

- The most common way managers fail at delegating is by not staying engaged to monitor progress. If you don't get a sense of how the work is proceeding once you've assigned it, you will almost always experience a serious implementation gap.

- When a project ends, you and your staff should reflect on results, draw lessons learned, and create accountability. You need your staff to understand that you mean what you say.

- How you apply all of these points will depend on the context. Consider the skill and will of your staffer as well as the difficulty and importance of the assignment, and adapt your approach accordingly.

Additional Reading

S. R. Covey, *The 7 Habits of Highly Effective People: Powerful Lessons in Personal Change* (New York: Free Press, 2004).

A. Gawande, "The Learning Curve," *The New Yorker*, January 28, 2002.

William Oncken Jr. and Donald Wass, "Management Time: Who's Got the Monkey?" *Harvard Business Review*, Nov.–Dec. 1999, pp. 2–7.

"Situational Leadership Theory," Wikipedia, http://en.wikipedia.org/wiki/Situational_leadership_theory and http://12manage.com/methods_blanchard_situational_leadership.html.

TOOL 2.1

DELEGATION WORKSHEET

I am assigning _____ the responsibility of _____.

Agree on Expectations

1. WHAT does success look like on this assignment? _____
_____

2. WHEN is the project due? How does this fit with other priorities? _____
_____

3. WHERE might the staff member go for resources? _____
_____

4. WHY does this work matter, and why is this staff person the one to make it happen?
_____

5. WHO else should be involved? The MOCHA for this project is:

   Manager: _____   Helper: _____

   Owner: _____   Approver: _____

   Consulted: _____

6. Tips on HOW to do it (if any): _____
_____

7. How will you make sure you and your staffer are aligned on key points and next steps?

   ☐ Verbal or written repeat-back   ☐ Project plan   ☐ Other _____

Stay Engaged

1. What specific products or activities (for example, outlines, data, rehearsals) will you want to review or see in action to monitor progress?

_____
_____

Create Accountability and Learning

1. When and how will you debrief how things went? Can you schedule that now?

_____

Adapt Your Approach

1. Given the difficulty and importance of the task and my staff member's will and skill for this task, my approach should generally be (circle one):

   Very hands-on   Moderately hands-on   Relatively hands-off

TOOL 2.2
SAMPLE PROJECT PLAN

Project: Host a panel on new climate change initiatives, raising our profile among groups working on environmental issues

Dates: October 20, 2011–January 15, 2012

This project will be a success if:

- We land four star speakers (major players) with a range of perspectives
- At least 80% of invitees attend, including reps from significant allies and at least three newcomer groups
- 90% are "highly satisfied" with the event
- 85% sign up to join our mailing list
- Smooth execution of all logistics (on time, all speakers briefed, enough food and drink, no technical issues)

Area of Work ("Stream")	Steps	Due	Stakeholders (MOCHA)	Status/Notes
Overall		Dec. 15	Owner = Sue! M = Dan, C = John and Rachel, H = Tina, A = Carlos	In progress
	Make the conference a smash hit	Dec. 15		Done
Panel discussion		Dec. 15	O = John (Sue = M, Carlos = H for making calls)	In progress
	Draft outline of topics we want covered in discussion	Oct. 28		Done

Think ahead of time as to who needs to be involved and in what capacity before starting the project.

Start with the deadline in mind, and work backward to determine the interim due dates.

It is often helpful at the start of large projects to list overall stages with deadlines.

Area of Work ("Stream")	Steps	Due	Stakeholders (MOCHA)	Status/Notes
	Identify potential speakers to join the panel and run by Carlos	Oct. 30		Done
	Draft e-mail invite for speakers	Nov. 3		Done
	Carlos signs off and sends e-mail	Nov. 7		
	Confirm list of speakers and arrange call with speakers	Nov. 17		Done
	Send speakers e-mail with info on other panelists, our publications, proposed outline for discussion	Nov. 20		Done
	Call with speakers	Week of Dec. 8		Thurs., Dec. 11: Carlos, Dan, Tina, me in small conference room
	Revise and send out final outline for discussion	Dec. 15		Append notes from call
	Confirm speakers' attendance; get special requests if needed	Dec. 18		
Invite		Dec. 8	O = Rachel; A = Dan	In progress
	Brainstorm session with team re: how to get the word out	Nov. 10		Done
	Draft invite	Nov. 19		Done
	Get comments from Dan on invite	Nov. 28		Done

Area of Work ("Stream")	Steps	Due	Stakeholders (MOCHA)	Status/Notes
	Revise invite based on Dan's input	Dec. 4		Done
	Finalize and send out	Dec. 8		Tina to track responses and check numbers periodically
	E-mail reminder to RSVP	Jan. 5	O = Tina	
Materials		Dec. 17	O = Sue, H = Tina, A = Dan	In progress
	Draft program and inserts	Nov. 20		See 2007 program
	Send materials to Dan	Nov. 20		Done
	Revise materials based on Dan's input	Dec. 12		
	Finalize and make copies	Dec. 17	O = Tina	Use heavy paper
Volunteer coordination			M = Dan, O = John, C= Sue and Rachel, H = Tina, A = Dan	In progress
	Confirm volunteers	Dec. 19		Need at least 4
	E-mail reminder to volunteers	Jan. 5		
Logistics			M = Sue, O = Tina, C = John and Rachel, H = Team, A = Dan	Pending

Area of Work ("Stream")	Steps	Due	Stakeholders (MOCHA)	Status/Notes
	Reserve large conference room and AV equipment	Nov. 17		Done
	Set up signs, chairs, welcome table	Jan. 8	H = volunteers	
	AV set up and testing	Jan. 9	H = tech team	
	Paper, pens, water bottles for speakers	Jan. 9		
After the event		Jan. 15	M = Dan, O = Sue, C = John and Rachel, H = Tina, A = Carlos	Pending
	Conduct debrief of event with Dan, Tina, Rachel, John, Carlos	Jan. 15		
	Send event summary to Dan and Carlos	Jan. 14		
	Volunteer thank-yous	Jan. 15		

CHAPTER

3

MANAGING BROAD RESPONSIBILITIES
Roles and Goals

In Chapter One we talked about how to set expectations, stay engaged, and create accountability to successfully delegate specific tasks or projects to your staff. For many managers, delegating even discrete projects will represent an important start to getting better results.

In the long run, though, managers will generate the kinds of results they need to, and free themselves up to take on the pieces that only they can do, only when they assign not just specific tasks but broad responsibilities to the people around them. Otherwise they'll find that they are still carrying the real weight of all the work, even if they're delegating specific tasks.

Jerry learned this lesson from Wendy Kopp, the founder of Teach For America. Like many other founders, when Wendy started the organization, she was on the hook for everything: she drove the fundraising, made sure the recruitment and training efforts were successful, oversaw the design of marketing materials, and on and on. She had people to help with each piece, but the real energy was coming from her and too much of the weight of responsibility was falling on her shoulders. Not surprisingly, this was exhausting for Wendy and, as she tells it, demoralizing for her staff.

Wendy came to realize that to better distribute the weight of ensuring Teach For America's success, she needed to have people truly in charge of each area of the organization and responsible for its progress. She needed a head of fundraising who would lie awake at night until she was sure the revenue would come in, she needed a head of programs to ensure that recruitment and training were top-notch, and she needed a head of communications to oversee marketing efforts.

As she set about doing this, Wendy made sure that staff roles were clear in each area and that each person had specific goals for what he or she would accomplish. Having staff members with well-defined roles and, in particular, clear, measurable goals became a key part of how Teach For America operated. To this day, they are an essential part of the organization's success.

In this chapter, we'll talk about how you can do what Wendy did: use roles and goals to distribute the responsibility across your team. We'll start by looking at how you can craft meaningful roles so that it's clear what each staff member is responsible for. Then we'll look at how you can use goals to describe what performing that role well will look like over a particular period of time. In doing so, you'll learn to hand off broad responsibilities so others can help drive significant pieces of your team or organization forward.

As you read this chapter, keep in mind that at their core, roles and goals are simply delegation writ more broadly. Instead of delegating a project or task, you're delegating broad responsibility but still using the same principles we set out in Chapter Two: setting expectations, engaging along the way, creating accountability and learning, and adapting all of these pieces to fit the context.

CREATING MEANINGFUL ROLES

Managers often define their staff members' roles in ways that use those staffers as helpers to the manager rather than giving them roles with real ownership. This leaves the manager bearing most of the emotional weight of ensuring the work is successful, including spotting what needs to be done and assigning the work, and leaves staff members feeling that they're responsible only for fielding the specific tasks the manager assigns.

This dynamic typically develops because managers craft roles that don't fully capture their expectations of what a great employee would do in the job. Instead, they tend to focus on specific activities like, "Check our inventory of supplies each month," instead of saying, "You're responsible for making sure everything runs smoothly."

By carving out more meaningful roles, you can transfer much of this weight and avoid having to identify, delegate, and manage every task that comes up. If you shift the weight of a role over to the staff member who holds that role, she should be the one responsible for obsessing over details and progress and driving the work forward, making her role more fulfilling and leaving you the time to focus more attention on other things (Figure 3.1).

To be concrete about this, one option is to create a one-page description of the role that considers both what the staff member should do and how she should approach her work:

The what: Each person on your team should be able to say what she is fundamentally responsible for. The traditional way to lay this out is in a bulleted list of responsibilities and tasks (in other words, a job description), ideally grouped in some

Before

After

FIGURE 3.1. *Handing Off Broad Responsibilities*

logical way. This can be a very helpful way to convey what's in your head about a particular role, but we're also fans of creating a memorable, overall "headline" for the work. After all, you're unlikely to think to include absolutely everything this person will do in your bulleted list, and you don't want your staff to think that if something is not listed, it's not their responsibility, so make sure you're clear on what the role is responsible for overall. For instance, the headline over your assistant's work might be "CEO of Ensuring That All Logistics Run Smoothly." (We like the "you are the CEO of . . ." construction as an easy way to communicate the essence of a role.)

The how: Since a written job description can never capture everything that will come up in the course of day-to-day work, you might also be explicit about how the staff member should approach her work, particularly if there are keys to success that are specific to the role. For instance, your role expectations for your assistant might include spotting and following up on new opportunities to increase efficiency or finding ways to make your days more effective. (To be clear, the how isn't about dictating the specific activities the staff member will use to do her work; instead, it's about the *approach* that you consider key to excelling in the role.)

Then, if your assistant knows the what and how of her job, you shouldn't need to ask her to check on that wire transfer or to be sure to get coffee for the afternoon meeting, because a great CEO of logistics is someone you can count on to handle those details without your needing to point them out. Moreover, that vision of the job is one that great candidates will be excited to sign up for!

Here are a few more points to keep in mind as you're creating meaningful roles for your staff:

- If you're overhauling the roles on your team or creating them anew, start by making a list of all the work that needs to be done, and then group it in logical buckets. Make sure that each category represents everything that needs to be covered, and try to avoid having any item in more than one bucket. Consultants call this idea MECE—mutually exclusive and completely exhaustive. That is, your division of labor should fully capture everything that needs to be done and not have overlap between areas.

- Think not just about grouping (the buckets of work) but also about linking (how the roles interact with each). While roles should be MECE, you don't want them to become closed-off silos where staff members never talk with each other. Consider what mechanisms will glue everything together to ensure people are cooperating and communicating to the extent needed (such as working groups, staff meetings, and e-mail groups).

- Establish clear, unambiguous lines of reporting. Dual reporting structures tend to cause confusion; instead, define a primary reporting line for each person. For management geeks: this means that if you're thinking about a matrix structure or dotted line reporting, you should ensure there's a solid line to one person who is fundamentally responsible for any given staff member's performance. For everyone: unambiguous lines of reporting means that you should not hide the fact that people in fact have managers. We recently encountered a client where the senior team was reluctant to tell the staff members that they had managers, even though there were clearly people responsible for hiring, supervising, evaluating, and firing them. Rather than feeling freed and empowered, the staff was confused and frustrated.

- Once you've captured what you expect from the role on paper, you can use this document in many places: incorporating pieces of it in job announcements, using it when orienting a new employee, pulling from it when conducting performance evaluations, and using it to capture expectations as they evolve.[1]

---

[1] Job announcements (what you use to advertise a job opening) are marketing tools to attract the right candidates, so they might be different from your internal job descriptions. Think about why your target candidate would be genuinely attracted to the role and make sure that comes across! You don't want to sugarcoat, of course, but you should sell the position and organization, showing candidates that the job is an incredible opportunity. While you'll of course capture the essence of the job, you might not need all of the nitty-gritty details.

EXECUTIVE ASSISTANT ROLE EXPECTATIONS

The "What"

Overall: You're the CEO of making sure everything runs smoothly!

Administration/operations: Office space is functional and everyone has what they need to do their jobs well

- Own all general/maintenance. Everything should be working well.
- Ensure we have appropriate space, layout, furniture, and supplies to do best work.
- Ensure all systems are working effectively (phones, Internet, mail, and so on).
- Support additional administrative needs of office (faxing, mailing, and PDFs, for example).

Calendar and internal meetings: Manage calendars and implement internal meeting structure

- Manage staff calendars to priorities (for example, surfacing questions, getting aligned on trade-offs, ensuring enough space and travel time).
- Implement internal meeting schedule (check-ins, monthly and quarterly step-backs, team step-backs).

Tech and systems: Technology is appropriate to meet the needs of a growing team and we have the systems in place and working to gather, share, and track information

- Ensure that all staff have the hardware and software they need for their work.
- Manage the e-mail vendor, and ensure we have capacity to handle e-mail demands.
- Ensure we have an appropriate data backup system and that it's working effectively.
- Spot opportunities to better track and maintain information.

Events and special projects: Own and help on other events and projects as needed

The "How": Keys to Success!

- *100 percent follow-through:* No dropped balls! Stay on top of all specific tasks and follow-up items and general areas of work; consistently meet deadlines.
- *Customer service orientation:* We're pretty busy here, and your job is to make it easy for staff to do their jobs. View your work as supporting the whole and integral to the team's effectiveness.
- *Attention to detail:* Everything going out (other than internal communication) is polished: accurate (for example, right content, no misspellings or grammatical errors) and precise (for example, reflects nuances, captures subtleties) and fits the situation (should have our "look and feel" generally but can be casual when the situation calls for it).
- *Positive attitude and flexibility*: Approach work with a spirit of yes; strike a positive tone; push work forward through obstacles and adapt quickly as things change, which they inevitably will.

GOOD ROLES SHIFT THE WEIGHT!

Some managers hesitate to truly shift the weight of a responsibility to a staff member because they rightly feel that they need to stay involved. But remember that MOCHA (from the previous chapter) allows you to stay involved as the M (manager), A (approver), or even H (helper), not the O (owner). By moving the ownership to your staff member, you move the weight but without bowing out entirely. Although your staff member is carrying the responsibility for the work, you'll stay engaged, monitoring progress, acting as a resource, and stepping in to correct the course if needed.

GOALS: ROLES PLAYED OUT OVER A DEFINED PERIOD OF TIME

Roles let you shift the burden of driving forward responsibilities that would otherwise fall to you. Goals are the next step in that process, making it clear what the staff member should accomplish in the role over a specific period of time. Put another way, while roles define the what and how of a staff member's responsibilities, goals define "how much."

After all, an executive director whose head of fundraising does not have a fundraising goal has essentially said, "Can you help me with fundraising?" But an executive director whose fundraising head has a goal of ensuring the organization raises $7.2 million this year has said, "You're responsible for making sure we raise our budget."

Goals, then, establish what success in a role looks like for a particular time period. For example, a development director might have goals like these:

- Increase fundraising revenue from $1.2 million last year to $1.6 million this year.

- Because they're key to our future growth, increase the number of individuals giving $5,000 or more from twelve to twenty-four.

Goals like these bring powerful benefits:

- *Alignment.* As you're transferring the weight of a responsibility, goals send clear signals about what is most important. For instance, in the example above, it should be clear to the development director that spending lots of time maximizing small-dollar donors is not a priority, since it is not one of the main goals.

- *Healthy urgency and tension.* Beyond being a tool for shifting weight, goals at their heart are an engine of progress. By setting goals that represent serious growth or impact, you make clear that you're not just going about the normal course of business, which is a recipe for mediocrity; you're striving to achieve more, and you instill a tension between the current state of affairs and where you're trying to get. (Management guru Peter Senge describes this as akin to the tension in a rubber band when it's extended.) Among the benefits this produces is a sense of urgency that permeates the organization and prevents distractions from creeping in. When a client comes to us complaining of internal "drama," one of the first questions we ask is, "What are these people's goals?" because we've found that when staff members are focused on reaching an ambitious goal, they rarely have time for drama.

- *Fresh thinking.* A related benefit of the urgency instilled by goals is the constant need to get better at what you're doing, which can lead to new thinking about tactics. For instance, in the example above, the ambitious goal of doubling the number of high-net-worth donors will require more than just incremental improvements; it will take serious thought to how to bring in more such donors.

- *Basis for accountability and reflection.* Setting clear targets against which success will be judged lays the groundwork to reflect on what went well and what could have been improved. It also establishes the basis for accountability, so that managers and staff alike know when someone has lived up to expectations and when they have fallen short.

- *Meaning and motivation.* The sense of accomplishment that comes from driving toward real progress makes most people's jobs more satisfying, which will help you attract and retain great people (as we'll discuss in Chapter Eight). For instance, the development director in the example might know that this year's growth is part of a three-year effort to reach a revenue base of $3 million, which would enable the organization to expand to other regions. What could otherwise seem a never-ending series of thankless tasks ("send a proposal to XYZ Foundation") becomes a path toward a broader purpose of expanding the organization's impact.

In the rest of this chapter, we'll discuss how to capture these benefits, first by describing the characteristics of an effective goal and then by discussing how you can set and use goals in practice.

SETTING SMART GOALS

While goals can confer powerful benefits, not all goals are created equal. Strong goals share a number of qualities, captured by the acronym SMART: strategic, measurable, ambitious, realistic, and time-bound.

Before we take a closer look at this, we want to warn you: some of what follows may look a little daunting at first. But know that every time you and your team go through the process of setting goals, things will get a little easier and a little more natural. So don't let the perfect be the enemy of the good. The important thing is to put clear goals in place and begin capturing their benefits, and then you can keep improving them over time.

Strategic

Goals are strategic when they reflect the most important dimensions of what the person responsible for them seeks to accomplish. Although this sounds obvious, we frequently see staff members set lofty sounding goals that don't actually reflect their most important work. For instance, we recently met with a client who manages the head of finance for her organization and was reviewing the finance head's goals. We asked the client to turn the draft goals over so she couldn't look at them and then asked her to tell us what she most wanted the finance head to accomplish in the coming year. Without hesitation, she told us that the most important thing was for the finance head to provide quick and accurate revenue and expense information to help shape the organization's decision making as it shifted resources from one area to another. We then turned the paper over and saw that the finance head's goals related to things like increasing the speed with which the finance department paid its bills. This was a classic case of reasonable-sounding goals that were not strategic.

In addition to reflecting the most important work of a team or individual, goals that are strategic are aligned at every level of the organization. Individual staff members have goals that add up to the department's goals, and department heads have goals that add up to the most important organizational priorities. Goals whose underlying objective is not connected in one way or another to the broad direction of the organization are not strategic and should be discarded.

Measurable

Consider the difference between an aspiring athlete who says, "I want to get in shape," versus one who says, "By the end of the year, I will be able to run six miles in under an hour." The former is a wish, the latter a commitment. Effective goals produce that sort of commitment by creating a clear finish line—a way to judge whether the goal has been attained.

What if your goals are hard to measure?

The easiest way for a goal to be measurable is for it to be quantitative, as in the runner example, but that doesn't always need to be the case. Coming to a qualitative agreement about what success looks like can be an extraordinarily powerful tool for managers when success is hard to quantify, as it often is in the nonprofit context.

A COMMON PITFALL: CONFUSING DATA WITH GOALS

Your team members might track a wide variety of data. Remember, though, that collecting data on something does not in and of itself make it a goal you should be managing to. For instance, it might be smart for your head of communications to look at your monthly Web site traffic to inform your strategies. That doesn't mean, though, that she should be expending effort to increase that traffic unless that is an explicit and deliberate aim that makes sense.

The trick in creating qualitative goals is to tap into the instinct that you would know success when you see it and to articulate the specifics beneath that instinct. For instance, an advocacy director's goal might be to generate significant attention to the organization's issue during a congressional campaign. The director might word the goal this way: "Our issue will become a salient issue in the congressional campaign, meaning that it will be included prominently in candidate materials, questions will be asked about it in debates and town hall meetings, candidates will mention it in ads and at events, and polls will show it among the top ten issues on voters' minds." Or your conference organizer might make one of her goals to "flawlessly execute our regional conference to present a highly professional image of Citizens for a Better World, provide high-quality training sessions that keep attendees engaged, ensure that all sessions and logistics run smoothly, and receive at least 90 percent positive feedback on evaluation forms from both presenters and participants." This is largely qualitative, but it still establishes a bar for expectations.

Activities Versus Outcomes

Measurability also raises questions about what exactly should be measured: activities or outcomes?[2] For instance, the advocacy director of a health care organization might set goals around activities and outcomes, such as the number of meetings held with legislators (activity) and the number of legislators who agree to support a bill (outcome). Activities tend to be easier to measure, and there is a direct correlation between the staff member's efforts and the metric. With outcomes, it can be harder to attribute the result to the staff member's effort. In this example, target legislators might decide to support the bill, but for reasons having little to do with the group's efforts.

Nonetheless, effective managers do push to set goals around outcomes whenever feasible. By doing this, they are articulating an answer to not just, "What do I want you to do?" but more fundamentally, "What do I want you to achieve?" When everyone within an organization is clear on the answer to this second question, they are free to think of new ways to approach problems. Continuing with the congressional example, if the staff member is clear that the real goal is to get eight legislators to support the bill, she might think of better ways to make that happen than holding direct meetings (perhaps persuading large campaign contributors to place calls instead, for instance). In this way, outcome-oriented goals can be an antidote to micromanagement because they let the manager and the staff member focus on what the result should be, with the staff member's job then being to figure out the best way to get there.

---

[2]For the sake of space and our readers' sanity, we've simplified a broader spectrum of terms that you may hear about. Most commonly, the full range goes from *inputs* ("spend $5,000 on publications") to *activities* ("write monthly e-mail updates") to *outputs* ("e-mail updates sent to 12,000 people each month") to *outcomes* ("at least $25,000 in donations generated by our e-mails") to *impacts* ("successful advocacy efforts in three states funded"). Of these, the most commonly used—and, we believe, the most useful—refer to activities and outcomes.

THE POWER OF GOALS

Specific and measurable goals are far more likely to be adhered to than more general ones. As *Time* magazine's Sanjay Gupta reported, "Investigators at Berlin's Free University found that people who set general goals, like 'I will exercise in my free time,' did a far worse job of sticking to that plan than people who made a firm commitment, like 'I will walk to my friend's house and back every Monday, Wednesday, and Friday.'" ("Stuck on the Couch," *Time*, February 22, 2008.)

Ambitious

While measurability means that goals must contain a clear finish line, "ambitious" here means that the finish line must represent significant progress. Goals should not simply be predictive, laying out what the staff member would be likely to achieve that year if she simply did what she always does.

Stretch goals—those that require staff members to reach far in terms of effort and tactics—can drive enormous progress within an organization. For instance, with the health care organization, if the advocacy director currently had secured the support of just three legislators, then a goal of adding fifteen more within a year might be a stretch goal. The director would need to focus significant energy here, leaving little room for distraction and requiring smart thinking about how to get there.

The habit of setting ambitious stretch goals is one of the key practices that distinguishes high-performing individuals and organizations. While others might go about the ordinary course of business each year, perhaps making incremental progress, organizations where staff members must think about how much progress is possible and set ambitious goals reflecting an aggressive sense of possibility often make dramatically more progress.

> "Why do we set goals? Because we take ourselves seriously."
>
> BLAKE DE PASTINO, EXECUTIVE EDITOR, AMERICAN INDEPENDENT NEWS NETWORK

Staff members who set stretch goals often worry about the consequences of not reaching them. The answer is more art than science because there is a delicate balance between rewarding risk and ambition, on the one hand, and ensuring that staff members take goals seriously, on the other. When a staff member sets a goal representing dramatic progress, there needs to be an implicit understanding that the task is difficult. Even in failing to meet the goal, the staff member could make significant progress, which merits reward rather than rebuke. At the same time, failure to meet a goal should cause reflection on what could be done differently going forward, and a pattern of failing to meet goals over time should be cause for concern.

From an external perspective, leaders might also fear that funders will cut support if goals aren't met. The key here is to communicate with your funders directly, perhaps flagging from the start that a goal is particularly ambitious so that you correctly set expectations. Ultimately, though, fear of what your funders might think should not deter you from setting ambitious goals. In our experience, funders are more likely to reward you if you make significant progress, and ambitious goals help you do that.

Realistic

At the same time that you want your people to have ambitious goals, implicit in the idea of taking those goals seriously is that they cannot be so ambitious that they simply represent wishful thinking; goals, in other words, must be more than purely aspirational. The best goals lie just at the intersection of ambitious and realistic (Figure 3.2). When goals are not realistic, staff members do not commit themselves to meeting them. The staff might mouth the words of the goal, but deep down they will not have decided to do whatever it takes to reach it, which is the type of commitment leaders need from their teams.

Making goals realistic has several important implications.

Goals Must Have Plans Behind Them

Setting a goal, especially a stretch goal, generally makes sense only if staff members have at least some sense of how they might reach it. Without that understanding, the goal is more of a wish than a commitment. So as goals are being developed, part of

Extremely Challenging

Ambitious

Bingo!

Realistic

Extremely Easy

FIGURE 3.2. *The Intersection of Ambitious and Realistic*

the conversation must be what tactics the staff member envisions using to achieve them. For instance, when setting annual fundraising goals at Teach For America, the directors of the local offices submitted plans showing a realistic list of potential sources of funds. No director would be able to set a goal of raising $1 million without demonstrating a realistic path to get there. Of course, your staff member's tactics may change during the year as she reacts to new developments and adapts her plans. But the important thing is to have thought through a plausible road map and had meaningful discussion about it before solidifying a goal. (We address plans more fully at the end of this section.)

Goals May Need to Represent Interim Progress

Particularly in advocacy work, sometimes the only realistic outcomes are interim ones. An advocacy director might have the long-term goal of getting a housing bill passed through the state legislature, but for this year, her realistic (but still ambitious) goal might be to get the desired bill out of committee in the state house or perhaps endorsed by the leading candidates for governor. These are still outcome goals because they capture the result of the organization's activities and not just the activities themselves, but they represent interim progress toward a longer-term end.

Sometimes Goals May Need to Change

In general, managers should be reluctant to change goals during the course of the year, because once a target is established, the team should commit to doing everything to reach that target. However, extraordinary circumstances may make reaching a goal impossible, in which case a leader would change the goal. For instance, an organization's advocacy director might have an ambitious agenda this year, but if a high-profile event, such as a major disaster, dramatically shifts the public's focus, she might have to recognize that significant progress this year isn't going to happen, regardless of her efforts. She might instead focus on laying the groundwork for the future, perhaps building a cadre of committed "grasstops" (that is, high-level) leaders who would speak on behalf of the issue next year.

Account for Unknown Variables

Don't get hung up on the presence of unknown variables in your goals. For instance, your regional director and her team might be engaged in state-level fights in eight states. She might reasonably argue that she will need to react to developments in the states to decide where to focus her efforts, so she cannot set meaningful goals specifying exactly how much progress will happen in each state. You and she might agree, though, that a successful year would include making significant progress in four states. Her goal then might be, "Of the following eight states, make significant progress in six."

Measurability Should Not Become a Project unto Itself

Being realistic about goals means examining not just the content of the goals themselves, but also the energy needed to measure them. Your advocacy director might decide that in an ideal world, she would set goals for the total number of activities that your grassroots members engage in: attending meetings, writing letters to the editor, selling tickets to fundraisers, and so on. She might, though, decide that the energy it would take to keep tabs on every member activity would be prohibitive and that a reasonable, more easily tracked proxy for total activity would be the number of members who attend meetings. In some cases, devoting significant energy to assessing progress toward a goal might make sense, but managers should use their judgment about how much effort is merited. In the end, your people should devote tracking energy appropriate to the importance of each goal, but not more.

Time-Bound

Being time-bound simply means that goals should contain not just a clear finish line, but also a deadline for reaching it. For instance, the goal, "Increase the number of donors giving at least $5,000 per year from fifteen to eighteen," should be accompanied by "before the end of our fiscal year" or "by June 15." In most organizations, goals are set annually, so the time is at least implicitly a twelve-month window. In situations where there's not necessarily a natural cycle (as there might be, say, with a school year), we've sometimes seen clients make faster progress by setting goals covering shorter periods, like six months.

Whatever the time period, once you have agreed on final goals, also ask your team members to establish milestones for interim progress, so that you and they will know throughout the year whether they are on track toward meeting their goals. There are two types of milestones:

- *Milestones that directly measure interim progress toward a goal.* For instance, if your development director's goal is to raise $100,000, she might agree that to be on track, she needs to raise $20,000 by March, $50,000 by June, and $75,000 by October.

- *Activity-based milestones.* Sometimes the only useful milestones are about completing activities rather than actual outcomes. For instance, your organization might receive the vast majority of its contributions in December, so your development director might not know how many people will end up contributing until the start of the new year. She might, then, set activity-based milestones, like having at least three "friendraisers" by July 1 and having follow-up meetings with fifteen donors by October 1.

What a SMART Goal Look Likes in Practice

Here's an example of a SMART goal with milestones for a training director:

Goal: Train 1,000 Student Leaders by December 31

Milestone 1: Develop an effective training manual and materials by February 1.

Milestone 2: Confirm partnerships with two national student organizations by March 1.

Milestone 3: Train 500 students by July 1.

Milestone 4: Complete new student outreach by September 20.

Milestone 5: Train 1,000 students by December 1.

And here's an example of a SMART goal for a chief operating officer in a context where measurability requires the use of a qualitative definition describing "how we'll know it when we see it":

> *Goal:* By March 31, all "low-performing" staff will have raised their performance significantly or left (with "low performers" defined as staff who only sometimes meet goals and rarely exceed them, who do not demonstrate our core values, and/or who would be relatively easy to replace with someone as good if they left).

How Many Goals Are Too Many?

In general, the number of goals for a person or department should be in the rough range of three to five. Going slightly over this (say, to eight) isn't a disaster, but having way too many (we've seen organizations in which one person will have thirty-two significant goals for the year) means that you can't truly focus on many of them.

In fact, having just a single, clear, overriding goal can be incredibly powerful. For instance, your development director might have several goals around adding new major donors, raising a certain amount from an event, and so forth, but ultimately you want her to be obsessing over a single bottom-line goal for dollars raised during the year.

In cases where a person does have multiple goals, consider indicating their relative weight. For instance, you might decide that while broadly educating the public on your issue is a goal, it represents only 10 percent of success for the year, and getting your curriculum adopted by a majority of school districts in your state is worth 60 percent and thus much more important.

> "If you can't tell me what your goals are without looking at a piece of paper, then you don't have real goals."
>
> JON COWAN, PRESIDENT, THIRD WAY

Goals Makeover

Take a look at how these goals were made over into SMART goals:

Before: Work with activists to build grassroots support for health care reform.

After: We will have quality grassroots activists (meaning they respond to the vast majority of our requests, they can articulate our messages, and they come off as "normal" people) working in twenty of our twenty-five targeted states by June.

Before: Manage publications schedule.

After: Ninety percent of our mailings and publications will be issued on time, and 100 percent will meet our quality guidelines.

Before: Maximize the amount of earned media coverage that includes our messages.

After: At least one-third of news stories on all major, national events related to our issue will have included our perspective. In addition, we will get an average of at least three letters to the editor published each month, reaching an average of at least 300,000 readers (based on average circulation) per month.

What About Plans?

Goals answer the questions, "What are we trying to accomplish?" and "How will we know whether we accomplished it?" Plans answer the question, "How will we get there?"

As we noted in Chapter Two, the basic ingredients for a good plan are:

* The key activities needed to reach desired goals

* A timeline for when those activities will take place

* An assignment of responsibility for each step

Put more succinctly, plans establish *who will do what by when.* Within those broad outlines, plans can take a variety of forms. In many cases, managers establish a high-level plan for the year, laying out the main tactics they plan to pursue and when they will implement them. A year is a long time to plan for, though, so many of our clients create annual plans to articulate general initiatives around their goals and then rely on quarterly plans for the specifics. For instance, a development director's annual plan might include the general tactic, "Expand circle of high-net-worth donors by convincing current donors to host friendraisers for us." Her quarterly plan, then, would be more specific: "By February 15, Joanna meets with Alan, Robin, and Marty to see whether they'll host events for us."

HOW TO CREATE GOALS

Let's now look at how you can develop and use goals. As with delegation, the key is to agree clearly on the expectations from the start and stay engaged to increase the chances of success and create accountability and learning at the end.

Lay Out a Timeline

Depending on the size of your team, there may be a lot of moving pieces to consider in a goal-setting process, so creating a timeline will help you keep the process on track. (See Tool 3.1 for an example of how this might work.) Your timeline should leave plenty of time for discussion between you and your staff members (and among staff members as well).

Engage Intensively

As your staff members propose their goals and tactics, you should engage rigorously to test their thinking, ensure the goals truly are SMART, and challenge the assumptions underlying them. For instance, if your development director proposes a goal of 50 percent growth in annual revenue, you'll want to understand what she will do that is different from prior years to produce that growth before you sign off on the goal. Without a plan to reach the target, the goal is merely wishful thinking and thus fails the "realistic" piece of SMART. Similarly, let's say your development director proposes a goal to increase the number of people who donate fifty dollars over the Internet. You, however, think the energy should be going to high-net-worth donors, so the two of you need to work that out. A significant part of the power of goals, in fact, comes not from the final words on the page but rather from the process of alignment that results from real discussion around what you expect your staff members to accomplish.

See Tool 3.2 for a useful goal-setting worksheet.

USING GOALS THROUGHOUT THE YEAR: TRACKING AND STAYING ENGAGED

Once goals have been created, they can be either an incredibly powerful tool for managers or an empty bureaucratic exercise that sits on a shelf gathering dust. To be meaningful, goals need to shape the regular course of business.

Managers and Staff Members Should Refer to Goals Regularly

All staffers should refer to the goals for which they're responsible on a regular basis. Ideally, at the end of each week, they review their own goals, consider what they need to do to remain on track, and then shape their plans for the following week to accomplish those tasks. Perhaps more realistically, as the manager, you can declare that at one meeting a month with each of your staff members, the two of you will look at the staff member's goals and assess the extent to which things are on track. (Chapter Five discusses how to conduct these monthly meetings.)

Managers Should Engage Meaningfully to Assess Progress

The best managers ask probing questions to get beneath the surface so that they can truly understand how things are progressing. For instance, instead of asking a simple, "Are things on track?" a manager might ask, "Can you review for me how you're moving forward in getting us established in Arkansas? What indicators do we have of whether we're on track? How many active members do we have so far? What are you worried about?" By using goals as the basis for regular conversations, managers can ensure their teams stay focused on what everyone has agreed is most important and can work with their teams to evaluate what's working and adapt tactics as needed.

Just as with delegation, in addition to asking good questions and looking at data on progress toward goals, managers should also see how broad priorities are actually

MANAGERS PLAY THE CRITICAL ROLE Throughout the process of creating and using goals, their success or failure will hinge on how well you as the manager use them. If you give goals only a cursory look when they are proposed, do not refer to them in the regular course of business, and do not hold your staff members accountable for meeting them, they may well be nothing more than a bureaucratic hassle. If, however, you reinforce their importance throughout the process, you will find that your staffers pursue them vigorously, taking on more and more ownership and freeing you to focus on new and higher-impact work.

playing out. For instance, if your IT department has a goal of providing same-day solutions to staffers' technical problems, you might sit in on some conversations between the IT staff and end users to observe the work in action. Or if your development staff has a goal of prompt, friendly answers to member inquiries, you might look through some of the member e-mails they've received and the replies they've sent. As with delegation, the aim is to shrink the implementation gap between plan and reality—between what you intend to make happen and what actually happens.

ASSESSING PERFORMANCE AGAINST GOALS: CREATING ACCOUNTABILITY

It sounds obvious, but too few organizations put it into practice: the extent to which your staff members achieve their goals should be an important component of their performance evaluations. We like to see managers evaluate their staff members on both what they did—that is, whether they achieved their goals and produced strong results—as well as how they did it. Frequently in the nonprofit world we've seen evaluations that focus only on the how component, commenting on whether a staff member collaborated well, showed up for work on time, or demonstrated particular skills. The how part does matter, but it should not overshadow the what. And if you want your staff to really work to achieve their goals, you must hold them accountable for the extent to which they succeed at that. (See the sample performance evaluations in Chapter Seven.) One specific implication of this is that if you set goals on a calendar-year cycle, your evaluations should happen around that cycle as well. We frequently see organizations with goals based on the calendar year but evaluations based on service anniversaries or dates of hire, which makes it next to impossible to include an assessment of whether staff members have actually met their goals for a given time period. (We realize that if you're not the executive director, this timing may not be up to you, so we encourage you to show this passage to your executive director or head of HR.)

Accountability for achievement of goals (or lack thereof) should include a learning component as well. By stepping back with your staff to assess their performance against goals, you can discuss why they succeeded or fell short, and you can work with them to draw lessons that will inform the pursuit of their goals in the next cycle.

GOALS AT THE ORGANIZATIONAL LEVEL

If you're leading an entire organization, setting goals for what the organization as a whole will accomplish can be as powerful a device as it is at the individual level. In fact, there's no conceptual difference between organizational goals and goals for an individual. Many of your organizational goals might in practice be goals owned by specific individuals. For instance, your overall fundraising goal might rise to the level of an organizational goal, but ultimately your development director might be responsible for it. (See Tool 3.3 for sample organizational goals.)

Just as with goals for individuals, you should have a relatively small number of goals for the organization as a whole that capture the most important work for a given time period. As with individuals, one way to think of good organizational goals is to answer the question, "If we accomplish nothing else, what would we need to achieve for this year to be successful?" Given that, you don't want to establish thirty organizational goals. Finding the most important three to five goals can be incredibly powerful. These goals often fall into two main areas: programmatic priorities, which are goals directly connected to the organization's mission, and capacity-building priorities, such as fundraising, staffing, or technology.

In order for your organizational goals to be strategic, they need to represent the broad direction of the organization. Organizations differ in how they establish this. Many engage in formal strategic planning processes in which they lay out a three- to five-year vision for where they want to be and how they plan to get there. Others might skip the full strategic plan but still establish longer-term goals—say, for three years— articulating how much progress they want to make. Finally, other organizations might feel they operate under so much uncertainty that setting longer-term aims is meaningless and may not look beyond more than one year.

In establishing organizational goals, consider these three components:

- *Process.* One way to think of organizational goals is to consider them the executive director's own goals, which they essentially are. In the same way a department head would create goals by taking the lead but involving her team, so too should the executive director create goals by driving the process but involving her staff. And since the executive director is the ultimate owner of the organizational goals, she should look at them frequently, assessing progress toward them and determining any additional steps that are needed. To ensure her team is fully invested in the goals as well, she might also make the organizational goals the basis for periodic step-backs with her management team.

- *Timing.* Organizations should align the goal-setting process with their budgeting process, since goals should inform decisions about resource allocation.

GOAL SETTING FOR START-UPS   If your organization is a start-up in its first year or two, is in a particularly "entrepreneurial" (read: chaotic) phase, or is in the midst of a fast-moving campaign, you might be operating in an environment that's changing quickly and you're still sorting out how you'll make the biggest impact. In that case, you might consider modifying your approach to goal setting in the following ways:

- Set and review progress against goals on a shorter cycle (every three or six months or even every month, depending on your context). Establish regular review meetings and simple tracking systems to support this faster cycle.

- Since you're operating with greater uncertainty, embrace subjective criteria for goals such as, "Maximize opportunities that come at us to . . ."

- If you're in an intensive building stage, your goals might focus more on activities than outcomes for the first year or two (for instance, "Get Web site up and running by November" versus "Build Web site into a hub that generates 20,000 hits a month").

- Recognize that shifts in goals may happen, but make the shifts explicit. Don't allow them to just happen on their own, and be sure to distinguish between distractions and true changes in direction that require adjusting your targets.

- *Accountability.* As with individual goals, there should be accountability around whether the organization as a whole meets its goals. One of the best ways to ensure this is through reporting to the board and to funders, both of whom can hold the organization and its leaders accountable. In the case of the board, an assessment of the organization's progress against its goals should form a significant part of the executive director's annual evaluation. Funders, of course, make up their own minds about whether the organization made significant progress toward goals, and act accordingly. Executive directors can create accountability internally as well by publicly sharing their assessments of progress with staff and openly discussing their thoughts on how the organization might improve in the future. And depending on the results, executive directors can also ensure that their organizations celebrate accomplishments, a critical step too often neglected in the rush to begin pursuing goals for the next cycle.

MISSION STATEMENTS

Whether or not your organizational goals are grounded in a longer-term plan, setting goals and managing to them presumes you know what broader end they're for: what your organization is trying to accomplish. That's where your organization's mission statement comes in.

If you've ever seen meaningless mission statements posted on walls ("Our mission is to delight our customers" hanging behind the counter of the local deli with the rude wait staff), you might approach the idea of mission statements with a bit of cynicism. We've found, though, that getting clear on your organization's fundamental purpose—its reason for being—can be incredibly powerful. For instance, one of our clients has struggled because half of his staff thinks the organization's fundamental purpose is to deliver a product, while the other half thinks the purpose is to train the people who deliver the product. That basic lack of alignment plays out on a daily basis in tension over how to prioritize activities.

What makes for a good mission statement? People approach this differently, but in our view, a mission statement should be a concise, action-oriented statement of your organization's fundamental purpose. The best mission statements we've seen begin with a verb (like *reduce* or *protect* or *make*) and then a description of the problem the organization leaders want to address or the conditions they want to foster—for instance:

- Make quality, affordable health services available to all Americans.

- Protect the rights of women to make safe and informed reproductive choices.

- Confront and end national and global cruelties to animals.

As a leader, you should use your mission statement constantly. When you describe what you do in your literature or to someone new, your mission statement should be a standard refrain, so that everyone has a shared, fundamental understanding of what you're about. And in deciding whether to take on major new streams of work for the organization, the first question you ask should be, "Does this advance our mission?" Fundamentally your mission should be the compass you steer by.

Once they've defined their fundamental purpose, organizations sometimes then add on a statement of strategies, which explains how they will go about achieving their purpose. For instance, the mission statement of the National Gay and Lesbian Task Force is "to build the political power of the lesbian, gay, bisexual and transgender (LGBT) community from the ground up [purpose]. We do this by training activists, organizing broad-based campaigns to defeat anti-LGBT referenda and advance pro-LGBT legislation, and by building the organizational capacity of our movement [strategy]."

SUMMING UP: EXPECTATIONS, ENGAGEMENT, AND ACCOUNTABILITY WRIT LARGE

Meaningful roles help you delegate fundamental responsibilities, and goals help you set clear expectations for what you want to see accomplished. Checking in on progress against the goals is your way of staying engaged, so that you maximize the possibility of success. Creating accountability around the extent to which your team meets its goals reinforces the importance of the goals and begins setting expectations for the next cycle. Simple, no?

KEY POINTS

• Meaningful roles fully capture expectations of what a great employee would do in the job, thereby shifting the weight of responsibility for success in a particular area over to the employee who holds that role, keeping the manager from having to identify, delegate, and manage every task that comes up.

• Roles define the what and how of a staff member's responsibilities, and goals define the "how much."

• SMART goals are strategic, measurable, ambitious, realistic, and time-bound.

• Goals should measure outcomes rather than activities whenever possible.

• To be effective, goals must be used in the normal course of business throughout the year. Staff should check them regularly, managers should hold regular meetings to check on progress, and executive directors should be deeply committed to doing everything possible to meet them.

• Goals should be aligned with other organizational processes, such as annual budgeting and personnel evaluations.

• Executive directors can use goals to set broad priorities and steer the direction of the organization.

Additional Reading

James C. Collins and Jerry I. Porras, *Built to Last: Successful Habits of Visionary Companies* (New York: HarperCollins, 1997), especially "Big Hairy Audacious Goals" (pp. 91–114).

David La Piana, *Nonprofit Strategy Revolution: Real-Time Strategic Planning in a Rapid-Response World* (New York: Turner Publishing, 2008).

TOOL 3.1

SAMPLE GOAL DEVELOPMENT PROCESS

This sample goal development process serves as a guide to help you design your organization's own process. The exact steps, dates, and duration for each phase will depend on your organization's size, its previous experience with setting goals, and the existence of a longer-term strategic plan, if any, that sets out priorities. The example here assumes an organization operating on a calendar-year cycle of January 1 to December 31.

I. Set Timeline

- Executive director (ED) drafts rough timeline for setting next year's goals (aligning them with budget cycle and performance evaluations) and shares with senior management team. (Aug. 20)

II. Identify Organizational Priorities Based on Broad Strategic Direction

[This phase may be substantially shortened or skipped if your organization has an existing strategic direction or plan (formal or informal) from which it can easily derive the upcoming year's priorities.]

- In one meeting or more, ED and department heads discuss and ultimately agree on a list of initiatives and areas of focus for the coming year, and identify high-level implications for each department. (Sept. 10–20)

III. Develop Departmental Goals and Plans

- With general organizational priorities in mind, department heads brainstorm on their own or with their teams to reflect on past year's progress and identify potential areas of focus for the year ahead. (Sept. 25)
- Department heads meet individually with ED to discuss department's progress from prior year, lessons learned, and goals for the year ahead. (Sept. 28–Oct. 10)
- Department heads take ED input and draft actual goals for the year ahead, getting further input from team members as desired, and ensuring goals are backed up by plans. Department heads send draft to ED.
- ED drafts goals and plans for any areas for which ED is directly responsible. (Oct. 20)
- Department heads and ED meet to review draft goals and plans. (Oct. 25–Nov. 5)
- Department heads make any revisions and send final version to ED. (Nov. 7)

IV. Finalize Key Organizational Goals

- ED pulls from departmental and own plan to create summary goals document, reflecting key areas of organizational focus for the year ahead. ED ensures key goals collectively add up to desired organizational progress toward strategic direction. (Nov. 10)

- ED discusses proposed final draft of organization's goals with board of directors. Board approves final draft (as is or with changes). (Dec. 1)

V. Create Individual Action Plans

- Department heads direct staff to draft individual goals and short-term action plans based on departmental goals and action plans. (Nov. 15–30)

Individual goals will become part of each staff member's performance evaluation.

- Department heads meet with individual staff to refine individual goals and action plans and ensure teams collectively cover areas of departmental responsibility. (Dec. 3–13)
- Department heads meet with staff for performance evaluations covering prior year. (Dec. 10–23)

VI. Roll Out Organizational Goals and Action Plans

- ED convenes full staff for meeting to discuss goals for the year ahead. One-page version of organization's key goals distributed in hard copy for easy posting and reference. (Dec. 5)

Potential funders will love the fact that you have meaningful goals.

- Development Director highlights organization's top goals in holiday fundraising drive. (Dec. 8–31)

TOOL 3.2

SAMPLE SUCCESS SHEET: SETTING GOALS

What will make this a great year?

Goals for This Year	Last Year Result (If Any)	Key Tactics (Emphasize New/ Improved)
Add at least 20,000 new subscribers to our e-mail list.	8,000	Promote list on Web site and on printed materials. Add a sign-up box to online action thank-you page.
Build relationships with key bloggers, so that we have at least 5 national, well-read bloggers we can call on for coverage.	NA	Identify 10 targets by Feb. 1.

Questions for Discussion

1. Are the goals ambitious enough? Do they represent significant progress?

2. How realistic are these goals? Do you have real plans to achieve them? Will the tactics listed be sufficient to drive the growth we'd need?

3. If we achieved these goals, would this be a successful year? Do they capture what we most care about?

4. Other questions we should discuss?

Reasonable people should be able to agree on whether you met your goal, so you should paint a clear finish line with numbers or qualitative descriptors—for instance, "get in shape" is not particularly measurable, but "lose five pounds" or even "develop six-pack abs" is. Also, rather than setting goals annually, you might use a shorter cycle, like every three or six months.

TOOL 3.3
SAMPLE ORGANIZATIONAL GOALS

State Health Care Now
January to December 2012

PRIORITY 1: Create significant traction for universal coverage legislation

- Goal 1: By Dec. 31, universal state health coverage bill introduced in one chamber with public support of either key committee chair or leadership.
- Goal 2: By Dec. 31, secure commitment of at least 75 percent of declared governor candidates to include universal state coverage in campaign platform.

PRIORITY 2: Intensify and broaden grassroots support

- Goal 1: By Dec. 31, quick grassroots response created (for three major calls to action, an average of at least 6,000 grassroots supporters contact state representatives and senators).
- Goal 2: By Dec. 15, 10 percent of existing (in database as of Jan. 1) grassroots supporters are "super activists," as defined by having forwarded each action alert to at least ten friends or having organized an in-person mobilization event such as a house party.

PRIORITY 3: Raise profile of state health care crisis in the media

- Goal 1: By Dec. 31, at least one major national media hit (estimated viewership or readership of 1 million or more) and at least five minor (state or regional) media hits generated.
- Goal 2: By July 31, editorial support received from at least one of the three major regional daily papers.

> *You should have only a few (ideally four to six) primary goals in order to focus your staff's efforts.*

PRIORITY 4: Strengthen our financial sustainability

- Goal 1: By Dec. 31, a total of at least $1,850,000 raised, including $1,600,000 in general support.
- Goal 2: By Dec. 31, 70 percent of 2006 donors renewed at same giving level or higher.

> *You should have long-term capacity-building goals in addition to programmatic ones.*

PRIORITY 5: Build strong staff and culture of performance

- Goal 1: All open positions filled by June 30.
- Goal 2: By Dec. 31, 90 percent of staff identified as high performers at start of year have committed to stay another year, and all staff identified as low or midperformers have raised performance significantly, are in the midst of performance improvement plans, or have left.

CHAPTER

4

MANAGING THE "IN-BETWEEN"
Building a Culture of Excellence

Up to now, we've addressed how to set and reinforce expectations so your staff can succeed on the specific tasks they take on and the broad responsibilities they are given. Along the way, though, whether as part of those assignments or just in the course of day-to-day business, your staff will perform thousands of activities that you may never see or even know about, from greeting visitors with a friendly smile rather than a curt, "Follow me," to making sure that e-mails to important stakeholders are typo free. Just as in other areas, here too you need to make sure staff members are clear about your expectations. In this case, your expectations are as much about how people operate as about what they do. The way you set those expectations is by creating and reinforcing a strong culture.

Culture is the invisible force that tells people "how we do things around here."

Culture is the invisible force that transmits messages about "how we do things around here." If you're wrestling with feeling that you have to tell your staff exactly how to handle every situation or aren't confident that they'll perform well in your absence, culture is likely the culprit—and the solution.

Whether you're managing a single team or an entire organization, culture is a powerful tool for shaping how staff members get work done. And whether you shape it deliberately or not, your team *will* have a culture, so the real issue is whether that culture is sending the kinds of signals you want it to.

This chapter looks at the kind of culture you might aim to create, how you shape and reinforce it, and how you hold people accountable for acting in accord with it.

ELEMENTS OF HIGH-PERFORMING CULTURES

First, let's talk about what you should be aiming for in your culture. Although no two cultures will be identical, we've been struck by how often we see the same elements on high-performing teams run by the best managers. These cultures blend a deep rigor about results with broadly shared engagement and positive energy.

Rigor and Engagement

Both of these elements, rigor and engagement, are essential. Cultures that emphasize rigor and accountability without positive engagement may get grudging compliance from their staff members, but they lack the spirit of possibility that can dramatically drive work forward. And because leaders in cultures that emphasize positive feelings over results don't push people to do better than they otherwise might, don't fire low performers, and don't make hard decisions that might be unpopular, they miss opportunities, and their organizations grow ineffective. High-performing organizations bring both elements to their work: a rigorous focus on results and positive engagement.

Here are some of the components that make up each of those elements:

Rigorous Focus on Results

- *Relentlessness.* High-performing managers run processes smoothly, but what they care most about is concrete achievement. When they're not getting the results they want, they persist until they do.

- *A high bar for performance.* In teams determined to make an impact, performance standards are high. There's often a sense that "not just anyone can work here," and employees know that the manager expects great, not merely good, performance.

- *Scrutiny of ideas.* That same high bar is brought to scrutiny of ideas. Regardless of the source, suggestions for improvement or new initiatives are subjected to rigorous examination and debate, rather than being allowed to take effect simply because the boss, or a junior staffer, brings them up.

- *Accountability.* On high-performing teams, staffers know that they need to follow through on commitments (that is, nothing just disappears) and that they'll be held accountable for their work. If they do a mediocre job on a project, they'll need to redo it.

- *Transparency and commitment to continuous improvement.* Because they're determined to be successful, high-performing managers are fairly ruthless when it comes to identifying ways their teams could perform better, and they put a premium on being open about their flaws so they can search for ways to improve. They're generally obsessive about learning from experience, incorporating lessons into practice, and adapting their approach to make it as effective as possible.

- *Mission integrity.* Leaders are focused on the actual impact of their work, not appearances. Their goals represent what they truly believe would be meaningful progress rather than just predicting results that would have come about regardless of the organization's actions. For instance, one high-performing organization we know had a goal of recruiting progressive candidates for local office. It wouldn't permit itself to count toward that goal candidates who likely would have emerged on their own, even though listing them might impress funders.

Positive Engagement

- *A shared sense of ownership.* Staff members feel deeply invested in the direction of the organization and assume responsibility for helping it succeed. They suggest ideas for how the organization could improve and serve as effective ambassadors for the organization because they feel it is partly theirs.

- *Positive energy.* Staff members are enthusiastic about their work and genuinely enjoy tackling the challenges that come with it. The overall mood in the organization is positive.

- *Teamwork and low drama.* There's a sense that everyone is working toward a common goal. People operate with cooperation and goodwill toward their colleagues, and unconstructive interpersonal conflict is discouraged. We love this story from Alyssa Mastromonaco, who was the director of scheduling and advance on the 2008 Obama campaign, which was well known for having relatively low drama. Shortly after she started working on the campaign, she became noticeably irritated at a colleague on a conference call. Right afterward, a campaign leader dropped by her office and told her, "This is a campaign where you need to respect other people's opinions." She says she quickly realized, "Oh, my God, these guys are serious!"[1]

- *Deep belief in mission.* Staff members genuinely believe their work is making the world a better place and their jobs are about much more than collecting a paycheck.

- *Trust in leadership.* Staff members trust that the organization's leaders care deeply about acting in the best interests of the organization. Staffers may not always agree with every decision, but they give leaders the benefit of the doubt, confident that they are acting out of the right motives and will exercise good judgment.

---

[1] R. Lizza, "Battle Plans: How Obama Won," *The New Yorker,* Nov. 17, 2008.

Authenticity

We can't say enough about the importance of all of these elements being authentic, because cultures are only as powerful as they are genuine. Although some organizations pay lip service to these concepts, on high-performing teams what we describe here is truly how things work.

> "A lot of the best organizations that I see are organizations where the role of the manager is primarily to reproduce the culture, because if people have that basic understanding of what the effort is about and how it's appropriate to pursue it, they can be freed up to make all kinds of decisions and take all kinds of initiative. There's a less intensive management workload with a higher return on investment."
>
> RICKEN PATEL, EXECUTIVE DIRECTOR, AVAAZ

CREATING AND REINFORCING A HIGH-PERFORMANCE, RESULTS-ORIENTED CULTURE

If these elements don't already exist on your team, how can you establish a culture where these are the defining characteristics? As with delegating tasks or using goals to assign broad responsibilities, the best approaches blend being clear from the start about what you expect, remaining engaged along the way, and holding people accountable to meeting those expectations. Here are some of the most effective ways we've seen managers do this.

Modeling

First and foremost, lead by example. Whether you're creating a culture from scratch or trying to turn one around, modeling by leaders is easily the most powerful way to transmit the cultural values and behaviors you want your staff to demonstrate, such as "always follow up on things" and "treat constituents with respect." In fact, your culture will reflect what you believe and how you act. For instance, if you mention in a meeting that you're going to e-mail a document afterward to everyone and then don't, your staff won't take their own next steps seriously either. But if in this case you send an explanatory e-mail—for instance, "I know I said I'd get this document out today, but I realized I should wait for input from our board chair, so it'll be tomorrow instead"—your staff will know they must demonstrate a similar sense of responsibility.

Explicit Articulation

Articulating the values you expect all staffers to live up to is a simple, worthwhile process that can send strong messages about how people should approach their work. However, in order to be worth doing, this must be authentic: we've all seen well-intentioned but laughable posters listing the alleged values of a poorly run business, often claiming that "customers come first" even as we're facing clear evidence that their customers decidedly don't come first. But if your core values are genuine, explicitly articulating them can help assimilate newcomers into your culture and reinforce the behaviors you want to see in your employees.

While this is most typically done at the organizational level, managers of departments or teams can do this as well. For instance, if you're an information technology director, your team might have a value around "Shockingly Good Customer Service" to describe what you provide to the rest of the organization.

Once you've established values you want staff members to aspire to, you can reinforce them through ongoing explicit discussions—for instance:

- When you're orienting new employees, discuss each of the values and what they mean in practice. You could even develop hypothetical scenarios and how the values would play out in them.

- Give feedback the moment that you see someone acting in a way that isn't consistent with your values. The same applies when you see someone exemplifying your values: praise people for strong examples of, say, persistence or commitment to improvement.

- Consider posting a list of core values in the office, and provide the list to your staff members.

- Periodically review and edit your list of values with your entire team or your most senior people. It's a great way to reinforce the meaning behind the words.

Tool 4.1 provides the core values for our organization.

Reinforcement During Hiring

You begin sending messages about your culture from the moment a job applicant contacts you: How responsive are you? Do you ask thoughtful, rigorous questions rather than typical interview fare? Do you convey a warm, positive tone during the interview, and maybe even make the candidate laugh? The hiring process is a microcosm of your culture, and smart candidates—exactly the people you want to hire—will be picking up loads of messages about how you do things.

In addition, we recommend including a discussion of your organization or team's culture as part of the interviewing process. You might also ask some of your staff members who best exemplify your culture to speak with top candidates to give them a better sense of your culture and to get input from your cultural stars about their sense of a candidate's fit.

Rituals

Rituals can be another powerful way to reach and reinforce shared values. A ritual might be a way you regularly share information, the ways you celebrate progress, or how you welcome new staff. For instance, one organization we know sends new staff members flowers when they're hired, which sends strong signals about culture ("we're a positive group and we value you!").

Any shared, regular, and positive experience can become a ritual, including something as simple as a champagne toast after major victories. We especially like rituals that have a substantive component tied to your work. For instance, the IT director whose team is committed to "Shockingly Good Customer Service" might present a monthly "Above and Beyond" award to a staff member who has received unsolicited praise from the team's clients. On a slightly different track, one group we know asks all staff members to read a particular article each week and then convenes a weekly hour-long meeting to discuss it. Not only do good ideas usually emerge from that discussion, but the ritual itself sends a message that new ideas are important to the organization.

Performance Evaluations and Consequences

One of the most powerful ways to reinforce values that you have articulated is to incorporate an assessment of how well staff members are demonstrating those values as part of your performance evaluations. You might list each of your values, and explicitly rate each staff member against them (in addition to measuring the extent to which the staffer met her goals).

If you're not in charge of the performance evaluation form you'll be using, this may be harder to do, but you can try to weave these elements in on your own. Or you can show this chapter to your executive director or head of HR and convince her that she should do it.

Having real consequences for performance (in terms of fit with your culture, as well as the results a staff member generates) sends strong messages about what is and isn't expected from staff members. High performers should see their behavior reinforced through positive consequences like promotion, additional responsibilities, lavish praise, extra pay, or some combination of these, and low performers should see consequences like serious warnings and terminations.

WHAT IT LOOKS LIKE IN PRACTICE

Apart from the specific methods we've discussed, most fundamentally your culture is shaped by hundreds of daily interactions. Here are some examples of what the type of culture we've described here looks like in the day-to-day course of work:

- You're the head of fundraising. You met your total revenue goal this year but missed your target for new high-net-worth donors. You celebrate hitting the big target, but you also hold a series of meetings with your team and your boss to brainstorm how your approach can be different going forward.

- A junior staff member proposes printing new T-shirts with a funny slogan on them. Although you like the staff member's creativity, you worry that the T-shirts don't reflect your organization's branding. It feels like a small thing to let slide in the name of encouraging staff initiative, but you don't shield this staff member from the rigor that is brought to decisions about the organization's image. You explain the constraints and why you're not going to run with the suggestion. You end by encouraging your staff member to come up with something that better fits the organization's brand.

- You're wrestling with whether to expand your program to a new state, which could lead to greater impact but might strain your resources. Rather than puzzling through it on your own or with several top leaders behind closed doors, you throw the question out to your staff members and offer them the chance to consider it and give you their thoughts while still being clear that the final decision rests with you.

KEY POINTS

- Culture is made up of and reinforces the hundreds of daily signals about "how we do things here."

- High-performing managers create cultures that blend a deep rigor (relentless pursuit of results, a high bar for performance, scrutiny of ideas, accountability, transparency and commitment to continuous improvement, and mission integrity) with positive engagement (positive sense of energy, shared sense of ownership, real sense of mission, and low drama). And it's all authentic; this is truly how things work.

- Powerful ways to reinforce culture include leading by example, explicitly articulating the core values you expect all staffers to hold, discussing those values during the hiring process, creating rituals, and having meaningful consequences for performing in accord with the culture.

Additional Reading

Jim Collins, *Good to Great: Why Some Companies Make the Leap . . . and Others Don't* (New York: HarperCollins, 2001).

James C. Collins and Jerry I. Porras, *Built to Last: Successful Habits of Visionary Companies* (New York: HarperCollins, 1997), especially "Cult-Like Cultures" (pp. 114–139).

W. Chan Kim and Renée Mauborgne, "Fair Process: Managing in the Knowledge Economy," *Harvard Business Review*, Jan. 2003.

TOOL 4.1

SAMPLE STATEMENT OF CORE VALUES

The Management Center Core Values	
Impact	We obsess about the results of our efforts, we are brutally honest with ourselves about what's working and what's not, and we constantly strive to do better.
Above and Beyond	We hold ourselves to a very high standard and do whatever we can to help our clients and to get results.
Realness	We talk like real people and make things as simple and straightforward as possible.
Humility	We are deeply on our clients' side and we approach them with tremendous respect for the difficulty of their work and appreciation for what they bring to the job.
Optimism	We bring a sense of possibility to our work, acting on the belief that change is possible and largely within our control.

CHAPTER

MANAGING THE DAY-TO-DAY WORK OF YOUR TEAM
Structures to Bring It All Together

This first part of this book has focused on managing work—more specifically, delegating specific projects, using roles and goals to hand over broad responsibilities, and using culture to manage all the things that fall in between the cracks. In theory, it's all pretty straightforward, but in practice, it can be a lot harder. You might have half a dozen staff members, and for each of them, you might have agreed on multiple goals and have added several specific projects for each of them. You want to follow the principles of setting clear expectations, staying engaged, creating accountability and learning, and adapting to fit the context, but what does that look like day to day when there's so much to stay on top of?

We've found that there are two very helpful tools that make it significantly easier to manage the day-to-day work of your staff members and ensure that it's connected to the big picture goals you want them to accomplish:

- *Weekly one-on-one check-in meetings*. Having a regular time to touch base with each of your staff members individually about their work keeps you focused on their results and creates a place for you to check on how projects are progressing, serve as a resource to them, and agree on prioritization. In short, regular one-on-one check-ins give you a forum for management.

- *Monthly step-back meetings.* Because it's easy to get caught up in the rush of day-to-day work, having a set time each month, or at least each quarter, to step back and talk about the larger picture will ensure that you don't lose the forest for the trees and neglect topics like progress toward big picture goals and development needs.

These two types of meetings can serve as the glue that holds together all the elements of managing work that we've discussed so far, so we'll spend the bulk of the chapter on them. We'll also touch briefly on a few of the more specific, and trickier, topics that arise: managing remote staff, managing other managers, and managing areas of work you know nothing about.

WEEKLY ONE-ON-ONE CHECK-INS

Check-ins, periodic meetings between a manager and a staff member to discuss ongoing work, serve a variety of purposes:

- *Advancing individual projects.* By spending a few minutes with each of the major items on the staff member's plate, the manager has a chance to ask probing questions, spot areas of concern for further work, and serve as a resource to the staff member. Often the manager's "one-level-up" perspective allows her to fairly quickly suggest solutions to problems that the staff member may have overlooked.

- *Balancing priorities across projects.* By looking across all the work on a staff member's plate, managers can help their staff focus on the most important pieces and can suggest areas that the staff member might deprioritize. Without check-ins, it's easy to overlook when a staffer's workload is too heavy or too light, when a staffer is focusing too much time on one project at the expense of another, or when a staffer is letting less visible tasks fall through the cracks.

- *Coordinating the team.* Managers can spot ways in which different staff members' work intersects and can ensure the different parts of the team act in concert. (Regular staff meetings can help with this too.)

- *Providing feedback.* In theory, managers should provide feedback in the moment, but it's sometimes easier to do this during a regular check-in meeting than in the rush of daily work. Check-ins give you a time to reflect on what's gone well recently ("Great report to the board—let's discuss why that went so smoothly!") and what didn't meet expectations ("Let's talk about what went wrong with the phone banking and what you might do differently next time").

- *Connecting personally.* Staff members need to know that you care about them as people, and having a regular time to meet outside the course of daily work gives you a better chance to ask about their morale, as well as their lives outside work.

WHAT ABOUT STAFF MEETINGS?   Staff meetings are best suited for communication and coordination, not individual management. Make sure your staff meetings aren't simply check-ins with one person after another; do check-ins individually, and save staff meetings for conversations that truly involve the entire group.

Putting Check-In Meetings into Practice

Putting check-in meetings into practice is easy: simply let your team know you plan to start holding them, and get them on the calendar. Here are a few details about how things might work:

- *How frequently should you have check-in meetings?* In our experience, a weekly check-in meeting works well for most employees, although more experienced staffers might need less frequent discussions. However, we wouldn't recommend meeting less frequently than every other week. During intense periods of work with tight deadlines or with newer staff, you might meet more frequently, even daily.

- *Who should attend?* Typically a check-in meeting is between just you and the employee. Unlike department meetings or staff meetings, where the goal is more about fostering coordination and communication across a team of staff members, check-ins work best when they are one-on-one.

- *How long should the meetings be?* The length of the meeting will vary, but in general, allow between thirty and ninety minutes per meeting, depending on the complexity of the staffer's work and her needs.

Making Check-In Meetings Effective

Check-in meetings are such a powerful tool that you'll begin to see better results just by implementing them as a regular practice. But here are a few ways to get the most out of them:

- *Think beforehand about what you want to get out of the meeting.* This sounds so obvious that we hesitate to say it, but few people actually do it. Taking two minutes in advance to think through what you are most worried about and what you want to focus on can have a big impact.

- *Use an agenda.* Again, this sounds obvious, but we see practices to the contrary all the time. Meetings are much more productive if you don't walk into them cold. Preparing for a check-in can run the gamut from asking the staffer to e-mail you an agenda beforehand to taking a minute at the beginning of the meeting to agree on what topics to cover. Tool 5.1 provides a sample check-in meeting agenda.

- *Stay focused.* Check-ins are one of your key management tools, so make sure to fully engage during the meeting. In fact, make sure everyone at the meeting puts their cell phones away. We've both been guilty of sneaking a glance at e-mail during a check-in, but we've also learned that resisting the temptation and staying focused saves us time in the long run.

- *Keep track of items you want to raise.* Although ideally the onus should be on the staffer to make sure you cover everything that needs to be discussed, it's ultimately your responsibility to make sure nothing is overlooked. Develop a system for keeping track of check-in topics that come up during the course of business. This could mean jotting them down on your weekly action list (see Chapter Eleven), or you might keep track in your electronic calendar. Not only will this help you remember important topics, but when your staff members see that you don't forget about things that are supposed to have happened, they'll feel more accountable and will keep better track themselves.

- *Make sure the next steps are clear.* Few discussions should end without an agreement about what should happen next, even if it's just, "Let's both think this over, and then you should bring it up again next week." It can be especially useful for your staffer to e-mail you a summary of everything that was agreed to, or at least for her to give you a verbal recap of next steps at the end of the meeting (just as you would ask for a repeat-back when delegating a single project).

- *Include a human element.* Take a few minutes to make a personal connection and find out how the person is doing generally. How is the person's life going outside work? Now is a good time to ask about significant others, kids, and nonwork interests.

- *Adjust your approach to the staffer.* Some staffers need you to be more directive and hands-on, whereas with others, you can switch into more of an ancillary mode, perhaps asking how you can be helpful. Or you may learn that one staffer needs help in not losing sight of the big picture, while another needs prompting about specific items that may be getting lost.

BIG PICTURE STEP-BACKS

Ideally your check-in meetings might include discussions of progress toward larger goals, morale, development needs, and lessons learned, but in reality, these larger topics often get pushed aside in the press of day-to-day business. So set aside one check-in each month to focus on these issues (some managers we know hold them the first Monday of each month). If monthly is too much, you might do them quarterly, but generally you wouldn't want to do fewer than that.

GETTING BENEATH THE SURFACE   As we discussed in Chapter

Two, you've probably had the experience of asking a staff member how a project is going and receiving a simple "good" in response. Where do you go from there in order to get beneath the surface and understand what's really happening?

If you simply run down a list of projects without digging deeper, you're likely to miss important information about what obstacles might be looming and how you might be a resource to your staff in avoiding them. Here are some questions that can help you get beneath the surface:

- What one or two things would make this week a success for you?
- How do you know you're on track?
- How are you checking to make sure that's working?
- How are you handling X [a specific element]?
- What seems to be working well? Why do you think that's working?
- What could go wrong? What are you most worried about?
- Have you thought about what you'll do if Y happens?
- What's most important out of all those things?
- What makes you say that?
- What kind of data do we have about how that's working?
- Roughly how much of your time are you spending on that?
- What's your timeline for that?
- Can you give me a specific example of that?
- Can we take one specific instance and talk through how you're approaching it?
- Why don't we role-play what that might look like?
- What does your agenda for that look like?
- What other options did you consider?

During these meetings:

- Pull out the staffer's goals and discuss how her progress is matching up against them. Is she on track to meet her goals? Where does she need to restrategize? What has she put aside while working on something else but should be moved to a more active status again, or vice versa? See Tool 5.2 for a handy check-in sheet to use here.

- What lessons has she learned from recent work, and how might she apply them in the future?

- What might you both be able to do to help the staff member develop further? (Chapter Seven discusses staff development in depth.)

WHAT ABOUT WRITTEN REPORTS?   We're not huge fans of written weekly reports that summarize a staff member's current and upcoming projects, because they can become a bureaucratic drain on valuable staff time. We'd rather see managers manage to big picture goals and apply the tips we've provided to get the most out of check-ins. However, we know some managers who swear by written reports, arguing that having a comprehensive list of everything on the staffer's plate can prompt both of them to ask questions or raise issues about tasks they might not otherwise think about.

If you do decide to use weekly reports, keep in mind that the goal is to put you and your staffer on the same page and make sure the staff member brings you up to date on priorities and identifies topics for later discussion, not simply require the staff member to document where her time went that week.

- In some cases, you might also check in on how the staff member is doing both personally and with the job. Is she happy? Frustrated? How is she feeling overall?

OBSERVING THE WORK IN ACTION

As powerful and important as weekly check-ins and bigger picture step-backs are, don't forget that they're not the only way to check on progress. You should get out from behind your desk and see things in action too. Often what you see looks different from what you pictured when you were just talking about it. Finding ways to observe the work in action can give you a much deeper understanding of how plans are really playing out.

SPECIAL CHALLENGES

Implementing regular check-in meetings and periodic big picture step-backs will make a dramatic difference in your ability to manage the work of staff members. However, what if your staff member isn't just down the hall but across the country or even on the other side of the world? Or if she is a manager of staff members herself? Or working in an area that you don't have much expertise in? Let's take a look at how to approach these additional challenges.

Managing Remote Staff

If you're managing staff members who aren't in the same physical location as you, give special consideration to how to make the relationship work smoothly. Here are four tips we've found that make remote management go more smoothly.

1. *Establish a clear system for communications and stick to it.* If you leave it informal, regular communication is less likely to happen than with someone who's physically

in the building with you. For instance, you might decide that you'll have one regularly scheduled phone meeting each week, won't rely on e-mail for complicated issues that arise between meetings and will instead will get on the phone to hash them out, and will have the staffer come to your headquarters for a few days at least twice a year.

2. *Create ways for remote staff to stay connected.* Since it can be harder for remote employees to know what's going on in the office, pay special attention to ensuring that they're included in communications.

3. *Create opportunities for in-person interaction.* This is key for building trust and getting to know each other. If you have an entire remote team, try bringing them together several times a year.

4. *Find ways to see remote staff in action.* You can do this by joining some of their phone calls, going on joint field visits, or shadowing them for a day in their own office. This is essential to know what's really going on in the field and to help you serve as a resource to your staffer. In addition, when your remote staffer knows that you've seen her world firsthand and that you understand its dynamics and challenges, it can dramatically increase the trust between you.

Managing Other Managers

Another challenge you may confront as you gain experience is managing others who themselves manage people. When the person you're managing is a manager herself, part of her job is to get work done through other people. Make sure, then, that you're managing her as a manager, not just as an individual contributor. This means that you should pay attention to the results her team is producing, and not solely to what she is doing directly herself, and that you should focus on building her skills in such areas as how she delegates work to others, how she hires and fires, and how she transmits your culture to her staffers.

So instead of, or in addition to, asking about how's she's spending her own time, ask about her team. Who is working on what? How is she managing Maria on that project? How is it going? How does she know? What is she doing to make sure Maria stays with the team for another year?

Here are more examples of the kinds of questions you might ask when managing other managers:

- How are you managing Josh on that?

- How are you making sure Josh is on track?

- Should we make sure you and I are aligned before you go back to him on that?

- What is Josh's plan for X?

- What are you most worried about in terms of how Josh will handle X? How are you taking that on?

- What are Josh's main priorities right now?

- What was your reaction to X [an event Josh pulled together or a plan he sent, for example]?

- Should we get aligned on X before you go back to Josh on it?

- Have you given Josh feedback, positive or negative, on X?

- What's your sense of how Josh is performing? What are his main areas for growth? How are you taking those on with him?

- [Where appropriate] What's your strategy for retaining Josh? Can I be helpful on that?

- Looking across your team, what are you most focused on from a management perspective? How are you taking that on?

And here too, getting your hands dirty will help. Be enough in touch with the people on her team that you have a good sense of what's going on, and consider doing a joint visit or meeting with the manager to observe the work of her team. However, be aware of the delicate balance you're striving for here: you want to understand what's going on without going around the manager or taking over the management functions that rightly belong to her (unless the manager has a serious performance problem, of course).

Managing Work Outside Your Area of Expertise

As you progress in your career, you might also end up in charge of areas you frankly know nothing about! If you're charged with managing an area of work outside your main expertise, such as information technology (IT), here are five ways to do it effectively:

1. *Get aligned about goals and have clear deadlines*—for instance, "We need an interactive Web site up and running in time for our big legislative push, which means tested, launched, and ready to use by February." This keeps you focused on the end product, and then you can ask questions about the process: "How will we know whether this is on track? Are there milestones you could set to hit along the way?"

2. *Manage by asking good questions rather than suggesting answers.* Even without knowing the substance, you can pose basic, useful questions like, "How do you know that XYZ is true?" or "What will you do if ABC happens?" or "What do other organizations do about DEF?"

3. *Use your ignorance to your advantage.* Try a lot of "Help me understand why . . ." questions, and probe the answers to make sure your staff member has thought through problems thoroughly. For instance, you might ask, "Help me understand why the network keeps going down when we have high volume on our site."

4. *Connect the person to her "customers."* Your staffer may be doing work that few others understand but where many know whether they're getting what they need. Often you find yourself in the middle between "customers" (staff members in other departments) who tell you they want something, and an "expert" whom you manage. Your job is to bring the two sides together. Make sure your managee is talking to customers and agreeing with them on what they'll have by when. Ensure there's an ongoing channel for communication and feedback, including periodic surveys or other means that let you and your staffer see how the customers feel. Where appropriate, make clear that producing customer satisfaction is part of the job.

5. *Judge by what you do know.* Often you won't have any clear idea whether 90 percent of what the person does is good because you don't understand the subject matter. You will, though, understand 10 percent of it even if it's just something like, "Did this person explain what she was doing in a way customers could understand?" or, with IT, whether your e-mail and networking are running smoothly. Extrapolate from what you can understand, and assume the 90 percent you don't understand is similar. If the small pieces you get seem great, it's reasonable to assume that the rest probably is, and if the piece you get seems off, it's likely that the rest may be too.

KEY POINTS

- Holding weekly check-in meetings with each staff member provides you a good forum for management. It helps you remain engaged in ongoing projects, ensure that problems are spotted and addressed, balance workloads, provide feedback, and generally check in with the employee about how things are going overall.

- Monthly step-back meetings ensure that you don't neglect topics like progress toward big picture goals and development needs.

TOOL 5.1

SAMPLE CHECK-IN MEETING AGENDA

EJ/RA Weekly Check-In: 7/19

This week will be successful if:

1. All materials for training are finalized and out the door by Thursday night.

2. The conference presentation is started and is on track to be done by the end of next week.

3. The newsletter draft is complete and ready for layout.

> *Weekly priorities should be few in number (two to four) in order to focus on the most important areas, and they should be presented as outcomes so it's clear at the end of the week if they've been achieved.*

---

1. Key Updates

   - Training: outline/agenda completed, materials for first training about to be finalized
   - Housing: new coalition members
   - Outreach: newsletter on schedule

2. Items for Your Thoughts

   - Program associate opening—*candidates/hiring process*
   - Coalition—*getting pushback from A.W.M.; would love to talk this through*
   - Conference talk—*touch base to check my thinking*

3. Lessons Learned

   - Quick debrief of house meetings (my view: pluses were great messaging, clear assignments on our team; main thing to improve was my checking in more with individual leads to make sure all was on track)

4. On Back Burner/Not Getting to Yet (FYI)

   - Grant proposal
   - Online advocacy center overhaul

5. Next Steps/Repeat-Back

TOOL 5.2
SAMPLE CHECK-IN SUCCESS SHEET

Paste your goals from your annual goals success sheet in [Tool 3.2 in Chapter Three] into the first column, and assess the extent to which you're on track.

Goals	On Track? (Y/N)	Update	Key Activities for Next Quarter
Add at least 20,000 new subscribers to our e-mail list.	Y	After Q1 we had 3,000 new people, but we've added new promotions and are adding at a rate of 6,000 for Q2	Promote on AFR's list. Free giveaway for sign-ups in May.
Build relationships with key bloggers so that we have at least five national, well-read bloggers we can call on for coverage when needed.	N	Mark W. is regularly covering our issue; Sam Z. reached out once for background.	Hold blogger lunch in May. Send at least one helpful (individualized) resource to each target each month.

Questions for Discussion

- What else needs to happen to achieve X?
- Is there anything you should be starting on now in anticipation of what's coming up in the next few months?
- For goals that are getting off-track: What's happened to throw us off-track? What are you doing to restrategize your plan for that goal?
- What could go wrong? What worries you? What can you do to plan now for those possibilities?
- Are there items that have been deprioritized that we should move to the front of our attention now? Are there items that we should be focusing on less now in favor of higher priorities?

PART

MANAGING
THE PEOPLE

Managing the work well is critically important, but having the right people to do the work in the first place might be even more important. Managers, though, often take the makeup of their teams as a given rather than proactively shaping them, missing perhaps their biggest opportunity to get great results.

To illustrate the flaw in this approach, let's talk sports. If you were coaching a basketball team and your job was to win, would you want to take players who were chosen for you and then work your hardest to shape them into a strong squad, or would you rather choose your players (at the risk of dating ourselves, let's say Michael Jordan and Scottie Pippen in their primes), even if it meant you couldn't do a thing to alter their performance once they joined your team? No matter how good a coach you are, you're never going to get a squad of Jerry Hausers and Alison Greens to beat Michael and Scottie.

The impact of having a team of high performers in the workplace is similarly dramatic. We're not talking about small gains in productivity and effectiveness, like 5 or 10 percent. We're talking about massive, startling gains. Think of the difference between the number of points Jerry would score versus the number Michael would (trust us on this; it would be big). We've seen that in a variety of situations, high performers outperform lower performers by five times or more. Consider:

- When Jerry was at Teach For America, he replaced one regional director with another, and in one year fundraising in the region soared from $43,000 to $285,000 (and within two more years, to $1 million).

- We've both had assistants who struggled to handle the volume of work and who swore that there was too much work for any one person to juggle. In each case, when that person left, the replacements were able to handle all of the duties and then some, to the point that we ended up loading them up with entire new areas of responsibility to make the best use of them.

- In the development department at one organization, a processing clerk couldn't keep up and created a six-month backlog of checks to process. A new person came in and within one month had processed the six-month backlog and was fully caught up.

We could go on and on with examples like this. One high performer can have the same impact as five or more lower performers—so imagine the impact of having an entire organization of people operating at this level!

If the right people make an enormous impact on your results and getting results is your fundamental job, then you should put significant energy into getting and keeping the right people and moving out the ones who don't meet that bar. The chapters in Part Two discuss how to do that:

- How to find and hire superstars (Chapter Six)

- How and when to develop the skills and performance of your staff (Chapter Seven)

- Ways to make sure your best employees stay (Chapter Eight)

- How to address performance issues, including terminating employees who aren't meeting your standards (Chapter Nine)

Managing the makeup of your team pays enormous dividends. When you have the right people with the right skills, you'll achieve dramatically better results.

CHAPTER

6

HIRING SUPERSTARS

Little about management is more important than hiring well, since you'll never get great results without having the right people on your staff. But we've found that even when managers say they know how crucial it is to have the right people, they often don't use the hiring practices that should stem from that belief.

To take one example, the key determinant of success for most hiring processes is the quality of the candidates a manager has to choose from. That is, most hiring mistakes occur not because managers select the wrong person, but because they don't have the right person to select to begin with. As we'll discuss in this chapter, the key to success lies in proactively building a strong pool of candidates. Many managers pay lip service to this idea but end up spending little energy doing anything beyond posting jobs on popular Internet sites.

This chapter explores how to do hiring the right way, so that you maximize your chances of ending up with a staff of superstars. We set out five key steps:

1. Figuring out who you're looking for by defining the critical qualities needed for the role

2. Building a strong pool of candidates

3. Gathering information about your candidates through interviews, exercises, and reference checks so you can make your hiring decision based on the *actual* rather than the *hypothetical*

4. Making your decision

5. Selling the position and making the offer

FIGURING OUT WHO YOU'RE LOOKING FOR

The first step in hiring well is to get a clear picture of who you are looking for. Who would your ideal candidate be? In order to answer this question and produce an effective job description for potential hires, you'll need to clarify the role and think critically about what skills and qualities you should look for.

Get Clear On the Job Responsibilities

First, organize your thoughts about what the person will do, creating a list for your own purposes (the job description comes later). As we discussed in the section on roles in Chapter Three, it's helpful to have a clear headline to keep in mind about the fundamentals of the role. Beyond that, think through specific activities that the person might be doing if she were in the role today. For instance, rather than saying, "manage our brand," your list of activities for your head of marketing might include "work with Jonah to design new recruitment brochure," "analyze Web data and draft a report to the board," and "conduct trainings at our October retreat so staff can identify messages that do and don't fit our brand."

Consider What Skills, Knowledge, and General Qualities the Position Requires

Once you're clear on what the person will need to do, consider what type of person would thrive in that work. What skills, background knowledge, and general qualities should she have? For instance, if you are hiring a research assistant who will gather information from multiple sources and then draft reports, key skills might include synthesizing data and writing clearly. You might also look for specific knowledge of the subject matter the research assistant will cover. As for general qualities, consider the specific job and your organization as a whole. What traits do the most successful people with whom you work share? Does your organization have explicit or implicit core values that the person must hold? For example, the nature of your organization's work and culture might require being able to operate in a fast-paced environment. If that quality is important, it should go on your list.

Separate "Must-Haves" from "Nice-to-Haves"

As you make your list, distinguish between what is a "must-have" for the role and what is a "nice-to-have." In doing this, consider what qualities tend to be inherent (the person either has it or does not) versus what can be taught or developed. Underlying talents like strong critical thinking, effective writing, a strong work ethic, meticulousness, or an ability to build strong interpersonal relationships are difficult to teach, so if they

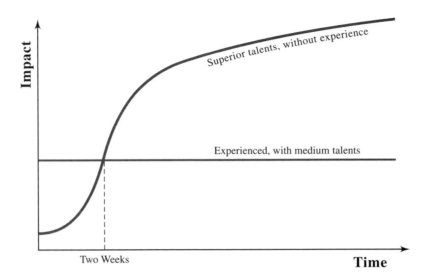

FIGURE 6.1. *Talent Trumps Experience*

are important to the job, they should go on your must-have list. More specific skills or knowledge, like mastery of a particular type of software, industry knowledge, or experience writing for a particular type of audience, can more easily be picked up along the way, particularly when more essential traits (in these cases, critical thinking and strong writing) are in place. There are, of course, times when prerequisite knowledge is essential—for instance, your chief financial officer needs to come in with an understanding of accounting principles—but in many cases, organizations overvalue specific skills or content knowledge and don't put enough weight on underlying qualities that are harder to develop. In the long or even medium term, underlying traits like critical thinking or initiative or assertiveness are much more likely to differentiate high performers than are things like specific experience in your sector (Figure 6.1).

Create a Job Posting

Once you are clear on your desired criteria, translate the list into a job posting, which should do three things: explain the job responsibilities, list the qualifications you're looking for, and sell the position and organization.

On that last point, remember that job postings are marketing tools. We often see job announcements for incredible opportunities that are filled with bureaucratic jargon that sucks the life out of the role. You want to attract people who will be excited about the work, so ideally your announcement will help your target candidates imagine what it would be like to work in *this* role at *this* organization, and to feel inspired by it.

That means that you might talk about some of the organization's recent successes and exciting challenges on the horizon, as well as how the person in this position will

WHAT ABOUT PASSION? Contrary to conventional wisdom, exhibiting a great deal of passion for your organization's issue should generally not be a must-have quality for candidates. In fact, we've seen no correlation between visible passion and effectiveness. Passion is certainly not a bad thing, but we've seen far too many managers use passion as a substitute for talent, hiring highly passionate candidates (or at least candidates who talk as if they're passionate) who end up not being well suited for the job. So beyond checking for a basic commitment to the objectives of the organization, don't let a candidate's enthusiasm about your work overly influence your thinking about her fit for the role. Ultimately, what you most want is a candidate who is passionate about getting results.

help address those issues. But it also has ramifications for how you talk about the job responsibilities and qualifications.

For instance, when you're explaining the job responsibilities, avoid internal jargon or getting bogged down with detail. You should convey the essence of the role and key details about it, but at this stage, sometimes broad strokes can more effectively convey what the role is all about. Remember that you want to get candidates excited, not make them think they've fallen into a dry internal processes manual.

In listing the qualifications for the job, make clear what traits are essential and what traits are less important so that the people with the traits you desire will recognize themselves in your summary. For instance, in the case of a research assistant, many potential applicants will assume you want someone with experience in your field. If you value general skills like strong writing more than industry-specific knowledge, you might say explicitly, "We care more about whether you're a great writer than whether you have experience in the health care field."

You also should think about the profile of the ideal person who would fill the role well. For instance, if you're looking for an executive assistant, do you picture hiring a career assistant who has a great deal of experience, or might a highly organized recent college graduate be well suited to what you want? If the latter, you might make a point of saying that prior experience is less important than being extremely organized and attentive to detail. Tool 6.1 provides a sample job posting.

BUILDING A STRONG POOL OF CANDIDATES

Now that you know what you're looking for, your next task—and, we'd argue, the most important determinant of whether you hire a superstar—is building your pool of candidates. As we noted in the opening to this chapter, most hiring mistakes occur not because managers select the wrong person but because they don't have the right person to select to begin with. Given this, the more energy you spend on building your pool of candidates, the more likely you'll be to find high performers.

Mass Marketing

Perhaps the easiest part of recruitment, and certainly the most commonly practiced, is mass marketing using techniques like Internet postings that reach multiple people rather than specific individuals. In this category, most organizations think to hit the obvious sources, such as posting on their own Web site, circulating announcements to e-mail lists, and posting on sites like www.idealist.org or www.craigslist.org.

In designing your advertising efforts, get creative and go beyond the obvious. For instance, if your ideal profile is someone with strong writing skills and you don't necessarily need prior experience in your specific field, post your job announcement at the English departments of local universities and on online job banks geared toward writers. If you're hiring an information technology staffer, send notices to IT consulting firms in your community.

Individual Headhunting

The most successful managers go beyond mass channels and bring their searches down to an individual level, basically becoming headhunters. They consider the ideal profile of the person in the role and try to think of anyone they know who might fit that profile, including current members of their staff. Besides being candidates themselves, your current staff can also help identify people to target. When there are important openings at one organization we know, the executive director gathers a small group of staff members, and in thirty minutes of brainstorming, they usually come up with a list of ten to fifteen good possibilities.

Recruit aggressively from your list of prospects. Rather than simply e-mailing them a job description and asking whether they're interested, make it harder for them to say no to the first step in the process. For instance, invite them out for a cup of coffee to talk about their future plans. This sort of personal interest is usually far more compelling than a quickly e-mailed job posting.

Finding Connector Sources

You should also think of connector sources—people who aren't right for the job themselves but might know others who are. Go through your list of contacts to identify people who are connected to your organization or are social acquaintances who might be good sources.

Here too, once you have a good source, you should try to speak with these people directly rather than e-mailing an announcement. You will be surprised how many more names you get when you spend a few minutes on the phone with these people. (This is why professional headhunters almost always want to speak to you on the phone rather than simply e-mail you an announcement.)

Striving for Diversity

For a variety of reasons, including the fact that many nonprofits have missions connected to promoting social, racial, or economic justice, many organizations strive to have a

THE PERMANENT CAMPAIGN You should always be looking for strong potential staffers, whether or not you have a current opening, noting interesting prospects you come across, and encourage your staff members to do the same. To ensure that good candidates readily come to mind when the time comes to hire, keep a running list of prospects. A simple document listing names, contact information, and one sentence of context about the person to trigger your memory works well. (See Tool 6.2 for a sample talent list.)

And do more than passively track these potential stars: reach out and cultivate them. Send the occasional e-mail with updates on your work, take them out for coffee and talk about their career goals and how your organization might fit in, or drop them a periodic e-mail to see how they're doing.

staff that is diverse in different respects. At a minimum, organizations should aim to have a workforce that reflects the relevant population in their community. The best way to reach this aim is to try to ensure through both mass marketing and individual headhunting that your applicant pool is diverse. For instance, at the mass marketing level, if you are looking for strong African American candidates, you might try to post your position on e-mail lists for black professionals in the area. On the personal headhunting level, if you don't have diverse networks of your own, reach out to others who do by finding sources who might be more likely to know of diverse candidates. The personal headhunting piece is key here; of the many organizations we know that have wrestled with how they can build a more diverse staff, the ones that have made the most progress undertook a serious effort to build and cultivate a strong pool of diverse candidates over time.

Ideas for Building a Strong Pool

Most hiring mistakes occur not because managers select the wrong person but because they don't have the right person to select to begin with. Here are a few tips to help you build a strong pool and avoid that trap.

Mass Marketing

- Post ads on your Web site and those of other friendly organizations.

- Send a message out to e-mail lists.

- Ask friends, colleagues, and staff members to circulate the announcement.

- Submit posts to job sites (including www.idealist.org).

- Use industry-specific online job banks.

- Post on social networking Web sites such as LinkedIn and Facebook.

- Contact the alumni and career services offices of undergraduate or graduate schools.

- Reach out to professional societies.

Individual Headhunting

- Go through your contact list and note potential candidates or sources.

- Hold a meeting of strong members of your staff and brainstorm ideas for candidates or sources. Setting a target is helpful: "We will not leave until we think of six good candidates and twenty good sources to call."

- Keep a running list of staff prospects, and review it when you have openings.

- Review your own staff list for candidates.

- Call peers at allied organizations and ask them to brainstorm with you.

- Identify pipeline organizations for your staff (such as service organizations, government agencies, or private companies) and call contacts there.

- Call former staffers and interns who were strong (either as candidates or sources).

- Hire an actual headhunter.

  Use Tool 6.3 for building an applicant pool.

SELECTING THE RIGHT PERSON

Once you've started building a strong pool of candidates, you'll begin the selection process, which typically consists of successive stages with cuts at each step along the way. The details will vary depending on the position, your organization, and the quality of applications you receive, but typically you'll begin by making a first cut after reading through candidates' résumés and cover letters, rejecting the ones who clearly aren't a strong match. You'll then do interviews on the phone or in person, often of greater length as the process goes on. Interspersed along the way, sometimes even before the first personal interview, ask candidates to complete exercises that assess the qualities you'll need them to demonstrate on the job. Finally, as you get more serious about a candidate, check with people who know her to find out their opinion about her fit with your role.

Let's take a look at the main steps: initial screening, interviews and exercises, and speaking with references.

Initial Screening of Candidates

To make your job easier at the initial screening stage, think carefully about what materials you ask applicants to submit. A résumé and cover letter are fairly typical, of course, but you can also ask for more. If a position involves writing, save yourself the

REJECTING CANDIDATES   Make sure to inform candidates when they are no longer under consideration, even if all they have done is to submit an application online. These candidates could be your future donors or supporters (or could be perfect for a job opening you have in the future), and how you handle rejections will give them an impression, good or bad, of your organization.

The fastest way to send a rejection is by having a standard e-mail template that you can adapt, depending on how much interaction you have had with a candidate (see Tool 6.4).

Managers (including the two of us) differ on whether a phone call is appropriate for candidates who have gone through an extensive process. If you do make a call, you can be direct without being insulting, telling candidates the ways in which you thought they were strong and the ways in which they might not have been the right fit for your position. For instance, you might say, "You clearly have a tremendous amount of knowledge about the industry. For this position, we were putting even more emphasis on the ability to network and bring in new supporters, and while I'm sure you could do that, it didn't strike me as your primary strength. I have no doubt, though, that you'll be a real asset to someone in the right position."

trouble of interviewing poor writers by asking for a three-page writing sample along with the résumé. If you're looking for a Web designer, ask applicants to submit links to several sites they created.

As applications begin coming in, you'll know immediately that some aren't right and you can reject these immediately (see the "Rejecting Candidates" box). For others, you'll need to scrutinize the materials more closely, looking for evidence of the must-have qualities you want in a role. For instance, if you need a go-getter who will take initiative without close supervision, look at how the candidate describes her accomplishments in prior jobs to see if there's evidence of going above and beyond the basics of the job. If you need a good writer, scrutinize the cover letter or writing sample.

Interviews and Exercises

Once you've chosen the candidates who seem promising enough to pursue further, you'll proceed to the get-to-know-you stage. In the typical process, a candidate who makes it to this point might have undergone two or more rounds of interviews, with a shorter first interview and a longer second (and often third or more) round. During the later rounds, the candidate might meet others in the organization, such as the hiring manager's boss, prospective subordinates if the person would be managing others, or a peer in the organization who would be working closely with the person. By getting others' perspectives, the hiring manager often surfaces underlying issues that she might be missing, and she also gives candidates a better sense of the work they might be responsible for and the culture of the organization.

However many rounds of interviews you do, your primary goal in an interview is to find out how well the candidate matches up with the list of must-have traits you developed earlier. If there's one thing to keep in mind as you try to glean this information, it's this: *Focus on the actual rather than the hypothetical.* In other words, the best way to gauge how people will act in the future is to find out how they have actually acted in the past or to observe how they actually act in the present. Too often, though, managers ask about the hypothetical, say, how a candidate might handle a difficult situation. For instance, if you want to figure out whether an assistant will be able to handle multiple tasks efficiently and without losing track of things, asking, "How do you think you would stay on top of everything?" or, worse yet, "Do you think you could handle the volume?" gets you little useful information (the first question tests more for critical thinking than efficiency, and the second tests whether the candidate is awake). Instead, ask, "How much volume did you have to handle in your last job? How did you stay on top of it all? Tell me about a time when the volume was at its peak. What did you do?" These questions probe the actual by looking at what the candidate did in her past. Alternatively, you can say, "Here's a pile of tasks to complete. I'd like you to figure out which order to do them in and then do them. I'll come back in twenty minutes," which probes the candidate's actual ability to do tasks quickly.

With this principle in mind, we urge you to use the following three methods of gathering useful information during the interview process.

Probe Prior Experiences Deeply

Focus on depth over breadth in your questions, because you will learn more by getting into the details of a few experiences than by covering every job listed on a résumé. In discussing a particular experience, start with general questions, but then probe for the specific traits you are interested in. Along the way, your main challenge will be to get beneath the surface of general descriptions and into the nitty-gritty of how a candidate actually operated. For example, if one of the key traits you are seeking is an ability to stay on top of a large volume of work, your line of questioning might go like this:

- Tell me about X. What did you do there?

- What was the project on which you spent the most time?

- That sounds interesting. How did you approach that?

- Was it successful?

- What was the biggest challenge?

- How did you deal with that challenge?

- I would think one challenge must have been staying on top of everything at once. Did you ever get overwhelmed?

- How did you stay organized?

- I know this is pretty nitpicky, but walk me through the organizational system you used. When you arrived at work in the morning, how did you decide what to start working on? As items came up during the day, where would you capture those so you didn't forget?

If your probing of specific experiences does not yield information about the traits you are looking for, you can also ask directly:

- Tell me about a time when you had to stay on top of a lot of work.

- How did you do it?

- What was hardest about that?

Be sure that you don't allow your desire to be nice to the candidate to prevent you from probing until you have a clear sense of her strengths and weaknesses. Pushing as much as it takes to get into the details is key to making an accurate assessment, and good candidates actually appreciate challenging questions.

Simulate Actual Job Activities

If you've hired even a few people before, you may know the terrible feeling of realizing after just a few days with a new employee that she is not going to work out. Having candidates complete activities similar to what they'd be doing on the job before they get hired can give you that insight before it's too late. Think of yourself as a football coach holding tryouts: you wouldn't ask a player whether he could make a tackle; you'd ask to see him do it.

For instance, if you are hiring a marketing director and want a candidate who can internalize your desired branding and help choose collateral that fits your image, you could have a candidate read your brand positioning statement and look at your Web site, and then ask for her opinions on whether the site fits your brand and how it might be improved. If you want someone who can write quickly under pressure, you might provide a candidate a set of talking points and give her thirty minutes to draft a press release. Or if you want a chief financial officer who can explain financial matters to other executives in clear terms, you might send candidates your financial statements ahead of time and ask them to explain them to you in plain English during the interview.

You can ask candidates to engage in these sorts of exercises at a variety of stages in the process. Even before granting first interviews for an assistant position, for instance, you could cull your pool by having applicants read a scenario about an upcoming meeting and draft a mock e-mail to a hypothetical executive at another organization. Once you're at the interview stage, you can weave activities into the course of the interview (by asking for a role play of a funder meeting, say), or you can have candidates complete them while they are on-site, or have them complete the tasks off-site and then send them back to you. You can also send background materials to candidates in advance of interviews so they can come prepared.

Close to the end of your process, you might even hire your top candidate in a consulting capacity to do a project for you, giving you much more substantive interaction to base your decision on. Or you might have her spend a half-day going to some of the meetings she'd attend on the job and then debrief with her afterward to hear her impressions and suggestions.

However you do it, finding ways to see the candidates demonstrate the qualities you must have in some kind of real-life situation can be invaluable in informing your decision.

Tool 6.5 lists some job simulation exercises, and Tool 6.6 provides a sample e-mail to candidates asking them to prepare for job-related activities.

Get to Know the Candidate

Many organizations focus almost their entire interview process on general "get to know you" questions, but you will find out more from exploring prior experiences and having candidates perform actual tasks for you, Nevertheless, don't entirely neglect this category of getting to know the candidate because it sometimes elicits useful information.

In this category, you might ask general questions about motivation and commitment, such as, "What are you looking for at this point in your career?" and "How does this role fit into your path?" You might also explore more specific questions about work preferences to help you understand a candidate's fit with your organization's culture, which is often one of your "must-have" criteria. Try questions like, "What drives you crazy at work?" and, "What was your favorite work environment and why?"

Keeping in mind the actual-versus-hypothetical rule, ask candidates to tie their answers back to specific experiences—for example, "You mentioned that you like having autonomy. Can you give me an example of a time you had that and how it worked?"

Pulling it all together, a good one-hour first interview might go something like this:

Introductions and small talk	3 minutes
Getting to know the candidate/general questions	5 minutes
Probing prior experiences	25 minutes
Simulating activities	5 minutes
Description of the job, culture, and organization, from you, followed by questions from the candidate, and questions about their questions: "You asked about a collaborative environment. How important is that to you?"	10 minutes total
Wrap-up; thank the candidate and tell her when she should expect to hear from you next	2 minutes

TRY BEFORE YOU BUY Since the best way to know whether someone is likely to succeed at a job is to actually see the person do it, in an ideal world you'd be able to do that before you commit to hiring someone. Think about whether your organization has ways to try people out more extensively than in a normal hiring process without actually offering them a staff position—for instance, by bringing people on to do short-term pieces of work or creating an internship program.

Tool 6.7 provides a full list of interview questions, and Tool 6.8 offers a worksheet on conducting interviews.

Speaking with References

As you go through your interviews, hopefully you have some idea of whom you want to hire. But complete one more step first: talking to references about the candidate. When done well, can save you from a bad hire or help you choose between two strong candidates.

Managers often find checking references to be the most frustrating part of the selection process, since it can be hard to get useful information out of what is usually a carefully selected set of people. Nevertheless, there are ways to increase your chances of getting helpful information from these conversations. (Tool 6.9 provides useful question for reference checking.)

Don't Limit Yourself to the Candidate's List of References

You don't need to confine your reference calls to the references provided by the candidate, especially since these people have likely been selected for their willingness to speak glowingly about her. If you know people in the candidate's circle, reach out and ask them about her. You can also ask candidates to put you in touch with specific people from their past. For instance, you can say something like, "I'd love to speak to your supervisor from that job you held from 2006 to 2009. Can you put me in touch with her?"

Make It Easy for the Reference to Tell the Full Story

In most cases, the reference will have a stronger relationship with the candidate than with you. Since references may feel disloyal or guilty providing negative information, your job is to make it easier for them to tell you what you need to hear. You can do this by making it easy for the person to tell you negative things as well as positives. For instance, you might pair positives and negatives by asking questions like, "What type of job would you hire X for? What type of job would X be less suited for?" or "What do you think X will excel in? What do you think we'd want to focus X's professional development on?"

Particularly when asking for downsides about a candidate, try to force the reference to give you something. Instead of asking, "Is there anything X could improve in?" to which references might respond, "Nothing comes to mind," ask, "If you had to pick two ways X could improve, what would they be?" You can also provide options where there is no obviously wrong choice that would make the candidate look bad and ask the reference to select the choice that sounds more like the candidate: "Some people thrive in fast-paced environments but might err on the side of losing precision, whereas others are incredibly precise but do better when there's more time to focus on their work. Which sounds more like X?"

You can also ask the reference to describe the candidate's greatest strengths or the words that most come to mind in describing the candidate, and listen for whether the key criteria you are interested in make the top of the list.

DON'T SEE 'EM SWEAT   Throughout the interview process, do everything you can to put candidates at ease so that you get a good sense of who they really are. You want to find out what candidates are like on a day-to-day basis, not what they're like in an interview. So be warm and friendly, and try to help candidates who seem nervous or tense to relax (unless of course "calm under pressure" is a trait you want).

MAKING YOUR DECISION

Once you have gone through these three stages, there's no magic to making the right decision. In general, assess the candidates against the criteria you established at the beginning of the process. If you have a clear sense of what you are looking for and a sufficiently strong and diverse pool of candidates and you have effectively gathered information about them, your decision might be straightforward.

In making the decision, listen to your gut: Would you be thrilled if this person came to work for you? If you have concerns or aren't excited about bringing the person into your staff, pay attention to your instincts. Both of us have ignored our instincts and ended up regretting it. Also, listen to the opinions of others who have been involved in the hiring process, and take seriously any warning signs that more than one of these people brought up.

If you're uncertain and think more information would help, modify the process to gather what you need. For instance, it is perfectly acceptable to explain to a candidate that you view this as a big decision and that you know she has already been through an extensive process, but you realized it would be helpful for her to

NO PHONE TAG   If you're having trouble getting in touch with references, put the burden on the candidate. Tell her, "I can't move forward until I speak with your old boss, but she's not calling me back. Do you think you'd be able to get her to return my call?" Often when the candidate hears this, she'll make sure you receive a call that day.

> **KEEP PEOPLE POSTED**   At every stage in the hiring process, make getting back to people quickly a priority. Not only do you risk losing good candidates by moving too slowly or not sharing information about your time line, but you also send the wrong messages about your culture. You want the person you hire to have begun picking up messages about "how we do things here," meaning being responsive and moving with a sense of urgency. And when there are delays, don't underestimate the power of sending a quick e-mail saying, "Although I told you last week that I would be scheduling interviews this week, I've had to push that back to next week. I'll be in touch by Monday."

meet with your board chair so that you could get one more opinion, or that you'd like her to give you one additional writing sample. You may never be 100 percent certain, but you should gather the information you feel you need to make the best decision possible.

And sometimes, after reading all of the résumés, conducting all of the interviews, and checking all of the references, you may realize that you are not excited enough about any of the candidates. If this happens to you, *no matter how desperately you need to fill a vacancy, rather than hiring someone you think might not be right, you will almost always be better off keeping the position open and searching for short-term solutions.* You might consider shifting responsibilities among your existing staff members to meet your highest-priority needs, bringing in temporary help to fill gaps, or as a last resort putting work on hold. In the long run, you will spend far more time and energy dealing with the consequences of a bad hiring decision than you will save by filling a vacancy with the wrong person.

SELLING THE POSITION AND MAKING THE OFFER

All along, you have been evaluating candidates, but once you're ready to make an offer, the focus shifts to the candidate's evaluation of you and the offer you will make. After all, two things need to happen to make a hire: you must choose the candidate, and the candidate must choose you.

Selling the Position Throughout the Hiring Process

The best way to ensure that this stage goes smoothly is to have been selling the position throughout the entire process, not just once you are ready to make an offer. This doesn't mean convincing someone at all costs to join you, but rather painting an authentic picture of the benefits of working with you so that the candidate can make a wise decision. In fact, you want to paint an accurate picture so that candidates who will not thrive can self-select out.

Some of this work occurs through the interview process itself. For instance, by meeting some of the staff during the process, the candidate will see what types of people work for you. In addition, one of the benefits of having the candidate complete activities that mimic the challenges of the position is that often the right candidate will be intrigued by the possibility of taking on that kind of work.

You can also talk about potentially enticing culture factors directly. For instance, Alison tells candidates during phone interviews, "One thing about our culture is that we hold ourselves to high standards. We strive for excellence in everything we do, the work ethic here is higher than anywhere else I've worked, and we're direct about addressing it when things aren't working out. Some people absolutely love that, but it's definitely not for everyone." Candidates who will fit in well with that culture become excited and more invested in the job prospect at this point, and candidates who aren't good matches tend to reveal that through their responses or drop out on their own.

Beyond the interview process, ensure that working at your organization is in fact an attractive proposition. Word-of-mouth about what it is like to work at the organization, and for you as a manager, may be the most important determinant of candidates' interest in the position (one of the many reasons *not* to be a tyrant, as we'll discuss in Chapter Ten).

In addition, you may want to make strategic decisions about your benefits package, knowing that building an organization of strong performers is generally the most important investment you can make. Among other things, consider salary levels (finances permitting, seek to have salaries that at a minimum are not a barrier to someone taking the job but that ideally might be an active selling point for the position), other benefits (including vacation time, which might be slightly more affordable than salary or other perks), and titles (which are cheap).

Perhaps most fundamental, you need to be able to communicate a clear story about your organization, the position, and the impact that the right person in the position can make. For people in the nonprofit sector, the most important benefit is often the opportunity to make a difference in the world, and you should communicate that opportunity to candidates throughout the process.

Making a Great Offer

Having sold the position throughout the hiring process, don't let it fall apart when you make the offer. Put yourself in the candidate's shoes: making the decision to join a new organization and team of people is anxiety producing, and having an offer conversation that is enthusiastic, organized, and thorough versus mechanical, unprepared, and uncommunicative can have an important impact on whether the candidate accepts the offer:

- *Create a sense of excitement.* Let your enthusiasm show when you make the offer. Tell her how excited you are at the possibility of having her work with you, why you think she will do a great job, and why you think she'll enjoy the position and organization.

- *Lead with a strong, clear offer.* Don't low-ball people on salary. Open with your strongest or close-to-strongest salary offer to show the candidate that you really want her. And if your budget allows it, be prepared to negotiate, within reason, so that you don't lose the right person over a small amount of money.

- *Give the candidate time to think it over.* Many candidates ask for time to think over the offer before giving you a decision; usually it's a few days, but sometimes it is longer. Although you don't want to rush your best candidate into saying no and you should always be willing to give at least a few days, your circumstances should inform your judgment about how much time you can give. If a top-notch candidate says she needs several weeks because her partner is waiting to find out if his company will transfer him to your city, that's a reasonable request that likely makes sense to accommodate. However, if you have an excellent second-choice candidate whom you might lose if you wait too long, you'll have to decide how much risk you're willing to tolerate in order to wait on the first candidate. A good rule of thumb is to be as flexible as you can while protecting your own interests.

- *Get a sense of the candidate's thought process.* Ask directly what factors she's considering so you can respond to them. For instance, when making the offer, you can say, "So, do you have any initial reaction?" and if you sense the candidate isn't sold, you can ask, "What, if anything, might make you hesitate?" This will help you understand the candidate's thought process so that you can tailor your discussions to address her concerns.

- *Make it clear you really want her to say yes!* If you really want to get the best people, you can't make an offer and then sit passively by waiting for the candidate to respond. Although you don't want to badger your potential new employee, you do want to make sure she feels valued. Call periodically to check in, offer to answer any questions, ask whether she has any hesitations, and convey your excitement. Find others to call and do the same as well. Calls from future peers, other senior managers, or the head of your organization or board chair can be remarkably persuasive. You can make it more comfortable to do all this by letting the candidate know that you might, saying something like, "Unless you object, I might pester you before the deadline we set just to hear any new thoughts you've had, and I might ask my board chair to give you a call because I'd love for you to hear her thoughts about your potential role here."

- *Wrapping it up.* Ideally the candidate will accept your offer and you will set a start date. But if she turns you down, try to find out why and suggest that you keep in touch in case other opportunities arise.

LEGAL ISSUES   Hiring can raise a host of legal issues that go well beyond the scope of this book. If you are at all uncertain about the legality of something you are doing in the hiring process, consider checking with a lawyer. That said, here are a few specific issues to be careful about:

- *Record keeping.* If a rejected job applicant sues you, you will need to be able to articulate why the person was not selected (and general statements such as "not the best qualified candidate" may not suffice). Establish a record-keeping system if there is not yet one that allows you to capture that rationale at the time you make your decision (at the minimum, begin a file for your interview notes, which you use to jot down your quick rationale). Be sure to preserve such records for the length of the local statute of limitations period.

- *Diversity considerations.* If you are taking race or sex or other similar factors into account in the actual selection (as opposed to recruitment) process, there may be significant legal concerns. Consult with counsel before you engage in this kind of a program.

- *Interview questions.* This area of the law has many gray areas, but the bottom line is not to ask questions that might create a suspicion that you are going to make your hiring decision based on an illegal criterion, such as the applicant's race, religion, marital status, sex, or national origin. In addition, do not ask any questions that may elicit information about a disability that is protected under the Americans with Disabilities Act. If you are not sure what is acceptable, check with a lawyer.

- *Disparate impact.* If you're using employment tests or selection criteria that might have a disparate impact on a protected category of applicants (such as members of a particular racial or ethnic group or applicants of a particular sex), consult with legal counsel about the possible applicability of the disparate impact doctrine.

TRAINING PEOPLE RIGHT FROM THE START

Congratulations on your new hire! But don't rest just yet. Now's the time to make sure that you prepare for and train your new employee effectively.

If you've ever started a new job and discovered your employer wasn't prepared for you the moment you walked in the door, you know that the impression you make on an employee's first day can send messages about culture and expectations from the start. By being prepared and organized when new employees start, you send the message from day one that you're organized and efficient and that you care about using employees' time effectively.

Here are three concrete ways to ensure your new staff member's first few weeks go smoothly, plus a bonus tip:

- *Create an initial training agenda.* Before your new staffer starts, develop an agenda for a series of meetings that lays out everything that you'll cover with her early in her tenure. Tool 6.10 provides suggestions on the types of topics you might cover.

- *Ensure logistics are ready in advance.* Make sure the staff member's computer, phone, and e-mail accounts are set up and working before her first day. Have a list of passwords waiting for her so she can immediately log in, set up her voice mail, and so forth, and ensure that her work space is clean and stocked with supplies.

- *Check in regularly.* Check in more frequently with your new staff member, not only to provide more detailed input than you'd give someone who has worked with you longer, but also to see how she's adjusting. What is she finding most challenging? What sort of help might she need?

- *Bonus tip.* Never, ever refer to this process as "onboarding." Your staff won't, or at least shouldn't, respect you if you use jargon.

KEY POINTS

- Managers often overvalue specific knowledge or prior experience and don't put enough weight on underlying skills or qualities that are harder to develop and in the long run are much more likely to differentiate high performers.

- The key to success in hiring is to build a strong pool of candidates in the first place. View yourself as a headhunter, and go after the people you want.

- The best way to gauge how people will act in the future is to find out how they have acted in the past or to observe how they actually act in the present, *not* to ask them how they might act in the future. Make your selection process about the actual, not the hypothetical.

- In making your decision, listen to your instincts. Would you be thrilled if this person joined your organization? If you have concerns, pay attention to your instincts. If more information would help, modify the process to gather the facts you need. If you don't have the right person, find short-term solutions rather than hiring the wrong person.

- Throughout the process, paint an authentic picture of the benefits of working with you. Candidates who are a good fit will become excited and more invested in the job.

Additional Reading

Marcus Buckingham and Curt Coffman, *First, Break All the Rules: What the World's Greatest Managers Do Differently* (New York: Simon & Schuster, 1999), especially "Skills, Knowledge, and Talents," "The World According to Talent," and "Talent: How Great Managers Find It" (pp. 83–104).

Jim Collins, *Good to Great: Why Some Companies Make the Leap . . . and Others Don't* (New York: HarperCollins, 2001), especially "First Who . . . Then What" (pp. 41–64).

TOOL 6.1

SAMPLE JOB POSTING

State Health Care Now: State Policy Director

State Health Care Now is seeking a full-time state policy director to lead our state advocacy activities, primarily by building and maintaining alliances among key actors throughout the state.

The ideal candidate will have a proven ability to foster coordination and cooperation among diverse, and even competing, groups. He or she will be committed to getting results in a fast-paced environment and able to handle a heavy workload. This position is an excellent opportunity to engage with policymakers, nongovernmental organizations, industry executives, and constituents to help bring about legislative change.

About State Health Care Now

State Health Care Now is a fast-paced nonprofit organization whose mission is to bring about affordable, meaningful health insurance to every state resident. We work closely with policymakers, advocates, and business leaders, and have built a reputation as one of the state's leading voices for health care reform. We plan to add twenty-four partners over the next two years and achieve universal coverage for all children in our state by 2015.

Job Responsibilities

The state policy director, who is based in X state and reports to the executive director, is responsible for the following:

- Building and maintaining strategic relationships with policymakers, nongovernmental organizations, industry executives, leading experts, and constituents
- Implementing our state advocacy agenda—currently, three major programs and one annual conference
- Supervising three state-based project staff and two to four consultants and volunteers
- Monitoring legislative proposals and trends
- Serving as a member of the organization's leadership team

Qualifications

We're seeking candidates who excel in relationship building, are results oriented, and have strong project management skills. You should have:

- A track record of developing and maintaining strong working relationships with and among a diverse group of stakeholders
- A demonstrated commitment to meeting a high bar and a history of getting things done even in the face of obstacles

- Experience managing multiple projects and the ability to oversee a cadre of staff, consultants, and volunteers

Knowledge of health care policy issues and prior experience in a legislative environment are both pluses but are not requirements.

Compensation depends on experience and is highly competitive.

How to Apply

Please send a cover letter and résumé to Pat Rodriguez, vice president of advocacy, at pat@statehcnow.org.

TOOL 6.2
SAMPLE TALENT LIST

Here's a template you can use to track promising potential staff members.

Name	Current Organization	Possible Fits	Contact Information	Notes
Liz Williams	Citizens for a Better World	Senior communications role	lwilliams@cbw.org	Savvy, energetic, responsible for CBW's 2009 media blitz, strong interest in new media
Mindy Menendez	Schools Now	Operations, midlevel	mindy@schools.org	Strong critical thinker, likes creating and making systems work, great interpersonal skills, not sure about writing
Talib Ali	Health Care for Kids	Political director, campaigns, senior level	tali@healthcare.org	Powerhouse campaign organizer, committed to staying at HCK through election, then wants to move East

TOOL 6.3
SAMPLE WORKSHEET FOR BUILDING
THE APPLICANT POOL

Most hiring mistakes occur not simply because managers select the wrong person, but because they don't have the right pool to select from. Use this worksheet to build a strong pool of applicants.

Job title: _____

1. Identify potential candidates and connector sources, or people who can put you in touch with other good applicants.

Categories to Draw From	Potential Candidates	Connector Sources
Your contact list	Sarah Smith (RJ)	
Your current staff		
Former staff		Jesse Lee (SK)
Peer or pipeline organizations		
Other		

Assign someone to pursue each lead, and put their initials in the parentheses.

Try conducting a brainstorming session with a set target: "We won't leave until we have six good candidates and twenty good sources to call."

2. Next, brainstorm ways to mass-market the job posting.

Mass Marketing Category	Places to Post Job Listing
Your own or allied organizations (Web sites, newsletters)	
Social networks	
Community or industry-specific listservs (idealist.org, indeed.com)	
Professional societies or associations (Association of Fundraising Professionals)	
Alumni/career services offices	
Other	

TOOL 6.4
SAMPLE REJECTION E-MAILS

This sample is to a candidate who didn't make it to the interview stage.

Subject: State Health Care Now State Policy Director position

Dear Josephine,

Thank you for applying for the state policy director position with State Health Care Now. We appreciate your interest in our organization and your commitment to sensible health care policy reform.

We received more than 200 applications for the position, and the hiring process has been a very competitive one. Although we were impressed with your qualifications, we have decided not to move your application forward. However, we greatly appreciate your interest in working with us and wish you the best of luck with your job search.

Sincerely,
Barry Ruiz
Chief of Staff

This sample is to a candidate who did have an in-person interview.

Subject: State Health Care Now State Policy Director position

Dear Dan,

Thanks so much for talking with Tracy and me last week about our state policy director position. We really enjoyed the meeting, especially hearing about your work with United Way, and we were impressed with your qualifications.

We've had a very competitive pool and have had to make hard decisions, and unfortunately I won't be able to advance you into the next round of interviews. I have no doubt, though, that you'll be a real asset to an organization in the right position, and I wish you the best of luck with your job search.

Best,
Barry Ruiz
Chief of Staff

TOOL 6.5

SAMPLE JOB SIMULATION EXERCISES

Having candidates complete exercises similar to what they'd be doing on the job can give you a good idea of how they would perform if hired. This list of sample exercises tests for specific qualities. Brainstorm activities for your candidates in the space below.

Position	Must-Have Qualities	Sample Exercise
Chief operating officer	Critical thinking, writing	Observe the organization in action (delivering a training session, staging a rally, holding a hearing) and propose recommendations for improvement in a two- or three-page memo.
Manager of programs	Strategic thinking	Read and analyze a set of goals and objectives and come up with recommendations to pursue.
Director of communications	Public speaking, judgment	Rehearse a press conference or a call with a reporter about a controversial program we support.
Manager of a small- or medium-sized department	General management, staff supervision	Simulate giving positive and corrective feedback to a supervisee.
Fundraising associate	Persuasive communication	Write a brief funding proposal or cover letter to a donor.
Special events associate	Organization or project management	Develop a project plan for an annual conference.
Director of policy and advocacy	Strategic thinking, interpersonal skills	Sit in on a meeting with a potential partner organization. Afterward, give feedback, including a recommendation on whether and how to engage with them.
Senior associate for policy and advocacy	Ability to explain complex ideas in a simple way	Produce a visual outlining key players in the health care industry and the relationships among them.

Position	Must-Have Qualities	Sample Exercise
Research associate	Strategic thinking, writing	Write a memo on how a specific change in legislation might affect state support for low-income families.
Trainer	Presentation and teaching skills	Make a short presentation teaching a skill of your choice (how to write a grant, how to create a work plan, how to plan a conference, and so forth).
Executive assistant	Fast paced, attention to detail	Complete a fifteen-minute scheduling exercise involving multiple meeting requests.

TOOL 6.6

SAMPLE INTERVIEW PREPARATION E-MAIL

This is a sample e-mail to a job applicant prior to a second interview.

Subject: Meeting on Tuesday

Susan,

I'm looking forward to speaking with you again next week about the state policy director position here at State Health Care Now.

As I mentioned on the phone, in addition to talking more about your prior experiences, I'm also hoping we can spend a portion of our time focusing on materials related to the position. Enclosed you will find:

- Monthly and quarterly goals. During our discussion, I'd love to get your feedback on these goals and hear how you might approach them.
- A newsletter and informational brochure from the Small Business Owners' Health Forum. As we discussed, you will be sitting in on Daniel's meeting with the forum's advocacy officer next week. I look forward to hearing your thoughts on how this conversation went and on whether and how you would structure a partnership with them.
- A list of our core values, a statement of expectations for managers, and a one-page version of our annual objectives to give you more background about our organization and where we are headed.

Thanks again for your interest, and I look forward to seeing you on Tuesday at 2:00.

Best,
Tracy Brown
Executive Director

TOOL 6.7
SAMPLE INTERVIEW QUESTIONS

The overarching key to each category is to listen carefully, probe to get beneath the surface, and focus the questions or activities around the key traits that you are most interested in.

Probing Prior Experiences

- Of your prior jobs, which do you think was the most significant?
- What was the part of your role you spent the most time doing [or, What was the most significant project]?
- What were you trying to achieve?
- How did you approach it?
- Walk me through your process. What did you do first? Why? What did you do next? What happened after that? What was the result?
- What was the biggest challenge there?
- What was your biggest achievement? What was something you accomplished that you think someone else in your role might not have gotten done [or, Where you approached it differently from how others might have, or where you went above and beyond]?
- It must have been hard to do Y. How did you approach that?
- On your résumé, you mentioned that you accomplished ABC. How did that come about? What was your specific role in it?
- Why did you leave X job?
- Tell me about Z job. What led you to work there? What was your role?

Direct Questions About Specific Qualities

Tell me about a time at X when:
- You were faced with a really difficult challenge.
- You went above and beyond to get a result.
- You persisted despite obstacles.
- You gave up or almost gave up.
- You had to put your ideas into writing.
- You had to deliver an important speech.
- You had to motivate someone to do something.
- You came up with a new approach for tackling a problem.
- You had to come up with a strategy for how to get to a particular outcome.
- You had to move a group to action (within or outside the organization).
- You had to stay on top of a large volume of work or had to multitask.
- You had to explain complex ideas in a simple way.

What did you do in this situation? What did you do next? What happened after that? What was the result? Would you do anything differently? Did you ever face another similar situation? How did you handle that one?

Personal Goals and General Fit

- What makes you want to work here?
- What leads to your interest in X issue?
- Where does that desire to improve things come from?
- What do you think is the most important problem facing our society today?
- Where do you see X [one of your organization's issues] fitting in?
- What are you looking for in your next job? If you could design the perfect job, what would it look like? Why?
- Some people are at a point in their career where work is their top priority and they're dying to immerse themselves fully in their work. Others are at a point where they want to do interesting work but it may not be the most important thing for them. Both are legitimate positions. Where would you put yourself on that spectrum right now?
- What was your favorite job and why? What was your least favorite and why? How do those things compare to what you're looking for now?

Note: Be careful not to ask about marital status, family, etc. here, though the interviewee might bring those things up. You are trying to figure out whether the person is looking for a job that might require going above and beyond, or whether they are looking for a 9 to 5 job, regardless of their external circumstances.

The following questions can be followed up by probing prior specific experiences: "So tell me about a time when that happened/when you demonstrated that/when that came up? What did you do next/how did you handle that?"

- What really frustrates you at work?
- What do you think it is that makes you outstanding at what you do? What do you think you need to get better at?
- If I were to talk to your colleagues or your managers, what would they say are the things you're best at? What would they say you need to improve in?
- What works for you in a manager? What doesn't work for you?

TOOL 6.8
SAMPLE INTERVIEW OUTLINE

Candidate: <u>Susan Smith</u>   Date/location: <u>9/18/2012, D.C. office</u>

Interviewed by: <u>Tracy Brown, ED</u>   Interview round: <u>1</u>

Key Must-Haves

- Relationship building
- Results orientation
- Project management skills

Nice-to-haves: Knowledge/experience related to our issue or legislative environment, good writing skills, ability to think strategically, belief in social issues

I. Introduction

I thought we'd start by having you share a bit more about your interest in the position and then dig into your background by discussing some of your past experiences. I'll then share with you more about where we're headed as an organization and what we're looking for in this role. At the end, we'll talk next steps. Sound good?

II. Warm-Up Questions

1. What led you to apply for this position?

2. What kind of role are you looking for at this point in your career?

> *Start off with one or two quick questions as a warm-up; then dive into the meat of the interview: probing prior experiences.*

III. Prior Experiences

General (seeking useful information keeping in mind all the must-have qualities)

1. I see from your résumé that you worked with Neighbors in Action. Tell me more about that.

   - What was the project on which you spent the most time?
   - What were you trying to achieve?
   - How did you approach the development of the campaign? Walk me through your process: What did you do first? Why? What did you do next? What other options did you consider? Why did you end up pursuing that route? What happened after that? What was the result?
   - Who else was directly involved with you in designing that campaign? What were some of the challenges in working together? How did you approach them?

- What other challenges did you face during the course of this campaign? How did you deal with them?
- What were the major victories? Would you say you met your original goals?
- How did the campaign conclude? Lesson learned?

2. What other job or project has been significant in your prior professional experience? Tell me about that.

Delve deeply into three or more prior experiences. Don't be shy about pressing for details and concrete evidence.

Direct (probing for evidence of specific must-have qualities)

1. *Relationship building:* More than anything else, this position involves a lot of relationship building. You mentioned partnering with a couple of other organizations when you worked on the Neighborhood Safety Campaign. Can we talk about another time when you had to build relationships with other actors?

   - How did you go about pursuing that relationship?
   - How did you gain access to their top level of management? Who else in that organization did you speak to? How often would you meet?

   Stick to real examples and avoid the hypothetical.

   - What were the major outcomes of that partnership? Is there a particular success in this area we could discuss? A challenge?

2. *Project management:* As the state policy director, you would be managing several projects at the same time, from our advocacy campaigns to monitoring legislation to building the statewide coalition.

   - Can you tell me about a project you managed that went well? What do you think made it successful? How did you plan it, and how did you manage to the plan?
   - What about a time when things didn't go so well? Was there ever a dropped ball on a project you were managing? What happened, and what did you do?
   - Have you ever had to manage multiple projects at once? How did you keep track of what was on your plate and what other people were doing?
   - In general, how do you stay on top of so many details? When you get into work in the morning, how do you decide what to do that day and where to begin?

IV. Exercises

We sent you a project plan before this meeting and would love to turn to that now.

- What did you think of the plan? Anything you would change or add to it?
- What do you think the likelihood of success is for this project as it's currently laid out?
- How would you manage to this plan if you were the owner of the project? What about if you were managing the owner of the project to this plan? How would you know things are on track?

V. General Information and Fit

General Information on Organization and Role

- Outgoing director moving to Iowa to oversee an expansion of our operations.
- Time of growth for us, and this position is key to our success: building alliances among a range of state players, conceiving and managing campaigns and other projects that move our issue forward, valuing results over process (public speaking is nice to have, but relationship building is key).
- Would work with national team and communications team and be part of the organization's leadership, reporting directly to me.
- Perhaps biggest selling point for our organization: our core values—continuous learning, excellence, and integrity—mean good people who like their work and are very good at it.

Questions About Personal Goals and Fit

- If you could design the position, how would you prioritize each of the areas of responsibility? What would be your favorite part of the job? Least favorite?
- At the beginning of this interview, you said your next position would ideally help you to develop "grasstops" advocacy skills. How do you see our organization and this particular position fitting into that goal?
- What are your concerns about this position? What questions do you have for me?

VI. Next Steps

Assuming the interview went well and you are interested in continuing the process, you might assign homework.

We find it useful to simulate part of the job in the interview process so that you get a taste of the role and we get to see you in action a bit. Assuming you're interested in continuing in the process, I'd like to start by giving you a homework assignment:

> Create a project plan for our spring advocacy day. Ideally it would include goals as well as a time line and key steps along the way. Here's a description of the campaign, the actors involved, and what we're aiming to achieve [provide the memo]. Ideally, you'd create a plan that would specify the path we'd take to get to April 15. Major constraints are a budget of $10,000 and a commitment to include all major stakeholders in key roles (see the overview for more detail). Would it be possible to send me a draft by next Tuesday? Also, if you have a project plan you've used for a past project, I'd love to see that as well.

Exercises can take place during or outside the actual interview. Starting with a homework assignment is a good first step if you know you want to advance the person to the next round or if you want more information.

I'll look forward to reviewing your project plan next week. Next-round interviews (and exercises) with me and our chief operating officer will be held the last week in September. I'll let you know about next steps either way by next Friday.

Specify when you'll follow up, whether or not you're advancing the candidate to the next round.

If the homework assignment goes well, you might bring the candidate back for a second-round interview and on- or off-site exercises.

On-site exercise testing for relationship building skills: Participate in a meeting between our outgoing director and the advocacy officer from the Small Business Owners' Health Forum. Give input/feedback on whether and how to partner with them.

TOOL 6.9
SAMPLE REFERENCE CHECK QUESTIONS

The fundamental challenge of checking references is that you want the person providing the reference to be candid with you, but this person probably feels loyal to your candidate and will avoid saying anything negative. It will help to use a conversational tone to put the reference at ease and to signal that this is not a mere bureaucratic exercise, and find ways to make it easier for references to talk about the candidate's downsides. For instance, ask bounded questions about weaknesses that are hard not to answer ("if you had to pick, what are two ways Susan could improve?") or posing neutral options where there is no "bad" choice.

Start by describing the role, which will help references give you better answers. For instance:

> I'm the legislative director at State Health Care Now. Thanks so much for agreeing to speak with me about your experience working with Susan. Before I ask you about her, would it be helpful for me to give you a bit of background about the role? We're a twenty-person advocacy organization committed to enacting universal health coverage legislation in the state. The organization is growing, and Susan is a finalist for our new state policy director position. This director must be a pro at working with a diverse group of actors and building alliances among them, have a demonstrated track record of getting results in a fast-paced environment, and be capable of managing multiple projects tightly without dropping any balls.

Then ask about the candidate:

- What parts of what we're looking for sound most like something Susan might succeed at? What makes you say that?
- If you had to pick out two pieces of where you think Susan might not be as strong or might need some development, what would those be?
- What do you think Susan's coworkers would say were her greatest strengths? What would they say Susan might need to work on?
- In my experience, I've seen some people who are more like A and some who are more like B. Which would you say Susan is? [For example, "In my experience, I've seen some people who are more uptight and organized, if a little prickly, and some who are more laid-back and friendly, though maybe not always hitting deadlines. Which sounds more like Susan?"]
- What was Susan's greatest achievement?
- Tell me about a time when you were not entirely thrilled with Susan's performance.
- Tell me about a time when Susan:
  - Was faced with a really difficult challenge
  - Went above and beyond to get a result
  - Persisted despite obstacles
  - Gave up or almost gave up

- Had to put her ideas in writing
- Had to deliver an important speech
- Had to move a group to action (within the organization or outside the organization)
- Came up with a new approach for tackling a problem
- Had to come up with a strategy for how to get to a particular outcome
- Had to stay on top of a large volume of work or had to work on several demanding projects at work
- Had to explain complex ideas in a simple way
- Had to motivate someone to do something

- What should I know about Susan if I'm going to manage her effectively? What should I get Susan to do a lot of because she's really good at it? In what area might I need to get Susan most to develop?
- What kind of job would you hire Susan for? What kind of job would you not hire Susan for?
- Overall, how would you rate Susan's performance?
- If you were thinking of hiring again for Susan's position, how would you describe your reaction if she applied, knowing what you know about her: would not hire, would consider hiring, would strongly consider hiring, would definitely hire, would move earth and moon to lure her back?
- How would Susan rank compared to people in similar positions? Would you say about average, a little better than average, top quarter, top 10 percent, top 1 percent, or the best ever? What makes you say that?
- Is there anything else you would want to know if you were in my shoes?
- May I call you again if I think of other questions?

TOOL 6.10
SAMPLE ORIENTATION OUTLINE

Having a written agenda for orienting a new employee not only helps you present information in an organized way, but also helps you think through everything that you want to cover. This sample lays out a plan for what topics will be covered, in what order, during the staff member's first days.

Position: Communications Director

Desired Outcomes

- You understand your overarching role and my expectations.
- We're aligned about logistics and how to work together.
- You feel settled in and know how to navigate the organization.
- You know what projects to prioritize initially.

Monday

I. Your Role

A. Getting our message into the news via pitching, interviews, op-eds, letters to the editor, news releases, creative stunts, and anything else you can think of

B. Ensuring our message and rhetoric are effective and on point; being the messaging guru

C. Related responsibilities:

- Setting our overall media strategy, both nationwide and in each state we work in
- Writing and editing various materials, such as talking points and briefing papers
- Managing department (work and staff)

D. Potential impact of your role = huge!

II. Working Together/Expectations

A. Some ideas on keys to success:

- 100 percent follow-through. Trust that when we say we will do something, we will do it (goes both ways!).
- Take initiative and be solutions oriented. Don't assume constraints.
- Spread a positive attitude, and be flexible in the face of a constantly changing environment.
- Complete open-door policy. Ask questions or raise suggestions without hesitation.

B. What you can expect from me:

- Initial period of heavier engagement for alignment (presumably less after that)
- 100 percent follow-through and responsiveness
- Good communication on expectations, priorities, and specific projects
- Interest in your development

C. Logistics and communications

- Hours: meetings 9:30 and 6:30; may extend beyond, but we try to avoid weekends.
- Our meeting: Regular weekly check-ins to review week ahead and discuss other topics (ideally, you bring any challenges/topics I can help with and you have suggested solutions, but don't feel obligated to wait on pressing matters for our check-in).
- Phone/voice mail: nonurgent = vmail at office; more pressing or quick response = cell. Try to flag with "this is urgent" or "not urgent—listen in the next day," etc.
- E-mail: also works well. Flag if time sensitive.

D. General principles

- Take good notes so you remember the subtleties of what we discuss.
- Let's do repeat-backs when appropriate so we're aligned from the start of projects.

E. Your goals/preferences/thoughts/quirks/questions?

III. Office Tour

- Supplies, front desk, conference rooms, copier, fax, etc. (with office manager)

IV. Orientation and Background Information

A. Review of mission (why we exist and what we do) and core values (how we do it)

B. Review annual plan: priorities and goals for this year

C. Confidentiality policy

D. Employee handbook—any questions?

E. Financial policies and procedures

V. Getting Started

A. Keys, phone/vmail, Internet/e-mail, and calendar (set up to be shared) (covered by office manager)

B. Timesheet basics: what and how to track (covered by office manager)

C. Upcoming meetings for you:

- Today: lunch with staff at 1:00
- Payroll, benefits, 403b, etc.: meet with Jim today at 2:00

- Tuesday: continue this meeting at 12:00
- Friday: lessons learned with staff on Fridays at 4:00

VI. Specific Initial Topics

A. Read as much as possible of assigned materials, and start getting comfortable with issues and our work.

B. Practice using all our systems as much as needed to be comfortable with them.

C. Meet department heads and learn about their projects.

D. Practice doing media interviews with Ryan.

E. Start on writing projects as needed (blog posts, drafting press releases).

F. Use press inquiries that come in to learn how to deal with these, find necessary information or referrals, etc.

G. Likely first media opportunity: New Mexico event, Dec. 14 or 15.

TUESDAY

I. Your Goals for This Quarter and for the Year

A. Setting three-month goals

B. Goals for full year

- Increase our news coverage by 20 percent over last year.
- Move our issue to the top of voters' minds in New Mexico.
- Garner significant positive coverage of the release of our fall report.

C. In two weeks, set up meeting with me to discuss in depth.

II. Learning the Issue

A. Reading list

B. Basic rhetoric training and talking points

C. What we DON'T say

D. Experts we can check with or send reporters to

III. Key Resources, Information and Systems

A. Media databases and directories

IV. Managing the Assistant Director of Communications

A. Amanda's duties; how work is split up

B. Amanda's strengths and weaknesses

C. Approving Amanda's work product, proofing and quality control

V. Working with Other Departments

A. Outreach

B. Membership

C. Campaigns

VI. Department Logistics

A. What you have the authority to do and what you need to seek approval for

B. Expenditures

C. What things need to be proofread

D. Department files

WEDNESDAY

- No meetings scheduled

THURSDAY

VII. Advanced Media Training with Ryan

A. Pitching—practice if needed

B. Appropriate spokespeople for various issues

C. Who is and isn't authorized to talk to the media and authorizing new people to talk to the media

D. Vetting and training spokespeople

NEXT WEEK

- Let's meet Tuesday and Thursday of next week to check in, then switch to weekly check-ins from there.

CHAPTER

7

DEVELOPING PEOPLE

Contrary to popular belief, you don't need fancy professional development programs, formal mentorships, or large investments in staff training in order to develop your staff's skills and performance. In fact, in our experience, the results of these programs often do not justify the amount of energy that goes into them. Rather, the best staff development stems naturally from strong, hands-on management. That's because serious learning and development happen when staff members pursue ambitious goals, are held to high standards, and reflect and receive candid feedback about what is and is not working along the way.

In this chapter, we discuss how to most effectively help your staff develop. We start with the threshold question of when it makes sense to invest significant energy in developing a member of your staff. Then, for situations where it does make sense, we look at specific methods to use.

WHEN TO DEVELOP PEOPLE—AND WHEN NOT TO

From a purely practical perspective, you should spend time developing people because it will get you better results: your staff will become more effective in both the short and the long terms, and your organization will become a more attractive place to work, thereby helping you attract great people who in turn will produce strong results. But because it's also a nice thing to do for your staff and many of us are drawn to management partly because we love seeing people develop, sometimes as managers we forget that developing people is not an end in itself. Rather, because it is a means to the end of producing results in pursuit of your mission, you should be strategic about when and how you spend time on staff development, balancing that time and energy with other priorities.

Keep these three principles in mind when deciding when to invest time in staff development:

1. Invest in your best.

2. Know what you can change and what you can't.

3. Distinguish between development needs and serious performance issues.

Invest in Your Best

Paradoxically, your best staff members are usually the ones who will grow the most. Strong performers are often more driven than weaker ones, and so their desire to take advantage of development opportunities is higher. They also tend to be generally skilled people who are able to take a small amount of assistance and put it into practice, whereas others may struggle to apply the help. Because of this, the payoff from spending energy on your strongest performers will greatly exceed the results from energy you spend on your lowest performers.

For instance, in the introduction to Part Two, we mentioned the new regional director with whom Jerry worked who increased fundraising in her area from $43,000 annually when she took over the position to almost $300,000 just one year later. Recognizing a star in its midst, the organization sent several senior staffers to spend a few days with her. An average employee might have leveraged the coaching into gains of 10 percent or so, but with just that bit of input, two years later she had tripled her total to over $1 million.

Know What You Can Change and What You Can't

As we discussed in Chapter Six, you can build staff members' knowledge and improve specific skills, but it is difficult to change talents and basic inclinations. You might teach someone to use a particular software program or to deliver an effective presentation, but talents (like good writing, critical thinking, or being able to connect well with other people) and inclinations (like having a strong sense of responsibility or pursuing goals relentlessly) build up over a lifetime and tend to be deeply rooted and difficult to develop.

For instance, you might have a regional director who frequently gives presentations about your program to external audiences. She is enthusiastic and knowledgeable but lacks polish and tends to read directly from her slides. In her other work, she is very strong and, among other things, has raised significantly more money than her peers have. This is a case where public speaking training, whether a formal program like Toastmasters or informal role playing with you, could pay off, helping her become a more confident and skilled speaker.

In contrast, if you have a legislative analyst who is shy and uncomfortable interacting with others, you might be able to get her to speak up a bit more, but she's probably never going to excel at networking and building coalitions.

Distinguish Between Development Needs and Serious Performance Issues

Fortunately, the meat of the shy legislative analyst's job is analyzing legislation and writing briefs, activities that don't require a lot of interaction with others. While it might be nice if she were more outgoing, her shyness doesn't interfere with her ability to do her job well. But in other cases, the behavior in question will have a negative impact on the staff member's ability to do her job at the level you need. In situations where the employee's basic talents and inclinations are at odds with the requirements of the job, don't allow development to become a distraction that prevents you from dealing with core performance issues.

A media director, for example, needs to have good judgment when talking to reporters and be able to represent the organization's positions clearly and compellingly. Perhaps your media director has been on the job for five months and has shown poor judgment in several cases—in one, speaking to a reporter calling about a delicate public issue without first consulting anyone and making comments that inflamed the situation, and in two others, confusing reporters to the point that they called the executive director asking for clarification. You also have noticed that she still doesn't give the standard spiel when describing your organization's work to reporters. These problems go to the heart of the media director's fit for the role. You might eventually succeed in drilling the basic spiel into her, but she lacks judgment, the ability to think on her feet, and perhaps even basic critical thinking skills. Development efforts might produce small improvements with her, but she will probably never perform at the high level you need.

In determining whether the problem goes beyond a simple development need, watch for the following signs:

- You've tried developing the person some but have not seen significant improvement.

- The issue is something fundamental to the job.

- You're busy and are unable to invest the amount of time that would be needed to guide the staff member to where you need her to be.

If one (or more) of these issues is the case, see Chapter Nine on dealing with serious performance issues and letting lower performers go.

What About Motivation?

If you have the right people on your team, you shouldn't have to spend lots of energy motivating them. It's important to create the conditions in which the right people will feel motivated, of course, by giving them meaningful roles with real responsibility, helping them feel as if they're making progress toward ambitious but attainable goals, giving them a sense that they're learning, reminding them of the bigger picture of what the work is adding up to, praising their efforts, and showing that you care about them as people. Managers also need to avoid demotivating staff, as we discuss in Chapter Ten. But taking someone who is not excited about a job and turning that person around is awfully hard, and generally a questionable use of energy. Therefore, the development techniques we'll talk about here focus mainly on developing skill, not will.

HOW TO DEVELOP PEOPLE

When it does make sense to invest in developing your people, how do you do it? Although formal training programs can help when they are aimed at specific, concrete skills, generally the best learning comes when employees stretch themselves in the pursuit of meaningful goals and when managers coach them through the process.

In fact, simply managing to a good outcome develops staff. For instance, imagine that you manage a grant writer who is responsible for producing a major proposal to an important foundation. Having read Chapter Two on delegation, you'll do everything we advised there:

1. You'll discuss your expectations and what makes a proposal good, and you may show your staffer a sample of a proposal that worked in the past.

2. Once you have agreed on the expectations, you'll review and discuss an outline and possibly even a draft of one section to make sure the tone is right. Then you'll make comments on full drafts until they are where they need to be.

3. After the proposal is in, you'll do a quick debriefing to talk about what went well and what could have gone better.

Through this rigorous process—even more than formal writing courses, or official development plans, or any of the rest—your staff member will almost certainly become a much better proposal writer. If you think about the times when you have most successfully learned a new skill, the same probably holds true: we'd bet that most of what you learned came from actually doing the work rather than from sitting in a classroom or reading a book on the subject.

Still, there are things you can do beyond simply managing to a good outcome to contribute to your staff's learning. We look at a number of them here.

Naming the Issue

Before you can address a development area effectively, you need to name the issue. We know this sounds obvious, but sometimes coming up with a label for a behavior you want to see can be powerful. For instance, if you have a general unease with the training workshops you've seen a staff member give, don't simply tell her that she

WHAT ABOUT DEVELOPMENT PLANS? Opinions vary on this, but we've grown skeptical about the value of separate development plans, in part because those plans can distract staff members' attention from pursuit of their substantive goals. When a staff member does have specific development goals, though, one option is to include them in a "key development areas" section at the end of her annual goals. This will remind both of you to revisit her progress in these areas while keeping the onus on the employee to drive herself forward. Here's an example:

Goal 4: Key Development Areas

1. Refine my meeting-running skills.

2. Learn our database software thoroughly so I can better spot opportunities for using its features.

3. Improve my ability to advise activists on strategy, incorporating more nuance and less one-size-fits-all advice.

needs to work on her presentation skills. Instead, identify specifically what the issue is, such as that she's using the same presentation for experienced participants as she is for less advanced ones. Once you've determined that, you'll be better able to name the issue for her—in this case, saying something like, "We need to work on how to adapt your message to fit different audiences."

Articulating Key Principles

Once you've named the issue for your staff member, you can break down the key principles behind how to perform the skill well even if they seem obvious to you. After all, if you're a successful and experienced presenter, adapting your message to fit your audience might feel like second nature to you. But it won't come naturally to someone with less experience, so be sure to articulate the principles that go into doing it well. After identifying for the staff member that you'd like to work on adapting her workshops to fit the audience, you'd then go on to talk about key elements of how to do that well, such as asking questions to gauge audience members' prior knowledge, modifying examples to make them relevant to the audience's work, and paying attention to the audience's body language and other cues.

Giving Stretch Assignments

Assigning a staff member a responsibility that requires her to apply new skills or old skills at a higher level (such as going from managing two people to managing eight) often produces significant growth. Because people learn by doing, you might produce more learning by asking your strongest staff members to do more.

WHAT ABOUT PROMOTING FROM WITHIN? Promotions can be a great way to recognize when a staffer has developed and is ready for new challenges, and promoting from within lets you avoid the uncertainties of hiring a relative unknown from the outside. At the same time, even when your staffer is outstanding in her current role, there are many cases in which a promotion isn't the right move.

When contemplating promoting someone, the most important factor to consider is not what sort of job the staffer is doing in her current position, but instead how strongly matched she is with the skills you need in the new position. Organizations often do the opposite of this: we have frequently seen outstanding staffers get promoted and then flounder because the skills that made them so effective in the first position aren't the same ones needed for the new one. Most commonly we see this with promotions to managerial positions, since the skills needed to get results through others are often very different from those needed to get results on your own. For instance, a grant writer might excel at writing winning grant applications, but when promoted to development director, she might need very different skills, such as the ability to articulate expectations, help people solve their problems, and judge talent.

We encourage you to create opportunities for promotion when they make sense for the employee and the organization. But don't feel that you need to promote employees in order to retain them. There are many other ways to keep good employees on your staff, which we address in Chapter Eight.

Introducing One Piece at a Time

Some staff members love an enormous new challenge and will rise to meet it, growing in the process. But others can be paralyzed. A complement to the stretch assignments approach, then, is to structure the process so that your staff member starts with easier pieces and gradually adds others. For example, in grooming someone to become a manager, you might first have her manage others on a particular project, without giving her overall responsibility for managing all of their work.

As part of this process of breaking down a large new skill into its steps, you can create an atmosphere of deliberate learning by using an approach of "discuss, do, reflect." First, you and the staff member talk through what she is going to do, then she does it (perhaps with you observing her in action, where appropriate), and finally she reflects with you on how it went and how to improve in the future. For instance, if your assistant already screens job applicants' résumés, you might ask her to go further and begin conducting initial phone interviews with internship candidates. In the discussing stage, you'd meet with her to talk about interview techniques and perhaps role-play several interview situations. In the doing stage, you might observe her conducting one or two of the phone interviews. And in the reflecting stage, you'd discuss how she did, identify what she found most difficult, and brainstorm alternate ways of responding in the future.

A similar approach is to emulate what classroom teachers do in almost every lesson: using a cycle of "I do, we do, you do." Here, you first demonstrate a new skill for the staff member, then you do some of the work jointly, and finally you step back and allow her to do it on her own. For instance, if you're teaching your staffer to create formulas in a spreadsheet, you might first do a few yourself while she is watching (I do). Then you'd talk through a few examples together and do them jointly (we do). Finally, you'd have her do a few on her own without any help from you (you do).

Modeling the Skill for the Staffer

Implicit in the "I do, we do, you do" approach is the idea that often people need to see a skill or approach applied before they can do it themselves. For instance, if you want a staff member to conduct external meetings more effectively, you might have her accompany you and watch while you do one yourself. In modeling the skill, be explicit with your staff member about what you are doing and why. For instance, in modeling an external meeting, point out to the staff member how you were careful to agree with the participants to an informal agenda at the beginning of the meeting.

Giving Feedback

One of the most powerful tools managers have for developing staff is providing direct feedback. Simply articulating areas in which you'd like to see a staff member develop can go a long way toward making progress. (Tool 7.1 provides a worksheet for preparing for a conversation on giving feedback.)

You should provide feedback on a constant, ongoing basis in order to reinforce behavior you want to see more of, prevent bad habits from becoming ingrained, and foster an atmosphere of open communication. Providing feedback regularly can also allow you to address potential problems while they're still small rather than telling a staffer that something she has been doing for months is wrong. While ideally you'd be providing feedback regularly throughout your interactions each day, some of our clients have found it helpful to have a triggering mechanism. One such system is the 2×2 system. Tool 7.2 provides a sample form for this system.

At different times, your feedback will be positive (recognizing where an employee is doing well), developmental (sharing ways a good employee could do even better), or corrective (things that must change in order for the employee to meet your expectations).

Positive Feedback

One of the best ways to shape your staff's behavior is to give positive feedback. Telling a staff member, "I loved the way you organized that spreadsheet; the categories made sense and you made sure it was easy to read on the screen," almost guarantees you'll be seeing more well-organized spreadsheets in the future. In addition, positive feedback is a form of creating accountability. If your staff member consistently does a good job but never hears from you about it, she may wonder why no one appears to have noticed.

At the same time, most people can see through sugarcoating, so give positive feedback only when you really mean it. And with good employees around, you should be able to find plenty of actions that warrant praise.

Developmental Suggestions for Growth

When you spot ways that a good employee could do even better, sharing these suggestions can help her take her performance to a higher level. This type of feedback isn't about serious concerns. Likely, the employee would continue to do a fine job even if she didn't implement your suggestion. For instance, if you notice that your Webmaster isn't at her most effective when explaining technical topics to nontechnical staff, you might say something like, "I wanted to talk about our meeting with the campaign team and share some thoughts about how you might get your points across to them better." You could then explain that while her agenda was well structured and her points strong ones, non-IT people don't know some of the terms she uses, and that using simpler language and stopping to check for understanding might help her communicate better with her audience.

Corrective Feedback

Unlike developmental suggestions for growth, where the staff member would still be doing a good job even if she didn't implement your suggestions, corrective feedback is about things that must change in order for the staff member to meet expectations. Most managers find this type of feedback the hardest to give, and some put it off out of discomfort. Don't fall into that trap. The longer you wait to give corrective feedback, the more the problem will take root, so get in the habit of giving this sort of feedback as soon as you can. As you do, be direct. Don't get so caught up in trying to be tactful that your message gets diluted or lost. For instance, if you're disappointed in your communications director's poorly written press release, say, "I'd like to talk about this recent press release. When would be a good time to do that?" Then tell her that the release did not meet your expectations. Point out the specific ways in which the press release fell short and suggest concrete ways she might improve it.

You might also use the example as a vehicle for delving into other issues that might be at play. For instance, you might say, "What's strange to me is that I know you are a better writer than this. Do you have a sense of why you didn't apply your skills as well as you might have here?" The employee might reply that she forgot to schedule time to write the release and wrote it at the last minute (an opening to delve into issues of time management), that she didn't think it was important to get it right because reporters rarely copy text straight from releases (responsibility), or that she honestly did give it her best shot and is frustrated that it didn't come out better (writing skills).

If the problem persists after talking about it directly, you may need to reconsider the employee's fundamental fit for the role. Chapter Nine has an in-depth discussion about what factors to consider in such a situation and how to have serious performance warning conversations.

A STRUCTURE FOR GIVING FEEDBACK

1. Describe the behavior you've observed in a short sentence: "I've noticed recently that when running meetings, you sometimes have trouble keeping the group focused on the agenda."

2. Provide two or three concrete examples to support your feedback: "First, in our meeting with X, and then with Y . . ."

3. State the impact of the behavior on you and, as appropriate, on your team, department, or organization: "We ended up not having time to reach conclusions and had to schedule a follow-up later, and we lost the attention of a couple of people when the topic we veered into wasn't relevant to them."

4. Make a recommendation: "Try allotting specific amounts of time to each item on your agenda to keep the meeting on track."

This structure applies for positive feedback as well (with the recommendation at the end amounting to, "Keep it up!"). For corrective or developmental feedback, make sure to do one additional step:

- Follow up. Make a note to revisit the topic a month or so later and discuss how it's been going. You might need to give additional guidance or correction, or you'll be able to recognize and praise the staff member's progress.

Providing Additional Resources

Particularly for help in developing specific skills or knowledge, you can steer staff members to books or articles, workshops, or other people you have found helpful.

Pulling It All Together

In practice, you'll often use more than one of these techniques at a time. You'll also choose different techniques for when you're helping someone develop a technical skill versus a behavior. For instance, writing effective press releases is a skill, while being consistent in work product is a behavior. You might use "I do, we do, you do" with the skill but would probably rely on naming the issue and giving feedback for the behavior.

Here are a few examples of development needs you might face and how you might approach them:

- *You want to help your program director run more effective meetings.* Start by naming the issue and giving her feedback on her technique, followed by some key principles for running a meeting well. Then you might have her watch you run a meeting and talk with her afterward about what she observed. Next, you'd watch her run a meeting herself, using the guidance you've been giving her, reflecting afterward on how it went.

- *Your database coordinator is quick, but, perhaps in the pursuit of speed, too often she makes mistakes in her work.* In this case, you'd name the issue and emphasize the need for accuracy. Then you'd check back a week or two later and provide feedback on her progress.

- *A manager is having trouble addressing a performance issue with one of her staffers.* In this case, modeling the skill might mean role-playing the conversation, starting with your playing her role so that she can hear what the conversation might sound like. Then you'd switch roles and have her play herself while you play her employee, allowing her to practice the tough conversation on you and allowing you to give her feedback on tone and language. She'd then speak with her staff member directly, and debrief with you afterward.

One thing the approaches in all three scenarios share is that developing is usually a process, not a one-time event. So in addition to surfacing the issue, a good developer of people will stay engaged to see how the staff member is progressing. Then she will ensure that a step-back conversation happens once the staff member has had a chance to improve to see how things are going. (Sound familiar? If you said, "This is just like the delegation cycle in Chapter Two!" then you're our favorite reader. If you've read ahead to our "Time and Systems" chapter and said, "Yeah, and I'd have to put a note in my calendar to remember to revisit this topic!" then you should come and work with us!)

LAUNCHING DIFFICULT CONVERSATIONS—CHOOSE YOUR MEDIUM
Conventional wisdom will tell you never to raise a sensitive or difficult topic over e-mail, and instead to always have such conversations face-to-face. We agree that's usually the ideal, but sometimes you might deliberately choose a different medium. For instance, sometimes you'll be raising an issue with someone you know will respond better if she has some time to absorb and process your feedback first. In that case, it can be both kinder and more effective to raise the issue initially in e-mail (or, depending on your culture, in a phone call or voice mail), before you discuss it in person. In other cases, you might be the one who has trouble raising an issue face-to-face, and so you might raise it in e-mail first in order to ensure the discussion happens at all.

We want to be clear: This isn't an excuse to avoid hard conversations; ultimately you will need to talk face-to-face. And in fact, make sure you include "let's talk tomorrow" in your message, so that the topic isn't left hanging. But sometimes surfacing the issue in an e-mail, phone call, or voice mail can help both parties.

"Earlier in my career, I hired someone, and it quickly became clear to me that he was so disorganized that we had made the wrong decision. In trying to reverse that decision, which is very difficult to do, I learned the limitations of trying to do things in a covert way. It doesn't work; it just backfires completely. I should have said, 'Here are the things you need to do to be more effective,' and had a rigorous process to evaluate against those things. Since then, I've realized that in that situation, you need to create extremely short-term goals that reflect the positive behaviors you want to see, things that are easy wins. If you do that in very short cycles, it clarifies whether the change is possible in a lower-stakes way than if you let the problems build."

DAVID BENNAHUM, FOUNDER, AMERICAN INDEPENDENT NEWS NETWORK

PERFORMANCE EVALUATIONS

In addition to giving feedback on a regular, ongoing basis throughout the year, you should also conduct more formal performance evaluations. These evaluations give you a vehicle to assess an employee's performance and progress against goals, provide suggestions for growth and improvement, let you find out how the employee is feeling about her job, and, in the case of lower performers, send clear messages about the consequences of failing to improve.

Effective Performance Review Processes

Organizations vary in how they structure performance review processes, but typically a manager provides a written evaluation to the employee and then the two meet to discuss it in person. Managers often ask employees to fill out self-assessments ahead of time as well, ideally using the same form that the manager will use for the assessment.

Most organizations conduct evaluations annually, sometimes with a second mid-year review. As we noted in Chapter Three, if you want your staff members to take their goals seriously, set the cycle for your evaluations so that you can assess whether the staff member achieved her goals for the relevant time period (as opposed to reviewing performance on staff members' anniversaries of employment). In addition, you should also conduct an evaluation with new employees two or three months after beginning the job in order to reflect on fit for the position and identify areas for growth. These can also include questions about how the employee is adjusting and what additional help she may need in the role.

What a Performance Evaluation Form Should Include

To be truly effective, a performance evaluation should focus primarily on the employee's results, how she got those results, and an overall summary and tenure considerations. A common mistake organizations make is focusing on how the employee did her work, to the exclusion of the actual outcomes she achieved, but in a results-oriented organization, the evaluation should start with outcomes:

1. *Results.* List the employee's objectives for the year and assess how well she met each of them. Take the context into account. For instance, if your development director didn't meet her fundraising goal for the year but it's because the stock market dropped 20 percent, acknowledge that. Conversely, if she met her goal but only because of an unexpected large bequest that she had little to do with, point out that she should have been able to vastly exceed the goal.

2. *Performance factors.* Next, assess how the employee approached her work. You might divide this section in two, first addressing organizational values that you expect all staff members to demonstrate (integrity, continuous improvement, persistence) and then assessing skills that are specific to this employee's role (say, public speaking, writing compelling briefing papers, building relationships with policymakers).

3. *Summary and tenure considerations.* In the final section, discuss how the staff member is performing overall. Are there any next steps for improvement she should take? In order to send clear, unambiguous signals about the staff member's performance, we strongly recommend using a rating system. You might also discuss the extent to which her continued tenure in the role makes sense. For higher-performing employees, the tenure question can be a sentence or two in which you flag the topic to be raised in your in-person discussion: "I'm excited to talk about what you're thinking about your future when we meet." But if you have concerns about the staffer's fit for the role, put that in writing here, noting that if she does not improve, she may face dismissal.

Elements of an Effective Performance Evaluation

Keep the following principles in mind when you're writing performance evaluations of your staff members:

- Ideally, nothing in a performance evaluation should be a surprise, because you've been giving the staff member feedback throughout the year. (But if that's not the case, don't let that prevent you from being direct now.)

- Be specific and use examples to illustrate your points when praising and when identifying areas for improvement. For instance, you could say, "You did a great job with the new inventory system," but it's more effective to say, "Your revamping of the inventory system has saved the organization money, and I've heard several people comment about how much easier you've made it to find the supplies they need."

- Pay attention to the overall picture you're painting. We've seen managers inadvertently write lukewarm evaluations for stellar employees whom they would be devastated to lose. And if the employee needs to make major improvements, make sure that comes through in the overall message. Think of the evaluation as a mini-essay, where you want to make sure that your thesis statement ("You're doing great!" or "I need you to reach the next level quickly") comes through. Tools 7.3 and 7.4 provide samples of completed evaluation forms.

- Resist the temptation to be overly influenced by recent events. If an employee has struggled with something all year but recently improved, or if she has done well all year but recently made a major error, be sure the evaluation reflects the whole year, not just the past few months. At the same time, if someone has struggled all year but improved recently, be sure to note that so the person doesn't feel her efforts went unnoticed.

- Consider getting feedback in confidence from others who work closely with the employee. You may find out aspects of the person's performance, both good and bad, that you didn't know about.

KEY POINTS

- Invest in your best, because your best staff members are usually the ones who will grow the most.

- Know what you can change (skills and knowledge) and what you can't (talents and basic inclinations).

- Distinguish between development needs and serious performance issues, and don't allow development to distract you from dealing with underlying performance issues.

- The best staff development stems naturally from strong, hands-on management: pursuing ambitious goals, being held to high standards, and being given candid and direct feedback about what is and is not leading staff members to reach their goals.

- Additional ways of developing staff members include naming the issue, articulating key principles, giving stretch assignments, introducing one new facet at a time, modeling, giving feedback, and providing additional resources.

- Provide feedback on a constant, ongoing basis in order to reinforce behavior you want to see more of, prevent bad habits from becoming ingrained, and foster an atmosphere of open communication.

- Conduct formal performance evaluations each year. To be truly effective, a performance evaluation should focus primarily on the employee's results, how she got those results, and an overall summary and tenure considerations.

- Promotions can be a great way to recognize when a staffer has developed and is ready for new challenges, but the key consideration must be how well matched the employee is with the skills needed in the new position, not how well she has done in the previous position.

Additional Reading

Marcus Buckingham and Curt Coffman, *First, Break All the Rules: What the World's Greatest Managers Do Differently* (New York: Simon & Schuster, 1999), especially "Spend the Most Time with Your Best People" (pp. 153–163).

TOOL 7.1
FEEDBACK WORKSHEET

I want to give _____ (name) feedback on _____ (skill/area).

Setting the Stage

I will set the stage for the conversation by: _____

_____

Probing Questions

If appropriate, some questions I might use to make this more of a conversation include (circle any you might use):

- How did you think that went?
- What do you think might be causing this?
- How could you approach it differently next time?
- What are some other approaches you could take?
- Why do you think that went so well?
- What are the takeaways from what you did that worked?
- What could have gone better?
- Do you have thoughts on how you might put that into practice?
- _____

Observations

Some observations and concrete examples that I will share:

Statements

Some statements I want to make around impact or what I need to see change:

Questions

Some questions I will ask or ways I will probe:

Suggestions

Some suggestions I could make:

Wrap-Up and Next Steps

I need/do not need a repeat-back. If I do, I will say this: _____

_____

I will follow up on this area in the future in this way: _____

_____

TOOL 7.2

SAMPLE 2 × 2 FEEDBACK FORM

The 2 × 2 system ensures that managers and staff members talk about how things are going in their work. The manager and the staff member each fill out two things she is doing well and two things she could do better, as well as two things the other person is doing well and two things that could be better. For the staff member, the focus is on her performance overall; for the manager, the focus is on her work with this staff member. You might build a monthly meeting around the 2 x 2 form, or you might incorporate it occasionally in your check-ins.

	Issue	Example
Two things I'm doing well [a]		
Two things I could do even better		
Two things you're doing well		
Two things you could do even better		
Example for a staff member	Persistence	You followed up the generic rejection from funder X and got us an in-person meeting.
Example for a manager	Giving clear guidance	I should have been much clearer about the time constraints around getting board materials out. We had a last-minute crunch that I could have helped prevent.

[a] If you're a staff member, list two things you're doing well in your work overall; if you're a manager, list two things you're doing well in your work with this staff member.

TOOL 7.3

SAMPLE COMPLETED EVALUATION FORM FOR A CORRECTIVE ASSESSMENT

STAFF EVALUATION FORM

Rating Scale

Exceeds expectations—Consistently delivers exceptional results; is a model for others to follow; rare.

Meets expectations—Consistently meets expectations in all areas.

Partially meets expectations—Meets expectations in some areas but needs improvement in others.

Does not meet expectations—Needs significant improvement quickly.

Employee name, position	Eric Bardwell, Technology Director
Manager name, position	Julia Torres, Managing Director
Review period	January–December 2011
Date of Review	December 5, 2011
Reviewed by	Self ☐ Manager ☑

SECTION I: GETTING RESULTS		
Mark important objectives and/or measures of success in bold		
Measurable Goal	**Result(s)**	**Rating** E: exceeds expectations M: meets expectations P: partially meets expectations D: does not meet expectations
Achieve high level of internal customer satisfaction, with 75 percent "highly satisfied" on year-end survey	62 percent highly satisfied	D
Complete Web site build-out and redesign on time and bug free by July 1	**Site launched three weeks late and there were four bugs reported over the first month**	P/D
Complete online application system on time and bug free with full functionality by October 1	Launched on October 3; three bugs reported and fixed in first week	P

Comments: To what extent did the staff member achieve objectives for the position this past period? Did the staff member complete the key steps necessary to reach objectives?

While you had some positive accomplishments this year, overall you fell short of our aims. Positive highlights include completing a number of the priority items we identified through the quarterly plans: getting the online application system up and running

> *Use a clear initial sentence to present the overall picture; then focus on specifics within that context.*

well and missing an aggressive deadline by just two days; and meeting a large number of recruitment and admissions needs (including enhanced reporting and helping trainings function at a higher level).

However, in several other key areas, the results were not what we would have wanted. Satisfaction is the most notable one. You'll need to improve those

> *Be honest and straightforward with negative feedback.*

numbers by doing more around some of the specific levers we've identified, including building tech capabilities for the regions more quickly and taking on regional connectivity and remote access issues more aggressively. The Web site result was mixed. It was an aggressive goal, but it might have been reachable if you'd prioritized hiring J.S. earlier in the year.

SECTION II. DEMONSTRATING PERFORMANCE FACTORS		
To what degree did this person demonstrate each of the core values and essential skills?		
Core values	**Description**	**Rating** E: exceeds expectations M: meets expectations P: partially meets expectations D: does not meet expectations
Relentless pursuit of results	We are determined to achieve ambitious, measurable results in working toward our vision. As a result, we continue pursuing our end goals despite the constraints or obstacles we encounter along the way, and we work toward those goals with a sense of urgency.	M
Good thinking	We push ourselves to think critically about all that we do, approaching each issue and decision with rigor and always searching for the best idea.	M
Collective impact	We assume responsibility for the success of our broader movement and contribute toward increasing our collective impact.	P

SECTION II. DEMONSTRATING PERFORMANCE FACTORS		
To what degree did this person demonstrate each of the core values and essential skills? *(cont.)*		
Constant learning	We reflect on and draw lessons from previous experiences and apply them to do even better in future endeavors. We also seek out feedback and resources to help meet our goals.	D
Respect and humility	We approach others in a way that demonstrates that we value them and their contributions and have high expectations of what they can contribute. We are cognizant of the limitations of our own experience and value others' perspectives.	M
Personal responsibility	We do our best in all that we take on and assume ownership for producing the best possible result in our area of work.	P
Positive outlook	We establish big goals and greet new ideas with a sense of possibility. We assume the best in others and treat them with a generosity of spirit.	M
Essential Skills	**Description**	**Rating**
Problem solving	Identifies issues, effectively structures problems, analyzes data to produce insights, and generates wise, actionable recommendations.	M
Communication	Produces strong written documents, edits documents effectively, engages in effective verbal communication— one-on-one and small group—and conducts effective large-group presentations.	P
Organization	Prioritizes tasks effectively, accomplishes tasks efficiently, follows through on all commitments, breaks down large projects to make them manageable, effectively manages complex projects involving multiple actors.	P
Management	Builds a team of high-performing staff members, appropriately structures jobs so that staff members can succeed, develops and motivates staff members, acts from the perspective of an organizational leader, manages other managers effectively to accomplish goals.	M

SECTION II. DEMONSTRATING PERFORMANCE FACTORS *(cont.)*		
To what degree did this person demonstrate each of the core values and essential skills?		
External relations	Serves as an effective ambassador, builds connections, and maintains relationships with outside constituents.	P
Staying current on latest technology	Stays up to date on latest technological developments and how companies can use them to improve performance and draws on this base of knowledge to address organizational challenges.	P

Comments: *In what priority areas of performance (values and skills) did the staff member excel? In what areas is improvement needed?*

As with the results you got this year, there are some positives here but also some important areas for improvement. I want to start by recognizing your improvement on respect and humility and positive outlook. I know you've been more conscious of how you approach others, including showing people that you respect what they bring to the table and making sure that you address problems head-on instead of leaving them to simmer, and I think your efforts have borne fruit.

Of all our core values, the area where I think you have the most potential for improvement is personal responsibility. You are sometimes good on this score, like last year when you got the servers up and run-

> Be as specific as possible about what success looks like.

ning quickly. But there are other situations, like with the Web site, where you seem content to have circumstances determine project outcomes. What I want to see—and the online regional reporting system will be a good test—is that you take full responsibility for making it a success. At the start, this means when people are vague about what they want, you ask lots of questions, show them examples of other systems, and insist on figuring out what they will and won't like so the end product works well. Then you'd need to plan backward to figure out what needs to happen by when in order to bring it in by the deadline. And in that plan, you should build in enough of a cushion so that when hurdles inevitably emerge, you have time to deal with them rather than allowing circumstance to determine whether you succeed. If you do that, I think you can get to where I'd like to see you get, which is making our technology work at an exemplary level.

On skills, one area to highlight is organization, where things seem to have improved, but there's still room for improvement. Personally I'm still not 100 percent confident you'll follow through when you tell me you'll do something. To flag a recent example, we had agreed you would send me your evaluation of S.T. before you conducted the meeting so we could touch base about the overall message, and that did not happen. This is a key area to improve in quickly.

> Where relevant, cite specific examples.

SECTION III. SUMMARY ASSESSMENT, NEXT STEPS, AND TENURE CONSIDERATIONS Overall performance rating:	
Exceeds expectations ☐	Meets expectations ☐
Partially meets expectations ☑	Does not meet expectations ☐

How is the staff member performing overall? What are the most notable areas of strength? What are the next steps for growth or improvement? To what extent does continuing in this role make sense?

As I said initially, your performance this year was mixed, and we need it to continue to improve.

Put the headline assessment up front, and, again, be straightforward and honest.

On the positive side, you have built a technology infrastructure that works well overall and helps people do their jobs much more effectively than they were able to before. You have also instilled a strong ethic in your team of responding to "client" needs and have adjusted your style to fit our culture, which has led to smoother communication all around.

However, we need more from you in order to maximize our effectiveness as an organization.

What I'd like you to focus on as you move forward is the personal responsibility piece I mentioned in the previous section. Probably the best place to start is with the online regional reporting system. Taking personal responsibility for that process would mean talking in the next month to the regional directors who tend to have the most to say about technology and getting their thoughts on what they would like to see. Then draw up a blueprint

Be specific about next steps where appropriate.

of a proposed system and get them on board early in terms of functionality, output data, interface design, and so forth. Then, if things shift along the way, make sure the regional directors have a chance to weigh in on the options. Doing all the little things to ensure that you build a reporting system people love won't be easy, but you have the skill, so it really will come down to taking personal responsibility for making it happen. If you commit yourself to taking this to the next level, I believe that you can do it.

I'm looking forward to our discussion on this, and let's also plan to revisit it again at the end of February.

TOOL 7.4

SAMPLE COMPLETED EVALUATION
FORM FOR A STRONG ASSESSMENT

STAFF EVALUATION FORM	
Rating Scale **Exceeds expectations**—Consistently delivers exceptional results; is a model for others to follow; rare. **Meets expectations**—Consistently meets expectations in all areas. **Partially meets expectations**—Meets expectations in some areas but needs improvement in others. **Does not meet expectations**—Needs significant improvement quickly.	
Employee name, position	Jesse Secrest, Development Director
Manager name, position	Julia Torres, Managing Director
Review period	January–December 2011
Date of review	December 8, 2011
Reviewed by	Self ☐ Manager ☑

SECTION I. GETTING RESULTS		
(Mark important objectives and/or measures of success in bold)		
Measurable Goal	**Result(s)**	**Rating** E: exceeds expectations M: meets expectations P: partially meets expectations D: does not meet expectations
Raise operating funding to $12.5 million	$12.8 million	E
Secure $2 million federal funding for following FY (2009)	**$1.8 million**	M
Increase number of individual donors giving at least $5K to 150	170	E

Comments: *To what extent did the staff member achieve the objectives for the position this past period? Did the staff member complete the key steps necessary to reach the objectives?*

> *Even in a strong evaluation, identify the path for the person to get to the next level.*

In short, I think your results were pretty spectacular. Even in a year when the economy was only so-so, we're on track to exceed our funding goal by roughly $300K. Not too shabby! We did this by focusing on key areas within regions, maximizing contributions from numerous national funders, and turning things around from the previous year in terms of ongoing funding at the federal level.

Going forward, in addition to just generally keeping up the great work and doing what you're doing, the main area I think you should focus on more is being out in the regions (physically and virtually), proactively engaging with and serving as a resource to regional directors. (To be clear, the regional directors all report that you're incredibly helpful, but in several cases it's also clear that deeper engagement would be valuable, especially for newer folks who are still learning.) Identifying the key levers that can take things to a higher level in particular regions will be valuable, particularly as our growth rate slows in more well-developed regions.

SECTION II. DEMONSTRATING PERFORMANCE FACTORS		
To what degree did this person demonstrate each of the core values and essential skills?		
Core Value	**Description**	**Rating** E: exceeds expectations M: meets expectations P: partially meets expectations D: does not meet expectations
Relentless pursuit of results	We are determined to achieve ambitious, measurable results in working toward our vision. As a result, we continue pursuing our end goals despite the constraints or obstacles we encounter along the way, and we work toward those goals with a sense of urgency.	E
Good thinking	We push ourselves to think critically about all that we do, approaching each issue and decision with rigor and always searching for the best idea.	E

SECTION II. DEMONSTRATING PERFORMANCE FACTORS		
To what degree did this person demonstrate each of the core values and essential skills?		
Collective impact	We assume responsibility for the success of our broader movement and contribute toward increasing our collective impact.	E
Constant learning	We reflect on and draw lessons from previous experiences and apply them to do even better in future endeavors. We also seek out feedback and resources to help meet our goals.	E
Respect and humility	We approach others in a way that demonstrates that we value them and their contributions and have high expectations of what they can contribute. We are cognizant of the limitations of our own experience and value others' perspectives.	E
Personal responsibility	We do our best in all that we take on and assume ownership for producing the best possible result in our area of work.	E
Positive outlook	We establish big goals and greet new ideas with a sense of possibility. We assume the best in others and treat them with a generosity of spirit.	M
To what degree did this person demonstrate each of the skills key to success in the position?		
Essential Skills	**Description**	**Rating**
Problem solving	Identifies issues, effectively structures problems, analyzes data to produce insights, and generates wise, actionable recommendations.	E
Communication	Produces strong written documents, edits documents effectively, engages in effective verbal communication—one-on-one and small group—and conducts effective large-group presentations.	E
Organization	Prioritizes tasks effectively, accomplishes tasks efficiently, follows through on all commitments, breaks down large projects to make them manageable, effectively manages complex projects involving multiple actors.	M

SECTION II. DEMONSTRATING PERFORMANCE FACTORS *(cont.)*		
To what degree did this person demonstrate each of the core values and essential skills?		
Management	Builds a team of high-performing staff members, appropriately structures jobs so that staff members can succeed, develops and motivates staff members, acts from the perspective of an organizational leader, manages other managers effectively to accomplish goals.	E
External relations	Serves as an effective ambassador, builds connections, and maintains relationships with outside constituents.	E

Comments: *In what priority areas of performance (values and skills) did the staff member excel? In what areas is improvement needed?*

As your exemplary ratings indicate, you embody our core values as well as anyone in the organization. A couple of particularly noteworthy areas:

Relentless pursuit of results: You continued pursuing every last channel relentlessly, turned around applications for funds at the last minute, etc.

> *Be detailed even in a strong review. It's a great opportunity to let a high performer know he or she is valued, which will be a big factor in retaining this person.*

Collective impact: H.G. said it well in her recent e-mail to you on this, where she alluded to your pushing us to pursue the additional channels "even though you knew it would create an added burden for the development team and despite the fact that it had nothing to do with your overall funding goal."

You're also operating at an exceptionally high level when it comes to skills:

Problem solving: It's hard to overstate your strengths as a thinker. On so many occasions over the past year, you've exercised great judgment about which levers we should pursue and how we should pursue them. One great example is the 2011–2012 funding memo you wrote, which I think does a great job of recognizing where we stand and what our realistic opportunities and constraints going forward may be.

Organization: I'd be interested to hear whether you think this has improved. My sense is that you have gotten better in terms of prioritizing work and that this area may come down to management and hiring the right people. The fact that things like end-of-year giving are rolling forward speaks well of your ability to take big projects and break them down. At the same time, you might think about whether there are any systems you could put in place to help guarantee that a big project (like the fund initiative) meets its deadline and stays on track, perhaps by setting up additional padding around deadlines.

Management: Your greatest management achievement this year was doing an outstanding job managing the makeup of your team, notably around transitioning out S.H., bringing on L.F. and H.W., and retaining M.K. Your team feels that you're an incredibly helpful, accessible resource. This is not a big deal, but just so I don't lose it: one person wrote that "it'd be helpful if he could provide more feedback, good and bad, on a regular basis."

SECTION III. SUMMARY ASSESSMENT, NEXT STEPS, AND TENURE CONSIDERATIONS	
Overall performance rating:	
Exceeds expectations ☑	Meets expectations ☐
Partially meets expectations ☐	Does not meet expectations ☐

How is the staff member performing overall? What are the most notable areas of strength? What are the next steps for growth or improvement? To what extent does continuing in this role make sense?

This should be pretty clear by now, but I think you had an outstanding year and that you're operating at an amazingly high level. You led us to spectacular results on overall funding and awards, you've made progress in areas for development that we talked about last year (management most prominent among them), and you've done even more to be an essential contributor to the broader discussions around the future of our organization.

In terms of areas to focus on going forward, the one thing I'd flag is what I mentioned in the goals section: engaging with RDs to identify key levers. I think that will be essential for us to continue meeting our considerable funding needs. Are you ready to sign the 2015 contract? ☺

Seriously, I know we'll be having lots of discussions re: your future plans as part of our planning around organizational capacity for the long-term plan, and I'm assuming we'll talk about this then.

> *With your superstar performers, use the evaluation process as a retention tool and an entry point into discussions about their future with your organization.*

CHAPTER

8

RETAINING YOUR BEST

So now that you have great staffers, you're set for life, right? Wrong. As it turns out, people leave jobs. And there's nothing worse for a manager than having a stellar employee tell you that she has accepted another offer.

As a manager, retaining your best people is a critically important part of your job. Since you're trying to get great results, and you know the right people are key here, you need to make sure that your best employees stay. You can't lock them to their desks (we've tried! but these are high performers—they can break locks!), but you can create a situation that they won't want to leave. You do this by being strategic about retention in the same way you'd be strategic about anything else you don't want to leave to chance, like fundraising or program design. Treat your retention efforts like as much of a priority as anything else you care about, and include retention on your to-do lists or in your quarterly plans. Even just writing, "Do everything I can to keep Miguel," on your plan for the quarter can help keep the goal at the front of your mind. (See Tool 8.1.)

Of course, as you develop strategies for keeping great staff members, make sure that you're strategic about which employees you focus those efforts on. Your goal is to retain your high performers, not the mediocre or low performers, so focus your efforts accordingly.

METHODS FOR RETAINING HIGH PERFORMERS

Contrary to conventional wisdom, retention isn't just about salaries and benefits packages. Although these do matter, retention most often comes from ensuring that high-performing staff members feel valued, have opportunities to grow, and have a manager who helps them focus on meeting ambitious, meaningful, and challenging goals.

However, as with most of the rest of management, adapt your approach to fit the context. Different staffers are motivated in different ways, so develop an individualized strategy tailored to each staffer you're trying to retain. Here are some of the potential levers you might incorporate in your retention strategy.

Meaningful Roles with Real Responsibility

Don't underestimate the power of being truly engaged in important work. Staff members who are able to have a real impact on the organization's success and who "own" their areas and its successes or failures are more likely to feel satisfied with their work and to stay focused on the challenges in front of them rather than seeking out new challenges somewhere else.

Sense of Progress

Inherent in the idea of having a real impact is a sense of movement and progress. To understand why this is so key to retention, imagine that you're hiking to the top of a large mountain. If you're seeing milestones along the way that let you mark your progress, you're going to stay focused on reaching the top; you're not going to be thinking about hiking a different mountain! But if your journey feels never ending and you're not seeing any signs of progress, you're more likely to give up. For instance, a staff member might be invested in a goal of getting her program to be 100 percent self-funded. Setting quarterly benchmarks of 25, 50, and 75 percent will help her feel the satisfaction that comes with making progress along the way.

PROGRESS: THE STRONGEST MOTIVATOR

One multiyear study found that progress is the strongest motivator of performance. The authors, Teresa M. Amabile and Steven J. Kramer, wrote in "What Really Motivates Workers" (*Harvard Business Review*, January-February 2010, pp. 44–45, "On days when workers have the sense they're making headway in their jobs, or when they receive support that helps them overcome obstacles, their emotions are most positive and their drive to succeed is at its peak. On days when they feel they are spinning their wheels or encountering roadblocks to meaningful accomplishment, their moods and motivation are lowest. . . . Making progress in one's work—even incremental progress—is more frequently associated with positive emotions and high motivation than any other workday event."

Growth

Don't let your best employees get bored, and don't make them go elsewhere to continue to grow in their careers. Here are three ways to avoid those pitfalls:

- *New challenges.* As great employees master an area, increase the bar so they are challenged to do better and better within that area. For instance, once your fundraising director hits her $5 million annual goal, you might agree on a higher goal for next year or even for three years down the road (tied, of course, to what the organization needs to accomplish in order to fulfill its mission).

- *Increased responsibility.* Aside from new challenges within existing areas of responsibility, you can add entirely new responsibilities to the plate of an employee who has proven she's ready for them. That said, be sure the strategy here is tailored to the individual. Some staff members see increased responsibilities as an affirmation of trust and a chance to develop new skills. Others, depending on where they are in life and what factors they're contending with outside work (such as a new baby or an ailing relative), might see them as a burden rather than a reward.

- *Grooming.* Sometimes your best performers may not thrive in a more advanced role. Others have the talents to move on to the next level, so give these staff members an idea of what their career development plan might look like if they stay with your organization. Think about what they can do in their current role to prepare them for the next rung on the ladder and then talk to them explicitly about that. For instance, if you are a communications director with a phenomenal marketing associate, you might have her attend higher-level meetings with you and explain that you want her exposed to the issues discussed there. You might also ask her to begin drafting some of the press releases you normally draft and give her feedback on them, again explaining that you want to help her prepare for the next step in her career. And you might even tell her explicitly, "In two years, I could see you taking on this role."

Direct Discussion

In our experience, few managers discuss the subject of retention with staff members directly. Take a valued staff member out to lunch or for coffee to talk about her future and ask her directly, "How can we make sure you stay for the next two years?" Even if you don't get an immediate commitment, having an explicit discussion and showing that you care enough to talk about it can go a long way.

Positive Reinforcement and Feeling Valued

Don't underestimate the impact of regularly making sure great staff members know you think they're great. Let them know that you notice their accomplishments and that you value everything they're bringing to the organization.

Salaries

Although retention isn't just about money, money can help. Your best staff members are probably not motivated by money, but they're probably not blind to it either. They will have many opportunities to make an impact in the world, and the reality is that money can sometimes sway their decisions about where they apply their talents.

Unfortunately, most nonprofits radically underinvest in salaries for their best people. Instead, they might pour as much money as possible into direct program work. While well intentioned, this can end up having the opposite of the desired effect: harming program activities by making it harder to attract and keep the people who will execute those activities most effectively. Your best performers get dramatically better results than the average—often five or more times better. If one high performer will get better results than several mediocre performers combined, paying your best staff members quite well can actually be an extremely economical move.

At a minimum, salaries should not be a reason people leave. Beyond that, ideally your salaries would be high enough that your best people know that while they might make more money elsewhere, they'll never make this much money *and* do work this interesting *and* contribute as much as they do with you.

In our experience, significant changes in salary can be game-changing, convincing employees who might otherwise have moved on to stay. For instance, at Teach For America, Jerry had a staff member he desperately wanted to retain but who was considering graduate school. He knew that a small salary increase would not change her mind. Instead, he offered her a 50 percent increase, which amounted to tens of thousands of dollars. She stayed, and the dramatically higher-than-expected salary increase changed her entire way of thinking about her position and future with the organization. She is still there as one of the top leaders of the organization, and the investment in her salary continues to pay enormous dividends.

Titles

Titles cost nothing and can be an effective way to recognize employees' development. For instance, your outstanding membership assistant might be rewarded for her achievements with the title of development officer, or you might recognize your superb communications coordinator's work by changing her title to assistant communications manager. You want titles to be accurate, of course, and as an organization grows, there is often an overall structure within which titles must be consistent. Nevertheless, there is often room to be creative in this area.

WHAT *NOT* TO DO, OR HOW TO LOSE YOUR BEST EMPLOYEES

Just as important as giving staff members motivators to stay is making sure you don't demotivate them through behaviors like yelling, creating a climate of fear, or letting serious problems go unresolved. (In short, as we discuss in Chapter Ten, don't be a tyrant or a wimp.)

Because a manager has such a pervasive impact on the day-to-day work environment, an employee's relationship with her direct supervisor is one of the factors that most strongly influences job satisfaction. As Marcus Buckingham and Curt Coffman write, "An employee may join [an organization] because she is lured by their generous benefits package and their reputation for valuing employees. But it is her relationship with her immediate manager that will determine how long she stays and how productive she is while she is there. . . . Managers trump companies."[1]

No matter how much a staff member likes her job or the organization, if she has a bad relationship with her manager, it will seep into her quality of life every day. Therefore, it's important to treat your staffers with respect and decency. This doesn't mean shying away from having tough conversations or delivering constructive feedback (to the contrary, great employees tend to want such feedback) but simply approaching your staffers as people, showing that you care about them (if you were Jerry's boss, maybe even laughing at his jokes), and treating them as you yourself would want to be treated.

Now that you're on the road to keeping your high performers, we'll turn to one of the hardest realities managers face: the unavoidable fact that you won't want to retain everyone. Just as you shouldn't leave retention to chance, chance shouldn't come into play when it comes to moving people out either. In the next chapter, we discuss how to transition out employees who aren't helping to propel you forward.

KEY POINTS

- If you want great results, retain your great (and only your great) employees.

- Different staffers are motivated in different ways, so develop an individualized strategy tailored to each person you're trying to retain.

- Retention strategies can include ensuring that staff members have meaningful roles with real responsibility and a sense of progress in their work; providing opportunities to take on new challenges; direct discussion; regularly providing positive feedback; having a strong, positive employee-manager relationship; and ensuring that titles reflect growth.

- Most nonprofits radically underinvest in staff salaries, which can harm program activities by making it harder to attract and keep the people who will execute those activities most effectively. Since one high performer may get better results than several mediocre performers combined, paying your best staff members quite well can end up being extremely economical.

---

[1] Marcus Buckingham and Curt Coffman, *First, Break All the Rules: What the World's Greatest Managers Do Differently* (New York: Simon & Schuster, 1999), p. 36.

Additional Reading

Teresa M. Amabile and Steven J. Kramer, "What Really Motivates Workers," *Harvard Business Review*, Jan.–Feb. 2010, pp. 44–45.

Marcus Buckingham and Curt Coffman, *First, Break All the Rules: What the World's Greatest Managers Do Differently* (New York: Simon & Schuster, 1999), especially "The Measuring Stick" and "Putting the Twelve to the Test" (pp. 25–36).

TOOL 8.1

SAMPLE RETENTION CHART

Taking just sixty seconds to think through your strategy for retaining your top performers and then transferring those actions to your to-do list can make the difference between keeping a star staff member long-term or losing her to another opportunity.

Who	How
Jaime W.	Be sure to praise his work at conference; ask the board chair to call and do the same Increase his responsibility over our northeast section?
Carla M.	Take her to lunch to discuss her future with us She's thinking about school; talk about what her impact will be here if she stays another two years

CHAPTER

9

ADDRESSING PERFORMANCE PROBLEMS AND LETTING PEOPLE GO

Even with the best efforts to hire well and develop your people, the reality is that you are going to have some staff members who simply don't perform at the level that you need. This is an unavoidable reality of managing, and one of the most important things you can do as a manager is to address it head-on. By addressing these situations in a forthright and matter-of-fact manner, you can sometimes help an employee get to the level you need. But when that doesn't work, you can lay the groundwork for letting the employee go in a way that is fair and compassionate to her. In this chapter, we'll talk about how you can move employees who aren't performing at the level you need "up or out"—successfully, fairly, and quickly.

A few words about the "out" part of this: we know letting someone go is difficult. We've both been guilty on multiple occasions of waiting too long to move out lower performers. It's especially tough when the staff member isn't flagrantly underperforming (or lying, stealing, or committing other ethical violations), but rather does contribute somewhat while still not getting you the results that you need. Because most people like to give others additional chances and don't like telling people they can't meet our required needs, managers too often shy away from firing when they should. As a result, most managers do not remove low or mediocre performers quickly enough or frequently enough.

Letting people go is hard, but it's also critically important. We've both been shocked after we let people go and brought in new staff by just how much more the new people accomplished. And of course, not being assertive in this area has particularly dire consequences in the nonprofit world, where having a weak link directly harms our ability to deliver on our missions to the communities we serve.

If you're serious about getting results, you will have to fire people. You can do everything else right—setting goals and expectations, delegating effectively, giving feedback, and retaining your best—but if you aren't willing to fire people who aren't performing at the level you need, you will never accomplish what you could.

In this chapter, we start with how to determine if a performance issue is a serious problem. Then we look at two methods for dealing with the issue: the textbook approach of progressive discipline (informal warnings, formal warnings, and letting people go) and the less traditional method of coaching out. In coaching out, you and the employee mutually agree that continued tenure in the role doesn't make sense and agree on a transition plan that leaves you both better off than progressive discipline might.

REASONS MANAGERS RESIST LETTING EMPLOYEES GO

The vast majority of managers err on the side of not firing when they should. Let's take a look at some of the most common reasons managers tend to resist letting low performers go:

- *Believing that everyone deserves another chance (and another, and another).* This belief is especially common in nonprofits, which are often staffed by people who highly value compassion and believe in giving people chances to develop. But as tempted as you may be to be lenient with struggling performers, don't lose sight of the fact that your donors are paying you to advance your mission and the beneficiaries of your work are counting on you to deliver. And no matter how personally kind it may be, a commitment to providing a job for someone mediocre is contrary to that mission.

- *Believing that you haven't invested enough in helping the person.* Yes, you should help people succeed—but within reason. You're never going to have done absolutely everything you could have done to create the optimal environment for every staff member to excel in. Take a look at what top performers have done in similar contexts. Would they have found a way to succeed with the same amount of resources and guidance?

- *Feeling overwhelmed by the amount of time it would take to bring a new person up to speed.* Managers tend to overestimate how much time it will take a new employee to become trained and start delivering value compared to the person currently in the role. Strong performers get up to speed far faster than you realize. Besides, even if this weren't true, wouldn't you rather have a short period of downtime followed by an all-out stellar performance, as opposed to years of mediocrity (or worse)?

- *Hoping that the employee will leave on her own.* A bad situation rarely gets better without direct intervention. You don't leave your fundraising or program execution to wishful thinking; you make decisions and take action. Why would you leave something as crucial as having the right staff to chance?

- *Feeling bad or feeling sorry for the staff member.* It's okay to feel sorry for the staff member; after all, getting fired is no one's ideal outcome. But if you handle the situation directly and honestly, she'll know that it's coming, she'll have had the chance to improve, and you can be kind as you help her move out of a job that she may never thrive in (and you can even help her brainstorm about other jobs she might be more suited for). Not only are you doing a disservice to your mission by keeping a low performer on staff, but you're also doing a disservice to the employee herself by keeping her in a job that doesn't fit her well.

- *Feeling nonprofits should be more egalitarian than for-profit organizations.* Sure, nonprofits have different missions from those in the private sector, but we're not different in our need for high performance. In fact, we should be *more* committed to high performance, because so much more is at stake.

Let's be honest: these are all excuses. Ultimately the most common reason people wait too long in these situations is about avoiding discomfort or hassle for ourselves. Just as with dating, putting off the day of reckoning (or trying to avoid it altogether by ignoring the problem or hoping the other person acts so you don't have to) is unfair to the person, who could be using this time to find something that *is* right. And unlike dating, as managers we get paid to handle difficult situations.

HOW TO DETERMINE IF YOU HAVE A SERIOUS PERFORMANCE PROBLEM

Sometimes it's clear you have a problem: your accountant repeatedly makes serious errors on financial statements or your membership coordinator isn't sending out renewal notices. Other times it's not as clear-cut: your lobbyist seems up-to-date on legislation but hasn't actually moved any. Or your communications director has creative ideas for generating media coverage but doesn't always follow through on the plans she forms.

Maybe there are good reasons that your lobbyist hasn't delivered any results. After all, legislators have their own priorities and outside factors can derail the best of plans. And perhaps your communications director's workload is so high that no one in her shoes could carry out all the plans.

Perhaps. But perhaps these things are true and you still have a problem. How can you decide?

Rule #1: Keep the focus on what the ideal staffer would do in a similar context.

Managers often tailor their expectations for a position to the person who happens to be inhabiting it. Certainly it's sound management to play to your team members' strengths and weaknesses, but this should not mean lowering your expectations about core results. The bar you use to assess performance should not be "the best this particular person could do," but rather a vision of what a truly high-performing staff member would be doing in the role.

Maybe your vision of a star lobbyist tells you that although she wouldn't necessarily be able to pass your model legislation quickly, she would still be able to build relationships that would allow you to tweak related bills and advance your agenda in less direct ways. In the case of the communications director, maybe you can't be sure that the workload isn't too great for one person. But you do know that an outstanding employee would handle a high workload differently by keeping the work organized, updating you about what isn't getting done, and not forgetting about projects entirely.

Rule #2: Determine if the problem is one of fundamental fit for the position or one that could quickly be resolved through more guidance.

Once you have a clear vision of what you expect from the position and how the person in it is falling short, determine whether the problem is likely to be correctable.

Begin by considering the employee's basic talents and inclinations and how well matched they are with the needs of the position. For instance, you want an assistant to be uptight about details and organization. If you have an assistant whose nature is simply more laid back, she may be able to improve but likely will never obsess about the details of your travel schedule at the level you need.

Be careful to avoid the trap of sinking too much of your own time or the organization's resources into remedial training. For example, you might believe that if you were able to spend several hours each week with a staff member working on her writing, you could get her to an acceptable level, but that might not be a good use of organizational resources.

Another area to consider is the extent to which you have clearly communicated your expectations to the employee. If you haven't already, you should talk explicitly

ASK THE RIGHT QUESTION   Imagine that you're in a relationship with someone who isn't quite what you're looking for. You like the person but know deep down that it isn't the right match for you. Most people would agree that it's kinder to be honest and end things than to continue stringing the person along. The question you ask yourself isn't, "Do I have enough reasons to break up with this person?" but rather, "Is this person so great that I want to stay with them long-term?"

But when it comes to employee fit, the picture gets much fuzzier for most managers. Managers tend to look at mediocre performers and ask, "Is this person really performing so badly that he should be fired?" when the question to ask instead should be, "Is this person performing so well that I should retain her?"

about those expectations now to try to get into alignment. That said, even when you have not communicated your expectations as well as you could have, sometimes there's still a question of fit.

You're never going to have done absolutely everything you could have to create the optimal environment for every staff member. Think about what top performers would have done in similar contexts: Would they have found a way to succeed with the same resources and guidance?

An extreme example of this is a client we worked with who hesitated to hold a staff member accountable after the staff member twice missed planes and trains to important meetings. The manager worried that perhaps he hadn't set clear enough expectations for the staffer: after all, he had never spelled out that the staffer needed to be on time for such things. Clearly a great performer (or even merely a reasonable person, in this case) wouldn't need that guidance.

Rule #3: Trust your gut.

In some cases, you may not be sure if your concerns are valid. Perhaps the employee's work is in a field far outside your expertise, like technology, or perhaps the position is a new one and so you haven't seen anyone else tackle the work.

In such cases, listen to your gut, because it's likely reacting to a larger body of knowledge than you realize. For instance, you may not feel equipped to judge much of your technology director's work because of its technical nature. But you have noticed that your e-mail network has more downtime than feels reasonable, the director doesn't react with a sense of urgency when things go wrong, and you're often told that problems "can't" be fixed.

If the small amount you do feel competent to judge is mediocre, it's likely representative of the rest. Don't be afraid to generalize from what you do know, and keep in mind that you don't need to prove your case with courtroom accuracy. The question for you is whether you're getting what you need from the employee, not whether you could convince a jury.

Rule #4: Pretend it would be easy.

Make your assessment independent of how difficult the next step may be to execute. Don't focus on the discomfort of having to tell someone she isn't meeting your expectations or the hassles of interviewing and training someone new. The main question before you is, "Is this the best person for the job?"

Time and time again, we see managers who know deep down that they should replace an employee but want to avoid the discomfort of addressing it head-on.

Here's a revealing test. Pretend that you have a red button that, if you pushed it, would lead to your staff member's being replaced instantaneously, without any accompanying drama or pain. Would you push it?

Another way to look at it is to close your eyes and pretend the staff member walked into your office and told you she was leaving to take another job. How did you feel? If your major feeling was relief rather than panic, then deep down you know that you would be better off letting the person go. Now you need to develop a plan to make it happen.

WHAT ABOUT HIGH PERFORMERS WHO AREN'T A CULTURE FIT?

What if you have a high performer who delivers when it comes to the meat of her job but is difficult to work with in other ways? An employee who is abrasive, unable to get along with others, or otherwise culturally off can be as disruptive as one who isn't meeting a performance bar.

Alison once worked with a research director who was highly skilled when it came to knowledge, research, and writing. His many years in the field had given him an almost unparalleled body of knowledge, and he had a unique talent for making highly complex subjects easily understandable by laypeople. However, he increasingly wanted to focus solely on his own interests and began swatting away ideas that weren't his own. Frequently when staff members inquired about getting research done to support a project another department was working on, the research director would cite a minor obstacle and respond that it couldn't be done. Only after much coaxing would he agree to do the work requested of him. He also scoffed at and shot down other people's ideas in meetings, something that was particularly corrosive on less experienced staffers who weren't confident in their ability to push back.

Staff members like this can be poisonous to both your culture and your results. Yet when the employee is producing good work, a manager may be hesitant to consider firing him.

Rarely are such cases solely a bad cultural fit. The results usually can be seen as performance issues as well. The research director's naysaying prevented the research department from tackling projects as vigorously as it otherwise would have, ate up the time of other employees when they had to convince him that it was worth doing the assigned work, and eroded the willingness of other staffers to contribute. Therefore, it would have been reasonable to decide that a can-do attitude and a willingness to explore new ideas were key requirements for a successful research director, and to hold him to that bar.

When you face a staffer who doesn't fit with your culture, try viewing the troubling behavior through the lens of substantive performance and consider if it might be about performance after all.

PROGRESSIVE DISCIPLINE AND COACHING OUT

Once you've determined that the performance issue is a serious one, you have two paths for addressing it:

- The more traditional path of progressive discipline

- A less traditional, but sometimes kinder and more effective, path that we call "coaching out"

Progressive Discipline

Progressive discipline consists of a brief series of increasingly serious warnings, culminating in dismissal if an employee fails to improve sufficiently. Typically there are

THE THREE STAGES OF PROGRESSIVE DISCIPLINE

1. Informal warning
2. Formal warning
3. Termination

Some organizations differ in how they apply progressive discipline, and in some contexts, you might skip the informal warning and move straight to the formal warning. Except in unusual circumstances, we don't recommend skipping the formal warning, lest your staff begin fearing being terminated without notice.

three stages: an informal verbal warning, followed by a formal warning with a written improvement plan, followed by termination if the employee fails to make sufficient improvement. At each of the first two points, the employee can make the necessary corrections. If she doesn't, you move to the next stage of letting her go.

Note that each step foreshadows the next ("If this doesn't get better, we're going to have talk about a more formal plan"), so that the staffer is clear about where she stands and isn't surprised by negative consequences. We've seen numerous situations where a manager gives lots of negative feedback to a struggling staff member but never explicitly says that the person's job is in jeopardy—and the staffer ends up shocked when she is fired. This is unfair to the staffer, who deserves to know the severity of the concerns. It can also create significant anxiety and a culture of fear among other staff members, who may begin to worry they're on the verge of being fired every time they receive negative feedback. A progressive discipline system, like the one in Tool 9.1, lets your staff know that they won't be fired without first knowing that their job is in jeopardy and having time to improve.[1]

FIRING WITHOUT USING PROGRESSIVE DISCIPLINE   Some

situations are so egregious that they warrant firing without moving through the stages of progressive discipline or attempting to coach the person out—for example, an employee who embezzles or physically accosts someone.

---

[1] Marcus Buckingham and Curt Coffman, *First, Break All the Rules: What the World's Greatest Managers Do Differently* (New York: Simon & Schuster, 1999). Nonetheless, from a legal perspective, progressive discipline procedures should be guidelines, not promises. You need to be able to act more quickly in unusual situations. Note the language in the sample policy in Tool 9.5.

Step One: Informal Warning

Let's say you've considered what a high performer would be doing in a given situation and have realized that you have a serious performance problem: a staff member whose performance does not reach the level you need it to. She must show significant improvement in order not to be fired. You may have tried some of the development techniques in Chapter Seven, like naming the issue, giving feedback, and even modeling, without result. What next?

The first step is to deliver an informal warning: an honest talk with the employee. Your goal is to let her know that her performance must improve, be specific about what improvements are needed, and be clear about potential consequences if she doesn't make the improvements.

This is different from the sort of corrective feedback we discussed in Chapter Seven: you're making it very clear that this isn't routine feedback. You're addressing a more severe problem that is holding the employee back and has the potential to become an even more serious problem if not fixed. In other words, the conversation has an "or else" attached this time. The staff member must improve, "or else" you will have to let her go.

Performance warning conversations need to have an "or else" attached, spelling out what happens if the staff member does not improve.

In some situations, the staff member will have recognized the problem and may feel relieved to discuss it openly. In others, the staff member may not have realized that the problems rose to this level, which of course makes the conversation even more important to have.

No matter what the outcome is, you will be doing the employee a significant service by speaking honestly about where her performance is falling short. Too many managers never put aside their discomfort about such conversations, and as a result, many employees never have the opportunity to learn how they could do better.

Let's walk through the informal warning process step by step (Tool 9.2 provides a sample script of how this conversation might go):

1. You may want to give your employee advance warning that you need to have a serious conversation about her performance. Consider, though, how much advance notice you want to give. Although you don't want her to be caught entirely off guard, too much advance warning can make her go through days of worry in anticipation of the meeting. Whether it happens a day in advance or at the start of the meeting, raise the subject by saying something like, "I want to step back and have a conversation about your performance."

2. At the start of the meeting, explain that you want to talk about changes you want to see from her. You might say something like, "As I mentioned in my e-mail, I'd like to talk about your performance lately. To be honest, your work is falling short of what I need from you."

3. Explain your general categories of concern, and offer specific instances to support your points—for example: "I'm concerned about the quality of your recent grant applications, as well as the fact that you've been missing deadlines lately. Your last several grant applications were disjointed, confusing in places, and didn't make a compelling case for funding our work. And you've missed three deadlines this month, including one that caused an important mailing to be held up."

4. Ask the employee to tell you how she perceives the issues. Say something like, "I'd like to hear your thoughts about what's causing these issues. What's your sense of what might be going on?"

5. As you would with corrective feedback, probe to understand what the root of the problem might be. Pick a few specific instances where the staffer didn't perform as you would have liked and delve into what happened. For instance, if you're concerned about poorly written grant applications, probe for factors that could be at work other than that she isn't a strong writer. Is she a poor time manager and writing at the last minute? Have you and she agreed on what a good grant application should look like? Is the fundamental issue one of responsibility, in that she isn't assuming ownership for ensuring that grant applications are as strong as possible?

6. If you're able to identify factors contributing to the problem, make suggestions you have about how the employee might do her work differently. For instance, if she has a time management issue, you might suggest she begin planning projects backward and set interim deadlines for herself to better structure her work. In some cases, you might decide it's worthwhile to make a one-time investment trying to help the person improve. With someone who chronically misses deadlines, you might spend time suggesting organizational systems and walking her through the basics of how to track projects and deadlines. At other times, you may decide that it's not reasonable for you to spend your time on this sort of intensive development. If you do decide to offer such help, be sure it's not unlimited. You can't afford to spend significant amounts of time hand-holding an employee who shouldn't need that level of help.

7. Regardless of the cause, be explicit about the standard you need the person to meet, and hold firm. For instance, say something like, "I need you to begin producing grant applications that are clearer and more compelling, using the samples I showed you as the standard, and which don't require more than minor editing from me. And I need you to start meeting deadlines right away. In the rare case that you do need to miss a deadline, I need to be informed ahead of time, not after the fact."

8. If you sense that the staff member believes that your expectations are too high or that she is doing the best that can be done, a good response is to acknowledge

that the bar is high while holding firm about your needs. For instance, you might say, "I know that the bar is high, but we need someone who can do this work and keep track of deadlines without a lot of supervision. I hear you that it's hard and I know it's a challenge, but in this context, we need someone who can handle a large workload and get the very difficult done with limited staff resources."

9. Most important, clearly state the consequences if her performance does not improve. Explain that the next step would be a formal improvement plan, and if that doesn't lead to quick improvement, you would have to let the staff member go—for example, "Assuming your performance improves and you sustain that level, then we'll just move forward. But if we're still seeing these issues in three weeks, I'll need to put you on a formal improvement plan. After that, if it doesn't improve, I'd need to let you go. So my concerns here are serious ones. I think you have a great deal of potential, but I also need you to be performing at a higher level."

As we describe later in the chapter, you might consider using the coaching-out option that we describe later in the chapter by asking the employee if she feels the role is the right one for her and seeing where the conversation leads. You might jointly agree to a solution that works better for both of you, giving the staff member time to search for a new job and you to look for a replacement without having a vacancy.

In some cases, the staff member will make the improvements needed after an informal warning. If she does, congratulate her, be specific about what's better and why, and make clear that she needs to sustain the improvement.

PREPPING FOR PROGRESSIVE DISCIPLINE CONVERSATIONS

1. Discuss the situation with your manager ahead of time, so that she is in the loop on the problems and your approach.

2. Prepare talking points. Treat the conversation the way you would an important presentation, outlining your points and how you will make them. Having a "script" to fall back on will make you more comfortable and make the conversation go more smoothly.

3. Use your manager, a friend, or a colleague to practice the meeting. Identify and repeatedly practice the hardest part—whatever it is that you find yourself most reluctant to say. Whatever you do, don't wing it!

4. Keep in mind that you are engaging in this conversation because you are acting in the organization's best interest. For you to be effective in your job, you have to develop a high-performing team.

Step Two: Formal Warning

When sufficient improvement doesn't happen, the next step is to move to a formal warning. Your goal here is to be explicit about the fact that dismissal is now a very real possibility and to give the staff member a final chance to make the needed improvements. Here is how the meeting might go:

1. At the start of the meeting, explain that you haven't seen the changes you discussed at the previous meeting and now need to put the staff member on a formal written improvement plan, setting areas for improvement and a time line.

2. Be explicit about the standard you need the staffer to meet and the time line for meeting it. Long, drawn-out probationary periods generally aren't necessary, since you should look for improvement in weeks, not months.

3. Clearly state the consequences if performance does not improve. Explain that the staffer will lose her job if she does not improve to the level you are specifying. We cannot overstate the importance of this step. Managers often find these words hard to say, and you may worry about damaging the person's morale with this warning. But however difficult it may be to raise the possibility of termination, it's far worse for the employee not to know that she risks being fired. Sometimes managers think, "Surely she knows her job is in danger given the serious talks we've been having and the level of my concern." Yet many people have a startling inability to hear negative input. In addition, if the employee has struggled professionally in the past, she may think negative feedback is normal and not realize that you, unlike her previous bosses, actually plan to do something about it. So fairness demands that you be explicit and never assume that an employee will figure out the severity or possible consequences on her own.

4. Establish the next steps. For instance, you might say, "I'd like you to come up with a system for better tracking deadlines right away. Send that to me by tomorrow, and then let's check back in two weeks to see how it's going, and we'll do the final review four weeks from today. If you've met and continue to sustain the level we just discussed, we'll move forward. If you don't improve, though, then we will have to let you go."

5. Follow up with a written summary of your conversation, like the one in Tool 9.3, laying out your expectations and the consequences for not meeting them. This is essential, so that there can be no doubt that the staff member heard the message and understands the key points and so that the consequences of not improving are in writing. As part of the document, include clear criteria for how you'll judge success. For instance, on an improvement plan for a struggling assistant, you might specify that success means no dropped balls over a three-week period and no more than one instance of inaccuracy (such as a meeting listed on the calendar at the wrong time).

WHAT ABOUT MOVING PEOPLE TO DIFFERENT ROLES?
Sometimes a manager, in a last-ditch attempt to salvage an employee, will move the person into another role in the organization. In our experience, this is rarely successful if it's done in order to address a problem. Someone who has failed to meet a bar for performance in one role within an organization often lacks the requisite talent or values to excel in other roles within the same organization. She may be able to survive in a new role better than in the old, but rarely will she be so strong that she will become the type of high performer you ultimately need.

Usually when managers try this, it's because they are uncomfortable making a decision that feels as difficult as letting someone go, so they take a less drastic course. But in doing so, they stretch out the problem.

That said, we have seen a limited number of cases where shifting roles has worked. In these situations, the staffer was a very strong cultural fit with the organization and had strong talents, but those talents were better suited to a different role. For instance, in one case, a regional director lacked the assertiveness necessary to move his region forward as quickly as was needed, but he was a great culture fit and an outstanding writer, so he was switched to a role where he could apply that talent, and he thrived.

Step Three: Letting People Go

By this step, you should either be seeing improvement or know that it's not going to work out. As you watch for improvement, don't get sidetracked by incremental improvements. Small improvements can feel promising, but hold out for your ultimate goal of outstanding performance. The staff member doesn't need to become great overnight, but you should see a steep climb in that direction. A climb to "barely acceptable" isn't what you're looking for here.

In some cases, the staff member will be able to make the improvements needed. When this happens, as at the informal warning step, be sure you tell her explicitly what you've noticed and what an improvement she's made. At the same time, the improvement must be sustained over time, so make sure she understands that if the problems recur, you will not go through the entire process all over again.

In other cases, you will not see the improvement you need. When that happens, it's time to move the person out. If you have followed the progressive discipline process, the employee has been clearly told about the problems and what needs to change, warned that the progress isn't what it needs to be, and explicitly told that her job is in jeopardy if specific changes don't occur. When the termination conversation happens, it's more of a wrap-up than anything else; it shouldn't be a surprise.

Here is how to go about this step (Tool 9.4 provides a sample script):

1. Decide ahead of time about logistics, such as whether you will offer severance and how much, and whether the person will be expected to leave the office immediately or will have until the end of the day.

2.   Some organizations have a third person in the room during a firing to corroborate what was said in case the employee later sues. Generally this is a human resources staffer or another manager above you. However, if your staff is small, it may be impossible to find a third party who could sit in without violating the employee's privacy and dignity.

3.   Begin the conversation with a statement like, "I want to have a conversation about your progress in the areas of concern we've discussed."

4.   Be direct and to the point. Announce your decision at the start of the conversation, because you don't want the employee to think she's supposed to be defending herself or thinking of an improvement plan when you have already made your decision. Say something like, "We talked last month about the fact that if these issues didn't change, I would need to look for a replacement. Unfortunately, although you have made some progress, it hasn't been enough, so we're now at the point where we're going to have to let you go, and today is going to be your last day."

5.   Be honest about the reason for the firing. Sometimes a manager will come up with a cover story for the firing, thinking the real reason will hurt the employee's feelings. (Often managers use a cover story because they haven't been direct enough about the problems earlier. You, of course, have followed the steps we have set out and won't find yourself in this situation.) Not being honest can come back to haunt you (we address legal issues later in this chapter).

6.   Be compassionate. It's okay to say, "I know this is hard" or, "I really do appreciate your efforts." Even if you've been incredibly frustrated with the employee, you can allow yourself to feel and express genuine compassion. When at all feasible, try to truly believe this is a case of a bad fit rather than that the employee is incompetent, unmotivated, or difficult. Going into the meeting with this mind-set will change the way you come across, which will help to defuse the situation and help the employee keep his or her dignity.

7.   Be clear that this decision is final. If the employee tries to change your mind, don't enter into prolonged discussion, which can make the employee think the decision is up for debate. Instead, say something like, "I realize that we see this differently, but the decision is final." In addition, ask for input from the employee only if you mean it. Don't ask questions like, "What do you think about this?" or "Does this make sense?" unless you mean to start a conversation. Present options only where there is a real choice. For instance, a staff member might be able to choose between different forms of a severance package but not about whether you are firing her.

8.   Consider a communications plan. Depending on the circumstances, you and the staff member might agree on a plan for explaining the change to the rest of the organization in a way that fairly reflects the situation and respects the staff member's privacy.

9. Cover all the details the employee may be wondering about, such as the effective date of the termination, COBRA benefits (which give employees the right to continue health benefits at their own cost), the final paycheck, and so forth.

10. When it's all over, debrief with your manager or a trusted advisor. As part of your commitment to continuous improvement, we recommend asking whether there's anything you can learn from the situation. While some number of terminations will always be unavoidable, it's worth asking some hard questions. Are there ways to improve your interview process to ferret out these sorts of problems before hiring a new employee? Did the choice result from hiring that person under pressure? Use terminations as a trigger for reflection and see if you might be able to strengthen your processes for the future.

Logistics. Organizations vary widely in how much time they give a dismissed employee to leave. Some expect employees to leave immediately, and others allow more time. Generally employees who have been coached out may stay for weeks or even several months, while employees who have been fired outright typically are expected to leave that same day. And if you have any cause to worry about an employee's reaction, you may prefer to err on the side of caution and have the person leave immediately.

In all cases, consider logistics such as disabling the person's access to e-mail and computer networks. You'll also need to arrange for the return of keys and any company property (such as a laptop, cell phone, or credit card), as well as establish with other staffers how the person's e-mail, voice mail, and computer files will be handled.

Severance pay. We're big fans of being as generous with severance payments as you can—not only because it's a nice thing to do for your staff member, but also because knowing that the staffer will receive severance pay may make you more comfortable moving forward with a transition. A generous severance package can save the organization money if it gives you mental permission to move aggressively rather than spending several months going through a performance warning process with a forgone conclusion.

In fact, you can also consider offering extended health care coverage and time to job search in order to ease the transition. (A lawyer would stress that it's key to treat similarly situated people similarly, but there's often room to find ways to help the person out in order to give yourself psychological permission to take action.)

However, if you do offer severance pay, tie it to a smooth transition. This gives you some leverage to prevent the employee from wreaking havoc before leaving. And in all cases, severance should be contingent on the employee's signing a general release agreement, forfeiting any future legal claims.

Coaching Out: An Alternative Approach

Sometimes you may determine that a progressive discipline process won't lead to the steep improvement that you need. Rather than drag the employee through a formal improvement process, knowing deep down that you'll almost surely be letting her go at the end of it, we believe that coaching out can be a far more effective and kinder approach. Coaching out involves an honest conversation about the employee's fundamental fitness for the role. It is aimed at convincing the employee that continued tenure in the role doesn't make sense and agreeing on a smooth transition plan. This allows her time to search for another job and you time to search for a replacement.

This approach is often the right choice for mediocre performers. These are people whose performance is not terrible—that is, you may not be able to document many egregious instances of poor performance—but whose performance doesn't reach the high bar you need in the role. It's also a good choice when you have a long-term, loyal employee whom the organization has simply outgrown.

In our experience, coaching out can turn a potentially difficult and unpleasant situation into one that ends with all parties satisfied. The key is to talk honestly and recognize that the employee may simply be miscast in the role, stealing a phrase from Marcus Buckingham and Curt Coffman in their *First, Break All the Rules: What the World's Greatest Managers Do Differently.* Buckingham and Coffman point out that poor performers often aren't untalented or unmotivated, but rather are in a role that is a fundamental mismatch with their true strengths. That belief is at the core of coaching out.

Buckingham and Coffman suggest thinking of it as "tough love": you're not going to compromise on your standards and what the organization needs, but you care about the employee and want to see her in a role where she'll blossom. You want to help her move out of a situation that is holding her back from true success and toward opportunities where her talents will be better used.

Here's an example of how this can work in real life. A few years ago, Alison had an employee whose work was good but not stellar. The employee frequently got frustrated and resentful over several demands of the job, snapped at people, and constantly needed to be calmed down. Numerous conversations hadn't improved things, so Alison tried a different approach. She sat down with him and acknowledged that he was frustrated by these particular things but that they simply weren't going to change because they were inherent parts of the job and that they couldn't be constantly battling over them. Rather than seeing him struggle in a job that obviously was making him frustrated and stressed, Alison wanted him to figure out if he could really be happy in the position, knowing that the things he was complaining about weren't going to change. She asked him to take a few days and think about whether he wanted the job in its current form, as opposed to the job he kept trying to change it into, and she told him that if he decided it just wasn't for him, there was no shame in that and she would help him in the transition out.

Several days later, the employee told Alison that he realized he should move on. During the next month, he worked on organizing his files and leaving his work in good order, he trained his replacement, and Alison helped him brainstorm about jobs he'd be happy in. On his last day, he confessed that he was shocked that such a potentially awful conversation had actually been pleasant. And since then, he's stayed in touch, periodically sending helpful leads and information.

In other words, coaching out can transform a situation that many managers would otherwise expect to be uncomfortable or even contentious. Here are some keys to making coaching out work smoothly (Tool 9.5 offers a sample coaching-out script):

- Begin a coaching-out conversation with a statement like this: "I want to talk with you about your fit for this role and some of our options for moving forward."

- Try to make the conversation as collaborative as possible. The overall tone of the meeting should be that you want to jointly figure out a way forward that will be best for both the employee and the organization.

- Focus on the high bar for performance you're setting rather than ways in which the staff member has truly messed up (because in the case of a merely mediocre performer, instances of a massive mistake may be rare). Frame the conversation by laying out what the ideal performer in the role would do, and then focus on the gap between the staff member's performance and that bar. Use a format similar to, "What we need is someone who can do X. I see your strengths as being more Y"— for instance, "We need someone who can forge new relationships where nothing existed previously. I see your strengths as more working with existing partners to develop programs that meet their needs."

- In some cases, the bar may be higher than in the past because of changed circumstances, such as organizational growth or the changing demands of the job. Prepare to tell the story of why that is the case: "We used to have people coming to us, so going out and starting new relationships wasn't important, but as we seek to grow to new parts of the region, we need to be more proactive."

- Depending on the circumstances, you might offer the staff member two options: pursue an improvement plan under your progressive discipline policy and try to meet the bar you're describing, with the understanding that she could be let go if she doesn't improve, or you can jointly form a transition plan that will give her time to search for another job while giving you time to look for a successor.

- Make clear why the joint agreement would be an attractive option. For instance, you might give the person more time to look for her next job than she would have otherwise, and she can say that she's still employed at your organization while she's looking. Be honest about your self-interest as well. It's okay to explain that this solution helps you because it prevents a vacancy in the role. In the case of a long-time, once-valued employee whom the organization has outgrown, it could be appropriate to soften this approach and steer the person away from the improvement process option altogether if you believe it's unlikely to be successful.

For instance, you might still offer the two options but say something like, "To be honest, I'm happy to give you a chance to pursue the improvement plan option if you want to, but I would hate for it to turn your experience here sour. I would much rather work together on a transition that meets your needs and ours."

- Give the staff member an appropriate amount of time to reflect and come back to you with her decision. Set a deadline for when you would like an answer—no longer than a week, since you want to make moving forward a priority.

- If the staff member chooses to pursue an improvement plan under your progressive discipline policy rather than agree to a transition plan, be sincere in your willingness to give her a chance to improve.

ISSUES SURROUNDING LETTING AN EMPLOYEE GO

What to Tell the Rest of Your Staff

After letting a staff member go, managers often wonder how transparent to be with other staff members about the circumstances surrounding the employee's departure.

Your staff will generally understand that you're not going to share every detail with them in cases like this. You might simply let them know, "August 4 will be Carla's last day." In many cases, the departing staff member might send out a message herself. For instance, the employee might explain that she's leaving to pursue jobs more closely aligned with her interest in communications, or that she's taking time to study for the LSAT. However, do be sure to share logistical details, such as how key responsibilities will be handled while the search for a replacement is ongoing.

Will a Firing Lower Morale Among the Rest of the Staff?

You might wonder whether a firing will lower morale among the rest of the staff. In fact, you will find that just the opposite occurs! In almost every case, keeping low or mediocre performers on staff is an enormous morale drain for high performers. If you've ever worked somewhere where shoddy work was tolerated, you know how frustrating and demoralizing it can be when a manager doesn't do anything about poor performers.

It's likely that your staff has spotted the problems and will be relieved when they are resolved. Good people want to work with other good people, and they want to know that their employer is discerning when it comes to results. Their quality of life goes up when they work in environments where standards are high, accountability is clear, and they can count on their coworkers to pull their own weight.

Even when employees are friendly with the staff member who is being let go, most people can separate personal affection from professional assessments. In fact, one client we worked with managed a man and a woman who were romantically involved. When he had to fire the man, the manager worried about how his girlfriend would react. Would she continue working for a boss who had fired her boyfriend?

Would her morale take a hit? But after the firing, the female employee approached the manager in confidence and told him that she agreed with the decision to fire her boyfriend.

As long as you are open with your staff about how you address performance problems so that they understand you don't make arbitrary personnel decisions, you will have a confident, motivated staff. Keep in mind that understanding is key. If firings occur without a general understanding on staff that employees are clearly warned and given a chance to improve before being let go, you risk creating a climate of fear where employees worry that they could be terminated at any point. So it's important to be open and honest with your staff about how problems are handled.

Unions

Although working with unions is beyond the scope of this book and very few nonprofits are unionized, the same principles apply. Hold a high bar and address performance problems clearly and forthrightly, even when your ultimate authority to fire may be more difficult to exercise or employees may be entitled to more formal processes than what is discussed here.

Legal Issues

You don't generally need to speak to a lawyer before dismissing an employee, but there are a few specific situations where you should consider consulting a lawyer in advance.

For at-will employees, that is, those without a specific employment contract (the vast majority of your employees), legal issues typically arise when there is evidence of illegal discrimination related to the employee being a member of a protected class (protected classes revolve around traits like age, gender, religion, race, or sexual orientation). When potential for such evidence exists, talk to a lawyer before taking action.

THE RIGHT KIND OF TURNOVER

Good to Great author Jim Collins notes that top-performing companies don't have any more or less turnover than other companies do. What differs is when the turnover occurs. He found that at top-performing companies, people either left very soon after starting or stayed for a long time. The best companies "did not churn more, they churned *better*," he writes. Great leaders "adopted the following approach: 'Let's take the time to make rigorous A+ selections right upfront. If we get it right, we'll do everything we can to try to keep them on board for a long time. If we make a mistake, then we'll confront that fact so that we can get on with our work and they can get on with their lives.'" (J. Collins, *Good to Great* [New York: HarperCollins, 2001]).

In particular, you should watch for situations where the following could pose issues:

- *Direct comments related to a protected class.* Remarks about an employee's age, gender, race, religion, or other protected status, even when meant as a joke, can give rise to legal claims. For instance, a birthday card delivered to a fifty-year-old employee about the horrors of aging could be used as evidence for an age discrimination claim.

- *Disparate treatment.* Evidence that similarly situated employees are treated differently can also give rise to claims. What "similarly situated" means is a complicated legal issue, but be careful if you are treating employees of comparable tenure, seniority, and performance level differently, particularly when they differ in race, gender, sexual orientation, disability, and so forth.

- *Pretext.* If you give false statements about why you are firing someone, a jury might infer that you were covering up real reasons that were actually discriminatory. Most commonly, this occurs when you have been giving someone positive feedback along the way (even if you didn't really mean it) and then, feeling that you don't have enough of a record to cite your real reasons, use a rationale that is not the actual cause for the person's dismissal. If the person argues that your true reasons were discriminatory ones, this sort of cover-up can make it much harder to defend yourself.

- *Retaliation.* If an employee has raised a complaint involving some kind of legal issue, such as a concern about sexual or racial harassment or about financial wrongdoing within the organization, the firing can look like retaliation, even if it is unrelated to the complaint.

In addition, situations that involve disabilities, including mental illness, or family or medical leave can raise tricky legal issues.

When one of the situations described here arises, it does not mean that you cannot dismiss an employee. But it does mean that you should proceed with caution and speak to a lawyer first. As a general rule, speak with a lawyer in any situation in which you are in doubt.

In addition, if you are concerned the employee you are firing may be litigious, be extra sure to document the reasons for the termination. This can be as simple as a detailed memo before or after the firing that sets out the reasons for the decision. The goal is to be able to demonstrate that you had performance-based reasons for the firing if the employee later alleges your reasons were discriminatory.

KEY POINTS

- Addressing performance problems and moving mediocre or low performers out of your organization is about a fundamental commitment to having great people.

- Most managers don't remove low or mediocre performers quickly enough or frequently enough, and their organizations suffer as a result.

- The bar you use to assess performance should not be "the best this particular person could do," but rather a vision of what a truly high-performing staff member would be doing in the role.

- Make your assessment of an employee's performance independent of how difficult the next step may be to execute. Pretend that you have a red button that, if pushed, would lead to your staff member's being replaced instantaneously. Would you push it?

- When you have a serious performance problem, you can address it through the more traditional path of progressive discipline or you can coach out the employee through a direct conversation.

- Progressive discipline is a series of increasingly serious warnings, culminating in dismissal if the problems aren't fixed. Typically there are three stages: an informal verbal warning, followed by a formal warning, followed by termination if the employee doesn't make sufficient improvement. At each point, the employee can make the necessary corrections; if she doesn't, you move to the next stage. Each step foreshadows the next, so that the staffer is clear about where she stands and isn't surprised by negative consequences.

- In coaching out, the aim is to convince the employee that continued tenure in the role doesn't make sense and agree on a smooth transition plan. The key is to talk honestly and collaboratively and recognize that the employee may simply be miscast in the role.

Additional Reading

Marcus Buckingham and Curt Coffman, *First, Break All the Rules: What the World's Greatest Managers Do Differently* (New York: Simon & Schuster, 1999), especially "The Art of Tough Love" (pp. 206–212).

TOOL 9.1

SAMPLE PROGRESSIVE DISCIPLINE POLICY

We strongly advise having any written progressive discipline policy reviewed by a lawyer, so that you do not inadvertently create a legal commitment to following the steps in this tool in every situation. You want to retain the flexibility to act outside your progressive discipline policy in particularly egregious or unusual situations, so be careful not to create a binding commitment.

Save the Trees is committed to a work environment in which employees receive clear messages when their performance needs to improve. We generally use a policy of progressive discipline to address performance concerns. Under this policy, employees who are not performing at the level they need to typically receive an informal verbal warning, followed by a formal warning and written improvement plan, followed by termination where sufficient improvement has not been made.

However, Save the Trees is an at-will employer and while it will generally take disciplinary action in a progressive manner, it reserves the right, in its sole discretion, to decide what disciplinary action will be taken in a given situation, including termination without prior warnings.

TOOL 9.2

SAMPLE SCRIPT FOR INFORMAL PERFORMANCE WARNING

The employee here is a staff attorney whose management of casework has been poor.

As I mentioned in my e-mail about our agenda, I wanted to talk about your performance lately.

To be frank, your performance has fallen short of what I need from you. I have concerns in two big areas: the quality of your written work and your interactions with our activists.

> *Frame big picture concerns at the start so the employee knows what to expect.*

In terms of written work, I've been having to rewrite significant portions of your draft filings in order to get them to where they meet our standards. For instance, on last week's reply to the motion to dismiss, your summary of the argument section was at least a page too long and didn't mention one of our three major points. In addition, the transitions from one section of the argument to another were abrupt and disjointed, and in at least two places, your parentheticals summarizing holdings were inaccurate.

> *Provide specific examples of where the person is falling short.*

So that's the written work piece. On the activist front, we continue to hear feedback that you aren't responsive enough when they try to get in touch with you.

I'd love to get your perspective on what's causing these problems. On the writing, do you have any sense of why the product hasn't been strong?

[We assume for this sample that the attorney says that she has been too busy to devote enough time to ensuring a quality product.]

> *Probe for insight from the employee. It's possible there could be an outside factor affecting performance that you should know about.*

I know what you mean about writing under pressure and without enough time. Unfortunately, though, I don't think the workload is going to get any lighter, and others on staff are handling comparable amounts of work. I could

> *Be empathetic as appropriate, but hold firm on the standard needed.*

see, though, how better planning in advance might lead to a better product. Should we talk about how you might do that, working backward from the deadline to ensure you don't hit a time crunch?

[The manager and staff member agree that better advance planning would help and that the staff member will send the manager a quick e-mail after each new piece of writing is assigned in which she lays out her time line for producing a draft.]

So better planning may help, and I'm happy to be a resource by looking over your initial time line. Over time, though, you'll need to be able to do that independently because I wouldn't be able to supervise everyone that closely in the long run.

> *Offer help, but make it clear that your staff member must be self-sufficient in the long run. Be specific about next steps where appropriate.*

Stepping back from this, I want to be clear about my expectations, and I also want to make sure we're both on the same page about what needs to happen and what the potential consequences are.

Going forward, I expect you to begin producing drafts of written documents that are ready to file with minimal editing by me, and by that I mean thirty minutes or less. Among other things, the arguments need to be clear, concise, and well supported and flow smoothly from one point to another.

Lay out a clear, specific bar that must be met.

In terms of activist relations, as you know, we promise a response time of no longer than two days. I know that can be hard when you have a lot of work with deadlines, but again, it's a bar we're committed to meeting and we can't have you continue to miss it.

In the short term, I want you to redraft the brief you sent me last night and have a stronger version to me by the end of the day tomorrow. I'm also going to put it on my calendar for us to check in on your performance in three weeks. Assuming it improves and you sustain the higher level, then we'll just roll forward. If it doesn't, then I'm going to have to put you on a formal written improvement plan.

Clearly identify next steps.

A formal written plan lays out areas for improvement and a time line, and as with this discussion, if you improve and sustain that level, things go forward. If you don't improve, then at that point we would have to dismiss you. So my concerns here are serious. I think you have a great deal of potential, but I need you to be performing at a higher level. Given our workload, I need someone in your position who can create strong written documents and respond to activists promptly and reliably. If you can't meet that bar, we would have to find someone else who can.

Be straightforward and clear about consequences.

Do you have any questions about how we're moving forward?

TOOL 9.3

SAMPLE FORMAL PERFORMANCE WARNING IN WRITING

The employee here is an assistant who hasn't been staying on top of her work.

Rachel,

Per our discussion, I wanted to capture how we're moving forward. As I mentioned, I realize that you've been trying very hard, but unfortunately your performance isn't where I need it to be, and without significant improvement I will have to let you go. That improvement needs to happen in the next two weeks, and then it needs to be sustained going forward.

> *Be clear from the beginning about where things stand in the process, and reiterate that if she doesn't improve, the consequence will be dismissal.*

My hope is that you will meet the expectations laid out in this plan and that I will be fully satisfied with the job you are doing. I've tried to be clear and specific about what these expectations are; please let me know if you have any questions about what follows, so I can clarify.

These are the main areas in which I need to see improvement:

1. 100 percent follow-through, in a timely fashion

I need you to take care of all of the items including meeting requests, issues raised by voice mail or e-mail, research requests, and other tasks that are part of the general course of business. As we discussed, this truly needs to be 100 percent. Because of the volume of issues, I can't check back in on every item, so I need to trust completely that when I hand you an item, it is as good as done. Everyone is human, and mistakes do happen from time to time, but over the next two weeks (and in general over any comparable time period) if more than one item slips through the cracks, then I'd deem that to be falling short of expectations.

> *Where possible, explain why the performance needs to be high.*

In terms of timeliness, it is hard to set an absolute rule, and the best guideline is that when you are in doubt, you should ask. In general, though, I would assume that you would handle most issues in your area that are not bigger projects—for example, printing documents, reaching out to others around meeting requests, replying to e-mails and voice mails—within one business day of receiving them, with many happening on the same business day. If for some reason you are not able to get to items that you normally would within this time frame, at a minimum I assume you will let the relevant person know that you are still on top of the item.

> *Be as specific as possible about the level of performance you're looking for and how you'll know if it's being reached.*

2. Quality/Accuracy

I need to be able to trust that when you do take something on, it will get done in the manner we have agreed to, and where that is not possible, you will brainstorm potential solutions and, as appropriate, communicate your options or recommendations back to us. Again, my expectation is that within a two-week span, there might be one instance of inaccuracy or one slip-up regarding quality, but not more.

3. Volume

Performing at a high level in this role means handling the large volume of items that come your way on an ongoing basis. I will continue to put things on your plate, and my expectation is that over the next two weeks, we will reach a steady state where there is no significant backlog of items that you are handling.

Consequences

As we discussed, we need to ensure that you quickly reach a high level of performance. That means that this improvement plan will be in effect for the next two weeks (starting today, Monday, October 20). We will check in at the end of next week to review your performance against this plan. If you do not fulfill the requirements of this plan, then I would need to dismiss you, with one week of severance pay.

Reiterate the consequences and be clear about the terms (severance pay) so there is no confusion about what's at stake or how it will happen.

My hope is that you will fulfill the requirements of this plan. If you do, you will no longer be on an official improvement plan. You will, however, need to maintain that high level of performance over time.

I've tried to be direct in laying out my expectations going forward and the consequences of this plan. What this memo does not do justice to, however, is how much I enjoy working with you on a personal level and how much I appreciate your commitment to this organization and all the hard work that you have put in up to this point.

You should not hesitate to be kind; just be sure it doesn't blunt the substance of your message.

Again, please let me know if you have any questions about what is laid out in this plan.

Anita

TOOL 9.4

SAMPLE FIRING SCRIPT

In this sample, an administrative assistant has already been placed on a formal improvement plan and has not shown the necessary improvements. He was warned in his formal improvement plan letter that if he did not improve, he would be dismissed.

As I told you yesterday, I wanted to use our meeting today to reflect on your progress against the improvement plan. We talked two weeks ago about the fact that if you couldn't meet the expectations of the job, I would have to let you go. We're now at that point, so unfortunately today will be your last day.

Refer back to the earlier agreement that you would need to replace him if sufficient improvements weren't made.

Be clear from the start about what is happening.

I know you've tried hard, particularly in terms of leaving a positive impression in your interactions with others. When I asked the rest of the team (as we had discussed that I would), I received a number of positive comments about your improvement.

Acknowledge any improvement that has been made . . .

But on the other two dimensions we'd spoken about—handling the daily flow of work from me and having no dropped balls— your performance isn't where we need it. I know you've been trying, but there have been at least three items that I asked you to handle more than two days ago that are still not complete: scheduling the meeting with Melissa, printing background materials for my meeting next Thursday, and completing my expense report. Unfortunately, we're now at the point where we need to move forward with someone else in the role.

. . . but be clear that it hasn't been sufficient and specify in what areas it has fallen short.

You can use today to clean out your desk, say good-bye to people, and finish any other items. I would really appreciate it if you would go through your e-mails and send me an update on where each item stands: whether you haven't gotten to it yet, if it's partly or fully done, and anything else I should know. This afternoon you should talk to Erica in human resources about exit procedures. She'll give you a list of other things that you need to take care of by the end of the day, like returning keys.

Be clear about the logistics.

Assuming all of that happens before the end of the day, then we'll be in good shape and we'll be able to give you two weeks of severance pay.

I know that this has been a challenging experience for you and that particularly over these past two weeks, you have been trying hard. On a personal level, I've enjoyed our interactions, and I really do wish you the best of luck.

Offer an opportunity for the employee to ask questions related to logistics, but not to argue the decision itself.

Do you have any questions about the exit procedures or what you need to do?

TOOL 9.5

SAMPLE COACHING-OUT SCRIPT

In this sample, the staff member, a director of technology, has been a reasonably loyal, well-intentioned employee whose skills no longer make sense for the position. The ideal outcome is for the staff member to agree to begin looking for a better-fit job in another organization, but the manager wants to give the staff member the choice of going down the progressive discipline process path. Therefore, the core of the manager's message is:

- *The demands of the role have changed, and you may not be a good fit for it anymore.*
- *You can choose to pursue the progressive discipline process route, but I think the alternative route makes the most sense.*

As I mentioned to you yesterday, I'd like to talk about how I see the director of technology role evolving. This is a tough conversation, because the bottom line is that I've started to have concerns about your fit for the role. I wanted to talk today about why that is and how we might move forward.

> *Be clear from the start as to why you're having the meeting so the employee understands the context for the conversation that follows.*

Let me start by saying that I know how much work you've put into this job over the past two years and that on a number of occasions you've gone above and beyond. For instance, last year when the servers shut down, you cancelled your weekend plans at the last minute to get them running again quickly. You've been great at paying attention to every last detail, fixing problems as they come up, and watching the bottom line. When we were starting up, you were great at working with vendors and driving a hard bargain to get us good deals on what we needed. Your attention to detail, that ability to look at someone's computer and diagnose what's wrong and fix it quickly, and your understanding of finances are real strengths.

> *Acknowledge your staff member's strengths and contributions to the organization.*

As our organization has grown, though, what we need in our director of technology role has changed. We used to be a small, single-site shop, and now we have multiple locations. Also, as we've added new programs, our database development needs have increased tremendously. We have a huge demand for new applications from the database, and those are things we have to do if we're going to maximize our impact as an organization.

As we entered this new stage, I realized we needed our director of technology to do a different set of things than we needed earlier in our evolution. When I realized that, I started to question whether you're the right person for the changed role, and whether in the long run, this is the job that is going to make the best use of your skills.

> *Tell the story of how and why the role has evolved.*

What we need in the director of technology role now is someone whose strengths are things like big picture conceptualization, communicating with the program staff about their needs, and project management. Take, for instance, the other day when the online advocacy team was

> *Explain the new bar that you now need.*

meeting about their strategic plan. We need someone who can sit in that meeting, understand fully what the team is trying to accomplish, translate that into a set of technological solutions that they don't even know to ask for, and then explain their options to them in terms that they can understand so that they can make an informed choice. Once we've decided on an approach, we need someone who can handle all the complexities of managing the development process with our staff members, account for the inevitable setbacks, and deliver a product on time that works and meets everyone's needs.

Candidly, I don't think those are your strengths. For instance, when we tried to develop the new database of our subscribers, there were quite a few issues, including the team's misunderstanding about what you were going to deliver and delays in completing the final product. I realize that there were problems on both ends of that process, but I need someone who even when the other team isn't performing perfectly will communicate the issues, help the other team understand what they need to do, and manage them to the deadlines they need to meet. I think that's a high bar, but it's also critical that we meet it.

> *Be clear in your assessment of the person's weaknesses as well as strengths. This is the first step in steering her toward the mutually beneficial process.*

So where does this leave us? I think we have two options. As you know, we have a formal process in place for staff members who aren't meeting expectations, and if you want, we can head down that road. This meeting would be the first step in that: it would be the informal performance warning, and we would talk concretely about how we would know over the next three weeks that your performance had improved. After that, if your performance didn't improve, there would be a written performance warning and improvement process, which would last another four weeks.

At the end of all that, if your performance didn't meet expectations, we would have to let you go and look for someone else. If your performance did meet expectations, then we would move ahead with you in this role as long as your performance stayed at the level we need. I want to be clear that this is a real option. If you choose to go this route, I promise that I'll work with you to set clear expectations and give you the reasonable help I can in developing your skills, given the constraints on my time. I would give you a fair chance to meet what I see as the new bar for performance.

> *Note that you're willing to follow progressive discipline steps.*

> *Be straightforward and clear about how you see the situation in order to steer the staff member toward the best possible outcome.*

All that said, from what I know of you and your strengths, I'm not convinced it would work. At the end of that process, we'd be giving you the standard two weeks of severance, and we'd be left with a vacancy in the tech role. I want to put forth another option for you to consider. If you agree that the role as I've described it isn't what you ideally want or think you're best at, then we could set up an arrangement that might work better for both of us. I think it would take me three months to hire a new head of technology from the time I started looking, and I'd rather not have the role vacant. I also know that you'd need time to conduct a job search, and I'd want to give you time to do that.

> *Offer a win-win path that would work for you both.*

So what I'd propose is this: we could agree now that you'll leave the role at the end of April. In the meantime, you'll continue ensuring our basic tech needs are met, but we won't expect you to take on any new projects, which will allow you to focus on a job

Preemptively address the preconditions of the offer.

search. We'd continue to pay you your current salary through the end of April. If you found a job sooner, then you could leave before that, but we'd stop paying you. All of this would be contingent on your continuing to perform as you have been, which means having a good attitude at work, keeping our basic infrastructure running, and so on. You'd also have to sign an agreement that our lawyers insist on. Knowing what I know about you and how you've operated, my sense is that this would work out.

I know I've just thrown a lot at you, but I wanted to put it all on the table. We can talk more about this now, or I can give you some time to think about it and then we can talk in the next day or two about which way you'd like to go. I do feel urgency around figuring this out, so I'd like to meet no later than Thursday to hear your decision. Do you want to talk now, or would you rather wait?

Give a clear deadline for deciding.

PART

3

MANAGING YOURSELF

As we've tried to make clear, management is how you get things done through other people. In order to do that effectively—to do everything we've explored in the previous chapters—you need to be personally effective yourself. If you're like many of our clients, you have a long history of being effective, though as a solo practitioner. What you may need to learn is how to manage yourself now that you're in a new role and the practices that might have worked for you before may no longer suffice.

The chapters in Part Three are all about what it means to manage yourself as a manager:

- How to exercise authority without being a wimp or a tyrant (Chapter Ten)

- How to figure out where your time should be focused, with specific tips for staying organized and managing your time (Chapter Eleven)

- The importance of your relationship with your own manager and how to work with her in a way that will maximize your results (Chapter Twelve)

- A look at the personal qualities exhibited by the best managers we've seen (Conclusion)

CHAPTER

10

EXERCISING AUTHORITY WITHOUT BEING A WIMP OR A TYRANT

Many new managers worry about something that sounds simple but can actually be the source of a lot of anxiety: how to act now that you have authority over others. You may feel especially awkward if you're managing people who are older, wiser, or more experienced than you.

Getting your style of authority right isn't going to make you a great manager all on its own, but getting it wrong can be ruinous. If you're too passive and shy away from using your authority, you'll end up a wimp. On the other end of the spectrum, if you use your authority too aggressively, you risk becoming a tyrant. Both wimps and tyrants drive away good employees and struggle to produce results.

The best managers we've seen aren't wimps or tyrants but are simply normal, assertive people. That might sound simple in theory, but in practice, it can be difficult to get the balance right—and even to recognize you have a problem in this area. In this chapter, we describe wimpy and tyrannical behaviors so that you can decide for yourself whether you fall on one side or the other. Then we describe how assertive management looks when it's done right.

WIMPS

Wimpiness in managers is typically rooted in a desire to be nice. We're big fans of being nice, but managers who are wimps allow that desire to be nice to trump their fundamental obligations as managers—obligations like holding the bar high and expecting people to adhere to them, warning them when they're falling short, and taking action when warnings don't work. Wimpiness can be fatal to the success of an organization because problems go unresolved and difficult decisions go unmade, which means the organization can't make nearly as much progress as it could if those obstacles were removed.

Ironically, while many wimpy managers are just trying to be liked, over time the opposite happens: as problems go unresolved and difficult decisions go unmade, staff members grow frustrated and complain, and the best among them leave.

Signs that you might be a wimp include:

- *Avoidance.* Wimps avoid conflict and tough conversations like the plague. Most frequently, this plays out in managers' not addressing performance problems or firing underperformers. But it surfaces in other ways as well. For instance, a conflict-averse manager may hesitate to insist on necessary course corrections midway through a project because she thinks doing so will upset her team.

- *Indirectness.* Wimpy managers often present requirements as mere suggestions. The result is that staffers end up confused about expectations, and managers get frustrated when staff don't act on those "suggestions." For example, an unassertive manager who wants to look at a letter before it's sent out might say, "Feel free to show me that letter before you send it out," leaving the staff member with the mistaken impression that the manager has no preference about looking at the letter.

- *Masking indecision as consensus building.* Because many nonprofits are working to achieve a more egalitarian, inclusive society, some managers feel that decisions should be made by majority rule or consensus, an approach that confuses everyone about whether they are just being consulted or actually making the decisions. While there are certainly times when building consensus is important for an organization, too frequently we see organizations in which difficult decisions don't get made and no one takes responsibility for moving work forward. Use your staff's input to inform your decisions, but remember that when it comes to making tough calls that will lead to good results, that's your job!

- *Overfriendliness.* Managers who are overly concerned with being liked by their employees can compromise their effectiveness if employees get mixed signals about the nature of their relationship. Ironically, this can lead from wimpy behavior into tyrannical behavior: if an employee starts taking advantage of the friendship, you may feel your authority is being challenged or undermined and end up reacting too aggressively.

Ricken Patel, executive director of Avaaz, an international nonprofit, says this about decision making:

> I used to think in order to get extremely talented people to work together, you needed their buy-in in terms of a decision-making structure, that you needed more of a consensual decision-making structure. What I've learned is that you can build an extremely dynamic team of these kinds of people while still having a hierarchical management structure in place. The mixture of a highly collaborative, transparent culture combined with a clear hierarchical structure has been the magic mix. Earlier in my career, I tried getting together the people I most respected and having everyone be codirectors and taking equal management and decision-making responsibilities, but we eventually realized that often it's best to have a single decision maker. Sometimes consensual processes place enormous demands on time and energy and sometimes result in compromises that are lower quality than following any single vision.

> A more structured hierarchy has been highly effective, and far from people feeling less bought in because they don't have equal decision-making power, people have felt more excited and more engaged because the team as a whole has performed better.

TYRANTS

Managers who are tyrants get things done through rigid control, negativity, and a climate of fear.

Most tyrants don't set out to be mean, but they don't trust that they can get the results they want any other way. However, tyrants aren't as effective in either the short or the long term. Staff members who are distracted by fear or anxiety won't bring up new ideas for fear of being ridiculed, and they won't be honest about problems. In addition, very few great people with lots of choices are going to want to work for a tyrant. We've seen this play out in many organizations where not only do good employees leave, but a manager who gets a reputation as difficult to work for finds it incredibly tough to attract the level of new talent the organization needs.

Signs that you might be a tyrant include:

- *Yelling.* We hear with surprising regularity about bosses who yell and scream. Managers who yell demean and humiliate the person being yelled at and diminish their own authority because they look out of control. In contrast, a manager confident in her own authority doesn't need to yell, because she has far more effective tools available to her. Our advice here is simple: don't yell.

- *Defensiveness.* Tyrannical managers often respond defensively when their decisions are questioned. They may also squash dissent, making employees less likely to suggest new and different ways of doing things, and they are prone to shooting the bearers of bad news, which means that staffers will avoid sharing negative information. When you're secure in your authority, you aren't threatened by dissent, and you might even recognize that—gasp!—others' ideas are sometimes better than your own.

> **THE WIMP/TYRANT COMBO**   Oddly enough, we see many managers who are both wimps and tyrants in one. Typically the manager starts out as a wimp, not being direct enough about what she expects or not addressing performance issues head-on. When her staff members don't properly interpret her too-subtle signals or don't deliver because they don't have the requisite skills, the manager gets frustrated and yells. Later she feels badly about yelling and tries to be friendly with her staff rather than correcting the underlying problems, and the cycle repeats itself.

- *Passive-aggressive criticism.* Rather than offering direct, constructive feedback, tyrants sometimes criticize in indirect asides, making it hard for the staff member to respond. For example, a manager given a memo only a minute before a meeting might walk in and say, "I don't know why I'm just getting this memo now, but I guess we should go ahead and talk about it." If you have feedback, make a note and talk to your staff member directly when the time is right.

- *Unreasonable demands.* Tyrants cross the line from holding their staffers to a high standard to pushing their staffers to the brink. For example, a tyrannical manager might insist that staff members work over the weekend to complete a project even if it isn't time sensitive, or might demand that a staffer do the truly impossible (such as getting a replacement part for a computer when all the stores that sell it are closed).

ASSERTIVE MANAGERS

Effective managers are neither wimpy nor tyrannical. They act with the confidence of their position: they directly lay out expectations and hold people to them; operate in a fair, positive, and straightforward manner; and back up their words with action. We'll call them assertive managers.[1]

Signs of assertive management include these:

- *Directness.* Assertive managers say what needs to be said in a direct and straightforward way. They don't shy away from difficult or awkward conversations, and they know that addressing problems head-on is a key part of their job.

- *Calm.* When giving an employee feedback or talking about a problem, an assertive manager may sound concerned but is rarely angry or hostile. For instance, in talking to a staff member who has been forgetting assignments, an assertive manager might

---

[1] In *Assertive Discipline* (Bloomington, Ind.: Solution Tree, 2011), a book about classroom teaching, Lee and Marlene Canter present a similar framework for teachers, distinguishing nonassertive, hostile, and assertive styles.

say, "I've noticed recently that some of the projects we agreed you'd take on fell off your radar screen, and that's a serious problem. I need to be able to rely on you to remember the assignments we discuss, because I can't check back in on every item. How can you make sure it doesn't happen again?"

- *Openness.* Because assertive managers know they aren't infallible, they're open to the possibility that they may be mistaken or that there may be a better way of doing something.

- *Fairness.* Inevitably conflicts among staff members will arise, and when they do, an assertive manager serves as a fair judge. We've seen managers who throw up their hands and say, "Just work it out on your own," which tends to create a Hobbesian state of nature in the office, where people's time on staff is nasty, brutish, and short. Rather than avoiding issues or appearing arbitrary in addressing them, an assertive manager's aim is to consider the situation calmly, fairly, and impartially so that she gets to the right answer. Because her staff members know that she's a fair judge, they're more likely to buy in to her decision, even when it doesn't go their way.

- *Comfortable in charge.* The best managers see their authority as simply one more tool for getting things done. It's neither something that makes them nervous nor something that they lord over others.

Let's look at one of these here, fair decision making, because it's so important.

When you're faced with tough decisions, it's a lot harder to get good outcomes if you don't get the process right. Here's what you *don't* want to do:

- Shy away from making decisions at all. (*wimp*)

- Let consensus rule every time. (*wimp*)

- Block out others' input in favor of your own counsel. (*tyrant*)

- Become defensive if others question your decisions. (*tyrant*)

You're most likely to reach the right decision if you welcome what others have to say, while simultaneously remembering that it may be your job to make the final call. What's more, your staff members are most likely to support decisions where they feel the decision-making process was fair. In this context, fairness means that when decisions affect them, staff members have a chance to be engaged by giving meaningful input on the issues. Fairness also means that staff members not only hear about the outcome of a decision, but about the rationale behind it in much the same way that judges often issue written opinions explaining the reasoning behind their decisions.

Suppose, for instance, that you're wrestling with whether to expand your field department. You might explain the context to your staff and solicit their ideas, engaging in rigorous conversation about the pros and cons—for example, "It's true that we could reach more people, but what about investing that money to beef up our development department, which might ultimately bring in even more resources for us?" After

WIMPS, TYRANTS, AND ASSERTIVE MANAGERS IN ACTION

A new receptionist is chronically late, leaving others covering for her.

What the wimp does: Very little. She may complain about the behavior to others or be silently irate, but she doesn't address it with the employee directly.

What the tyrant does: Calls the employee into her office and says to her loudly enough for others to hear: "This is not hard! How do you function in life? If you don't get your act together, you're gone!"

What the assertive manager does: Addresses the person privately as soon as it's clear there's a pattern: "Kate, you've been late four times in the past two weeks. When you're late, Alex and Jill have to cover for you. I need you to make sure you're here by 9:00 from here on out. Can you commit to that?"

A manager is growing concerned that a field organizer is falling short of her recruiting goals for the year.

What the wimp does: Hopes to herself that the field organizer gets back on track by the end of the year.

What the tyrant does: Comes down hard: "Do I have to do your job for you? Do you really not know how to get this done?" or is passive-aggressive: "We'd have a better chance to win this campaign if our organizer would organize a house party with more than four people."

What the assertive manager does: Addresses it directly: "I'm concerned that our recruiting numbers are lower than they should be at this point in the year. Let's meet this afternoon to talk about what you could do differently to get back on track toward this goal."

A communications director scores an editorial endorsement for the group's legislation from a major newspaper.

What the wimp does: Responds more like a friend than a manager: "Sweet endorsement!"

What the tyrant does: Barely acknowledges it, if at all, or possibly takes the credit.

What the assertive manager does: Quickly praises the communications director for the victory and the work that went into it: "Great coup! All that outreach to the editorial board and the pitching you did really paid off."

spending some time thinking it over and making the final decision, you'd then come back to your staff and explain how you arrived at it: "I thought about Julie's point about increased workload next year and José's concern about resources already being stretched thin, but in the end, I became convinced that we need to seize the momentum now and add these regions while we can." In this way, no matter what your ultimate decision is, your staff know that they were heard, you considered their input, and you made a thoughtful decision. (For a fuller description of this approach, read the article by W. Chan Kim and Renée Mauborgne that we list at the end of this chapter in the Additional Reading section.)

JUST BE NORMAL

Ultimately our advice to you is to just be normal. That is, be yourself and don't over-think it. If you use humor in your personal life, don't be afraid to use it in your work life too. If you're on the quiet side, you don't need to lead office cheers. Just be normal.

Of course, one response to this advice is to say, "Well, I *am* kind of a tyrant [or a wimp], so if I'm supposed to be myself, I'm going to be tyrannical [or wimpy]." But people are rarely tyrants across the board. What's more common is selective tyranny. Few people are tyrants toward their own bosses, for instance, or toward funders, or toward their loved ones. So perhaps the rule of thumb here is to be yourself within the confines of bringing out the right pieces of yourself.

KEY POINTS

- The best managers we've seen aren't wimps or tyrants but simply normal, asser-tive people.

- Managers who are wimps often get that way by allowing a desire to be nice to trump their fundamental obligations. These managers, who avoid difficult decisions or topics, are uncomfortable asserting authority, frame requirements as suggestions or overvalue consensus, or create environments in which problems go unresolved, no one takes responsibility for moving work forward, and good staff members get frustrated and often leave.

GENDER DYNAMICS AND AUTHORITY   Women managers may at times confront the reality that authoritative women will sometimes be seen as "bitchy," while men displaying the same behaviors are seen as resolute, strong leaders. In our experience, this is a very real, and unfortunate, dynamic. But until society changes, our advice to female managers is to do precisely what we recommend throughout this chapter: be normal, be assertive, and be neither a tyrant nor a wimp.

- Managers who are tyrants generally don't trust that they'll get the results they want any other way. These managers, who get things done through rigid control, negativity, or a climate of anxiety and fear, create an atmosphere where staffers won't raise new ideas or be honest about problems and where good employees won't stay long-term.

- Effective managers act with the confidence of their position: they directly lay out expectations and hold people to them, operating in a fair, positive, and straightforward manner and backing up their words with action. They are open to feedback, have a matter-of-fact attitude toward being in charge, and treat people as they themselves would want to be treated.

- You're most likely to reach good decisions—and receive your staff members' advice—by assessing all sides fairly and impartially, and sharing the rationale for your ultimate decision.

Additional Reading

Lee Canter and Marlene Canter, *Assertive Discipline: Positive Behavior Management for Today's Classroom* (Solution Tree, 2001), especially "Response Styles" (pp. 25–38).

Jim Collins, *Good to Great: Why Some Companies Make the Leap . . . and Others Don't* (New York: HarperCollins 2001), especially "Level 5 Leadership" (pp. 17–40).

Joseph Grenny, David Maxfield, and Andrew Shimberg, "How to Have Influence," *MIT Sloan Management Review,* 2008, *50*(1), 47–52.

W. Chan Kim and Renée Mauborgne, "Fair Process: Managing in the Knowledge Economy," *Harvard Business Review*, Jan. 2003, pp. 3–11.

CHAPTER

MANAGING YOUR TIME AND STAYING ORGANIZED

It's the unspoken secret among managers: we all struggle with the seemingly simple job of staying organized and using our time well.

If you're like many managers we know (and us on bad days), this may describe a typical day for you. You arrive at the office and begin sorting through your e-mail. A staffer drops by with some questions about a project, and just as she leaves, you get a phone call from a volunteer with feedback on a recent event. When you're done talking to her, you begin reviewing a draft of a mailing, but when you're halfway through, you're interrupted by a stressed-out staffer who needs help prioritizing her workload. Before returning to the mailing, you check your e-mail and find a handful of urgent messages to respond to. The day continues like this, and by its end, you haven't managed to touch the two biggest things you had hoped to get to.

Sound familiar? When you become a manager, the flow of stuff coming at you increases exponentially: e-mails, reports, questions, meetings, materials to review. As a result, systems that used to be adequate for juggling it all may no longer suffice.

How you manage yourself and your time and how you stay organized will have a serious impact on the kind of results you'll get. There are many good books that delve into organization systems with more justice than we can do here, so in this chapter we'll simply synthesize what we've seen work best. We address how to think about where your time should go (and how to make sure your intentions don't get crushed by circumstance) and then move into some specific tips for managing your time and staying organized. And we end with some thoughts on how to tame the e-mail beast.

FIVE WAYS FOR WHERE TO SPEND YOUR TIME

There's no magic bullet to managing your time; if you were busy before reading this, you're probably going to be busy afterward. The key, though, is to make sure that you are spending your time on the right items, and the way to do that is by clarity—clarity about what you're trying to accomplish. Yet in the hustle of daily work life, with a steady flow of demands coming at you, it's easy to lose sight of the most important ways for you to spend your time.

In this section, we look at five ways you might think about where your time is best spent:

Tip 1: Focus on the big rocks.

Tip 2: Use comparative advantage, the time management principle that will change your work life.

Tip 3: You're a manager, so spend time managing.

Tip 4: Manage your calendar; don't let it manage you.

Tip 5: Know when you should get more involved.

Tip 1: Focus on the Big Rocks

The biggest time management mistake that most managers make is spending their time on what's immediately at hand or what's most comfortable to work on rather than what's most important. If you don't make time for the important work first, you may never get to it, as this parable from Stephen Covey illustrates:

> One day, an expert in time management was speaking to a group of business students and, to drive home a point, used an illustration those students will never forget. As he stood in front of the group of high powered overachievers he said, "Okay, time for a quiz."
>
> Then he pulled out a one gallon, wide-mouthed Mason jar and set it on the table in front of him. Then he produced about a dozen fist-sized rocks and carefully placed them, one at a time, into the jar. When the jar was filled to the top and no more rocks would fit inside, he asked, "Is this jar full?"
>
> Everyone in the class said, "Yes." Then he said, "Really?" He reached under the table and pulled out a bucket of gravel. Then he dumped some gravel in and shook the jar, causing pieces of gravel to work themselves down into the space between the big rocks. Then he asked the group once more, "Is the jar full?"

By this time the class was on to him. "Probably not," one of them answered. "Good," he replied. He reached under the table and brought out a bucket of sand. He started dumping the sand in the jar, and it went into all of the spaces left between the rocks and the gravel. Once more he asked the question, "Is this jar full?" "No," the class shouted.

Once again he said, "Good." Then he grabbed a pitcher of water and began to pour it in until the jar was filled to the brim. Then he looked at the class and asked, "What is the point of this illustration?"

One eager beaver raised his hand and said, "The point is, no matter how full your schedule is, if you try really hard you can always fit some more things in it."

"No," the speaker replied, "that's not the point. The truth this illustration teaches us is: If you don't put the big rocks in first, you'll never get them in at all. What are the 'big rocks' in your life? Your children, your loved ones, your education, your dreams, a worthy cause, teaching or mentoring others, doing things that you love, time for yourself, your health, your significant other? Remember to put these big rocks in first or you'll never get them in at all. If you sweat the little stuff (the gravel, the sand) then you'll fill your life with little things you worry about that don't really matter, and you'll never have the real quality time you need to spend on the big, important stuff (the big rocks). So, tonight, or in the morning, when you are reflecting on this short story, ask yourself this question: What are the 'big rocks' in my life? Then, put those in your jar first."[1]

Although this story is about getting priorities straight across all the realms of your life, it applies at work as well. You could easily fill most of your days with small things and never get to the big picture priorities that will significantly move your work forward. How often have you agreed to spend an hour at a meeting that wasn't crucial for you when your to-do list was filled with high-impact but less urgent needs, like checking in on a project you've delegated or talking to an employee about a performance problem?

To avoid this, figure out what one or two items are most important to accomplish on any given day and make those your priorities. Whenever possible, do them first, before other things have the chance to intervene. The details will fill in where there's room for them.

One of the best ways to free up time to focus on the big rocks is by delegating anything else you can. Let's talk about what that means.

---

[1] As related in Stephen R. Covey, A. Roger Merrill, and Rebecca R. Merrill, *First Things First* (New York: Free Press, 1994), pp. 88–89. Reprinted with permission.

"The question you need to ask yourself is not, `Am I getting everything done?' but, `Am I getting the most important things done?'"

RICKEN PATEL, EXECUTIVE DIRECTOR, AVAAZ

Tip 2: Comparative Advantage, or the Time Management Principle That Will Change Your Work Life

It's one thing to say that you should delegate more; it's entirely another to put it into practice. If you're like most managers, the idea of delegating work that you think you could do better yourself makes you very, very nervous. And, you might think, if you have time to do everything yourself and you're still achieving all your big goals, then you can skip right through this section. But assuming that you routinely don't have time to get to everything or that you feel stretched too thin, then you're going to need to delegate more.

Painful, we know. But here's the thing: if you don't deliberately choose what not to spend your time on, then those things will get chosen for you by default—or, rather, by the limited number of hours in the day—and they may not be the right items. Most frequently, the work that gets pushed aside so that you can focus on all the items coming at you right now are the big picture items that could more powerfully drive your work forward than all those little items combined. So while you might do a great job of drafting newsletter articles or proofreading documents, if that will keep you from reaching out to major funders or cultivating a highly promising prospect for your team, then it's not the right use of your time.

If you took Economics 101, you might remember the principle of comparative advantage. You might be a bit better than your assistant at proofreading, but given your experience and role, you're probably far more effective than she would be at talking to the media, cultivating donors, and hiring a new head of the communications

(ALMOST) NEVER STUFF AN ENVELOPE   Don't feel silly or awkward about focusing intensely on the areas where you bring the most value and not spending time on the areas where you don't. For instance, some nonprofits have an ethos that everyone should pitch in on projects like stuffing envelopes. This may be egalitarian, but it's not a good use of resources. Your budget will go further if you hire temps to stuff envelopes while you stay focused on the higher-level work that only you can do. If you feel uncomfortable about this, explain that it's not about pulling rank but about responsible use of limited resources.

In rare cases, pitching in like this can send a nice symbolic message that you're all in the work together, but this should not become something you do on more than the very infrequent occasion.

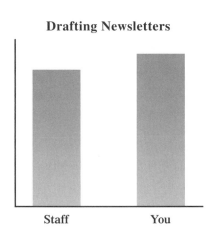

Drafting Newsletters

Staff   You

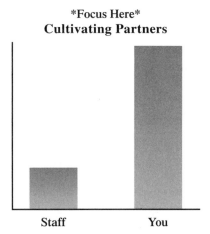

Focus Here
Cultivating Partners

Staff   You

FIGURE 11.1. *The Law of Comparative Advantage at Work*

department. You should be spending your time in the areas where you're much better than your staff, because the payoff will be greater (Figure 11.1).

Of course, this doesn't mean that you should accept mediocre work. Continuing with the proofreading example, you should use the delegation principles we discussed in Chapter Two and make it clear to your assistant that when she's done proofreading, there should be no typos, and you should spot-check her work and hold her accountable. And if she wasn't a better proofreader than you to start, hopefully over time she will become that.

So this is the simple principle for knowing when you should delegate something: if you *can* delegate it, you *should* delegate it. In other words, work should flow downward to the lowest-level person who can do it well enough. That's right: we said "well enough," not "perfectly."

One executive director we know described his feelings this way: "I've been told that I should let my staff take the calls from most of our volunteers and activists. But I feel like by doing it myself, I'm panning for gold. All sorts of nuggets come out of those conversations, and I don't want to miss those." Although we like the fact that the executive director was getting his hands dirty enough to know what was going on in the field, in spending his time taking all of these routine calls, he was letting entire gold mountains go unexplored because he greatly cut into the time he had available for overseeing strategy and raising funds. He has since shifted out of this mode and generated several sizable contributions that might not have otherwise happened.

Tip 3: You're a Manager, So Spend Time Managing

The corollary of delegating as much as you can is that while you do less, you should guide more. And guiding takes time. Whether it's reviewing drafts and giving feedback, having check-in meetings to help your staff members sort out their priorities, visiting the field so you can see how your team's work is playing out in real life, or preparing for a coaching-out conversation, a sizable portion of your work now is to help shape the work of others.

Many new managers fail to make the shift from doing to guiding. They spend just as much time as they used to on their own work, and they try to squeeze in managing others between the cracks, almost treating that part of their job as an inconvenience. They end up in a vicious cycle, where work they delegate gets done poorly because they don't invest the time to manage it well. So they take on the work themselves and then have less time to supervise other work they have delegated, which in turn goes poorly, so they take that work on too.

Avoid the trap of the manager who doesn't manage: change how you allocate your time so you can get the benefits of having others working for you. It's simple leverage: if you have a team of five people and you can make each of them successful, you'll get much more done through them than you will if you try to do all the work yourself.

Tip 4: Manage Your Calendar; Don't Let It Manage You

Your calendar can fill up with meetings and other obligations to the point that you don't have any time left to work on your biggest priorities. Rather than just hoping time will become available, review your calendar regularly and make sure you have time carved out to work on whatever is most important for you to spend time on.

Two specific techniques can be quite helpful here. First, schedule time on your calendar for specific pieces of work, particularly things you need to do yourself (most people are reasonably good at scheduling meetings with others when they need to, so think of this as a meeting with yourself). For instance, if you know the next step in filling the vacancy on your team for a field organizer is for you to draft the job description, pull out your calendar and block off 10:00 A.M. to 11:00 A.M. on Monday just as you would for a meeting, and write, "Write job description." That way, even if you end up having to move the time for a "real" meeting, you know that you better block off another chunk or the job description may not get done.

Beyond blocking off time for specific projects, a second good practice is to schedule work blocks into your calendar: two three- or four-hour blocks of time each week to do your most important work. Depending on the nature of your work in any given week, you might use these blocks to discuss a key project with your staff, write an update for the board, reach out to an important funder, or whatever else best meets your needs. Having that time set aside helps you avoid filling your calendar so full with other meetings—some important, some not—that you never have time to actually do the things that might most move your priorities forward.

Once you set up regular work blocks, make sure you preserve that time. Although in general you want your staff to err on the side of asking you a question when one arises (because you can often save a staff member hours of struggling by providing a few minutes of advice), it's also important to feel comfortable protecting your time when you need to. If you're interrupted with something that isn't urgent, it can be fine to say, "I'm in a work block right now, so I'd love to save that if we can unless it's urgent."

And if constant interruptions are disrupting your ability to focus on your priorities, you might look at whether you've delegated broadly enough and given most of your staff sufficient ability to move priorities forward without constantly checking in with you.

Tip 5: Know When You Should Get More Involved

Despite everything you'll do to protect your time, there are occasions when you should get more involved than you would in the normal course of business. You may recall the story in Chapter One of the manager who stepped in to do the job of his regional manager when that person was not moving as quickly as he needed to. Like that manager, you don't want to be hands-off if there's a crisis or something important going awry. One manager we know describes this approach as the helicopter theory: you circle the land in a helicopter, watching to make sure everything is moving along smoothly. When you spot what looks like smoke, you swoop in to engage.

Of course, when you need to swoop in like this, you should be examining why you need to be so involved. Is it because you're short-staffed? Is there a problem with a particular staffer? For instance, if you see that an event coordinator is letting important planning elements drift, you should involve yourself to whatever extent necessary to ensure that the event is a success. But you should also make sure the coordinator knows you shouldn't have needed to be involved at that level and that she isn't meeting the bar you need from her.

ESTABLISHING STRONG SYSTEMS

In addition to using your time well, you need to find a system for organizing the many pieces of information, to-do items, and requests that will be coming at you throughout the day.

If you're like many managers when we first encounter them, you have a full calendar, multiple to-do lists, sticky notes on your computer and phone, thousands of e-mails in your in-box, and a code-red stress level from the need to remember numerous items stored in your head.

As you are likely painfully aware, it's pretty tough to see beyond the day-to-day and be a resource to your staff members when you're struggling to stay afloat among the daily demands of your own work. Fortunately, there are systems that will organize the overwhelming morass and allow you to comfortably handle all the important information in a way that will free up your time rather than demanding more of it.

MAKE THE MOST OF AN ASSISTANT   Having an assistant is an incredibly powerful tool for making yourself more efficient—if you use the role effectively. Here are five ways to maximize the position:

- In our experience, the best assistants tend not to be career assistants but less experienced workers who are smart, hyperefficient, energetic, and ambitious. They usually won't stay in the position for more than a year or two, precisely because of the talents that make them excel in the role. But because a really good assistant will learn the job in just a few days, it's worth it to accept some turnover in the position every year or two.

- Be explicit from the start that it will be crucial for the assistant to have airtight systems that ensure 100 percent follow-through so that absolutely nothing can fall through the cracks. In order to rely on her to the extent you're going to, you need to have perfect faith that once you transfer an item from your plate to hers, it won't disappear.

- Be explicit from the start that you're going to delegate to her plenty of things that you could do yourself. This is important, because managers often feel embarrassed to ask an assistant to do small tasks that they could easily do themselves, such as printing documents, formatting a letter, or scheduling a meeting. So set the stage from the beginning. You can even say that you feel awkward about it but are going to force yourself to do it anyway, since you're a bottleneck in the organization and therefore need to delegate anything that isn't something only you can do.

- Scheduling and setting up meetings often takes a lot of back and forth. Use your assistant for scheduling anything but the most uncomplicated appointments.

- Maximize the organization's use of the assistant. We've rarely seen an efficient assistant who wasn't able to support multiple executives.

Criteria for a Good System

There are lots of systems that work well (and plenty of books and office supply stores that stand ready to sell them to you), but any good system should meet these five criteria:[2]

1. Every piece of information should have one designated home. And floating around your head does not (we repeat, does not!) count as a home. A good test of whether your system meets this standard is whether you can answer questions like these:

   - A colleague calls you in the middle of a meeting and you say you'll call her back. How will you ensure you do?

---

[2] We like David Allen, *Getting Things Done: The Art of Stress-Free Productivity* (New York: Penguin Books, 2001).

- You have an idea over lunch that you want to follow up on when you get to the office. Where do you capture it?

- A friend recommends a good book that you want to read next summer. How will you remember?

- You receive an e-mailed agenda for next week's staff meeting. What do you do with it?

2. Your system should funnel all the things coming at you into as few places as possible. If you have eight lists to consult, you'll inevitably stop consulting all of them and things will get missed.

3. Your system should be easy to maintain and should make your life easier, not harder. You don't want a system that is a project unto itself.

4. Your system should focus you on the most important work at any given moment.

5. If you travel for your job, the system should be portable and accessible on the go.

The Three Homes System

You'll want to come up with a system that works well for you. But if you're stumped or if you want to see an example of one system that works well for many people, here's one that meets the five criteria above and has saved the sanity of many a harried manager!

The system is built on three basic types of homes, paper or electronic, that capture all the pieces of information that come across your desk (Figure 11.2):

- A list, which keeps track of all action items and helps you identify what you should be spending your time on at any given moment

- Folders, to store the key materials you need to do your work

- The calendar, which captures every item with a date and feeds into your lists

STORAGE   Your folders will contain the materials you need for current and upcoming action items. Everything else should be kept in files that are easy to access. Adopt a categorization that works for you (alphabetical, grouped, or whatever else makes sense) and resist the temptation to overstuff your files: if you can't find something easily or drop something in a file, you are less likely to use your system.

Given the volume of information and requests you receive every day, funneling each item into its proper place and keeping your lists up to date will require a bit of discipline. But we can't overstate the value of organizing your work to make the most effective use of your time. Try this system for at least three weeks, tweaking it to meet your needs. Whether you stick with this system or find another, we guarantee a good system will help you get better results and make you less stressed because you won't have to worry about what you may have forgotten.

Lists

Lists are the essential element of this system, and there are only two of them: a daily, which is simply a list of things you'll do today and the only list you look at more than once a day, and the weekly-plus, a separate list that captures projects you'll work on tomorrow or later. (Tools 11.1 and 11.2 provide samples of these two lists.) The separation keeps you from constantly reading over things you have to do in three days, which may not be relevant for today's work and can easily become a distraction or source of stress. These lists can be electronic or on paper; the key principle is that they're always with you in meetings and you can take notes and add to them.

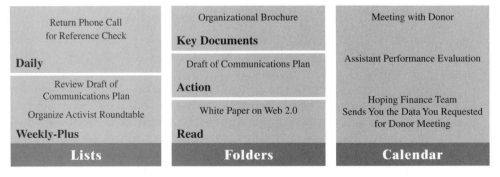

FIGURE 11.2. *The Three Homes System—Before and After*

How to use the daily. The daily list is the backbone of this entire system. Everything else funnels into it, so it is the one, and the only, place you'll check throughout the day to stay on track. In other words, no more flipping through pieces of paper or stickies or your e-mail (or your memory!) to remember what you need to get done today; you'll just consult your daily list to stay on track.

Before you finish at the end of the day or first thing when you start work in the morning, spend five minutes revising and updating this list for the day ahead. You can do this by pulling from your weekly-plus list and looking at your e-mail and calendar.

Once you've created your daily list, highlight, bold, or underline the two or three big rocks of the list and do them first. (To help identify your big rocks, ask yourself this: If you were going to get only two or three things done today, what would they need to be for you to feel reasonably good at the end of the day?) You can add a section on your daily for "quick to-do's," or items that you can take of in just a couple of minutes, such as forwarding a document your colleague asks you to send or making reservations for a lunch meeting.

One helpful tool for your daily is the "waiting for" (w/f) section.[3] W/fs are items that are due to you, in contrast to items that require action from you. Reports you request, work you delegate, and phone calls you're expecting fall in this category. By getting your w/fs on a list and out of your head, you can better track items you're waiting for and have a lot less anxiety about things falling through the cracks.

How to use the weekly-plus. The weekly-plus list is a list of items you plan to accomplish at some point in the future, just not today. Its focus is on work you need to tackle this week, but it should have a separate section to capture longer-term work at

YOUR DAILY LIST IN ACTION

- Your colleague calls you in the middle of a meeting and you say you'll call her back. To ensure that you do, add a quick note to your daily as soon as you hang up the phone.
- Later that day, you ask a scatterbrained colleague in another department to send you some data you'll need by the end of the day, and you're not confident he'll remember. Write "w/f data from Josh" on your daily list so that if you don't receive the data, you'll remember to pester him.
- You have thirty free minutes between meetings. Pull out your daily and find your most important remaining item that you can make progress on in that time. Spend your time on that rather than flipping through e-mail.

---

[3] Ibid., pp. 149–150.

YOUR WEEKLY-PLUS LIST IN ACTION

- In a meeting, you agree to write a memo about the fundraising plan for 2013. You know you won't get to it today, so you add it to your weekly-plus list. At the end of the week, you think through a couple of specific steps you can take to move the project forward ("schedule meeting with Carla to get her input; ask Priya for sample plans").

- Making sure that your communications assistant commits to stay on your team for another year is a "big rock" for you this quarter. Under the "Team" section of your weekly-plus, write, "Retain Miguel! Invite to lunch; brainstorm talking points and run by Jason in advance."

- One of your colleagues insists you read an entire series of teen vampire books. You're not ready to commit to doing it, but you at least want to remember that she made the suggestion to you. You add the item to the Someday/Maybe section of your list (perhaps toward the bottom).

the bottom (so that you can avoid having a third separate list for items that are further out in time). You'll update this list every week, drawing from your calendar, project plans, and goals for the year and thinking critically about what you can do in the near future to move work forward.

You also might take time every couple of months to review your goals for the year and make a list of your key priorities to accomplish over the next two months. You can then paste that short, bulleted list of priorities at the top of your weekly-plus, so that as you're making plans for each week, your actions align with those priorities. To keep the rest of the weekly-plus from being one long list of items, you also might divide it into buckets of work, with sections for different projects or areas of responsibility. This demarcation helps you think through what you need to do to move each of those areas forward.

One challenge on the weekly-plus, or any other list of longer-term actions, is that big projects can sit on the list for a long time when there aren't clear next steps to move them forward. For example, writing "plan gala dinner" is less helpful than breaking the item into a few initial steps such as "gala dinner: call printer for cost estimates on invitations; call hotel to confirm date; set up meeting with John to discuss program." (That said, if it's a complicated item with a separate project plan, it might be easier just to write, "See project plan.") In general, when you have big or unwieldy items, taking the time to figure out even a few specific, actionable next steps can be immensely helpful.

One more piece that we've found helpful for the weekly-plus list is the "someday/maybe" section.[4] This is where you capture items you aren't committed to acting on

---

[4] Ibid., pp. 167–170.

yet but that you want to remember and consider later. Recommended reading, interesting projects, and random ideas that strike you in the middle of the night go here.

Finally, as with your daily list, your weekly-plus can have a w/f section for things you're waiting for—in this case, items that are due beyond the current day. Remember to look closely at this list only when updating your daily each morning (or evening) so that it keeps you on track day-to-day but doesn't distract or worry you.

> "Learning simple tools like making a weekly to-do list and starring the most important items, and checking in with yourself at the end of the week, tracking whether you're being overly ambitious or hitting your targets, has made an enormous difference. I get to feel much more satisfied, because at the end of the week, I'm able to look at a work plan and feel comfortable that I've accomplished it. If you lay things out that way, and can say you've accomplished the things that were prioritized, you can enjoy your weekend without having to worry about the things you didn't get done."
>
> RICKEN PATEL, EXECUTIVE DIRECTOR, AVAAZ

Folders

As a manager, you're probably in and out of meetings, sometimes in the office and sometimes not. You don't want to carry around a pile of materials, but it's essential that you always have what you need at your fingertips. The solution is to create a few key folders to funnel things into and take them with you everywhere. These folders don't need to be paper ones; they might be electronic folders stored on your computer or electronic tablet.

- *Key documents.* The key documents folder stores the few documents and materials that you reference often or want to keep close at hand. It might contain a list of your annual goals, your weekly-plus list, and, if you have a lot of external meetings, a one-page overview of your organization.

- *Action.* The action folder is where you file all the materials you need for current and upcoming work as those materials come in. Don't hesitate to put something for the holidays in this folder when it's only July. You'll want it at your fingertips come December rather than have to go digging through your computer or desk to find it. If your action folder gets too full, which it probably will, split it into two: one that holds projects and meetings for that week ("action—this week") and one with material for future weeks ("action—longer term").

- *Read.* Create a read folder for, well, things to read. (If you're using paper folders, carry it around so you can take advantage of your commute or downtime between meetings.) However, be honest with yourself about what you will actually read. Be ruthless about deleting e-mails that you might read in an ideal world but that you really don't have time to do (like your aunt's four-page e-mail about her trip to Savannah).

YOUR FOLDERS IN ACTION

- You receive an e-mailed agenda for this Tuesday's staff meeting. Put it in your "action—this week" folder.

- A vendor gives you a document that you'll need when filling out an expense report next month. Put it in the "action—longer-term" folder.

Calendar

In addition to lists and folders, the only other piece you need is a calendar to record everything with a date attached. Start with the basics, recording all your meetings, trips, and deadlines in the calendar. Add in the blocks of time we described earlier in the chapter: specific "meetings with yourself" to work on priority projects and general work blocks so you know you'll have time outside meetings to focus on what matters most. (See Figure 11.3.)

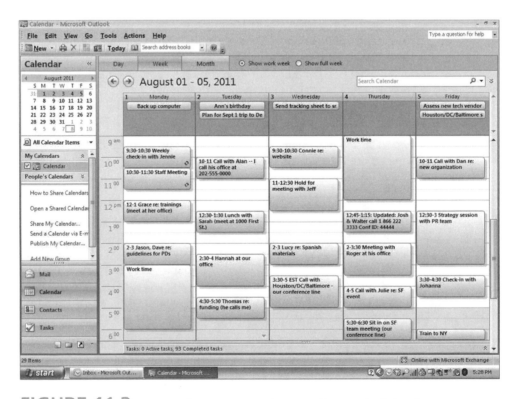

FIGURE 11.3. *Capturing Key Items in Your Electronic Calendar*

Beyond that, use your calendar to trigger actions with any sort of time frame, even ones not associated with hard dates. For these items, enter them as "all day events" (in most electronic calendar programs) and they will show up in the space above your scheduled appointments for the day. For example, you know that in roughly mid-February, you need to kick off your team's search for summer interns. Pick a random date in early February, and add, "Kick off intern search in middle of month—ask Jesse to convene team meeting, and then assign owner," to your calendar. Ensure that items from your calendar regularly funnel into your action plan by reviewing your calendar each day as you prepare your daily list.

TAMING THE E-MAIL BEAST

Answering e-mail could sometimes be a full-time job in itself if you let it. We've seen managers drowning in e-mail with no system for processing it: an in-box with thousands of unanswered (or even unread) e-mails, a constant worry about what might be in those messages, and a feeling that as soon as one e-mail is dealt with, five more arrive to take its place.

Here are some tips to get control of your e-mail:

- Check e-mail only at defined periods. Consider turning off your "new messages" indicator so you aren't tempted to cheat on this.

- Apply the two-minute rule: if you can do a task in two minutes or less, do it now! Reply right away, forward it to someone else to deal with, put it in your "read" folder, delete it, or otherwise figure out what next action to take to move it forward.

- Don't create work for yourself. If you ever look at the number of e-mails you get while you're on vacation, you'll notice that the total (apart from spam) decreases significantly with each passing day. You might get 120 on the first day, then 100,

YOUR CALENDAR IN ACTION

- You hire a new staff member and need to remember to have a three-month review meeting, but your schedule is too uncertain for it to make sense to pick a hard date now. Flip ahead a couple of months on your calendar and add, "Schedule step-back with Janene for early March," to the all-day section on a random weekday.

- You have an important trip in September. Mark a day in mid-August to plan for it.

- You edit a letter for your development director and cross the task off your daily. Add "w/f revised draft of letter from Julie" to the top of your calendar for Friday, and you'll remember to follow up if you don't receive a new version before the end of the week.

- Every month you're supposed to turn in your expense form. Record a monthly reminder, and set it to recur on the fourth Thursday of every month.

then 80, then 40. This is a sign that when you're around, you're creating work for yourself. Reply to e-mails in a way that makes clear who should drive what steps and how you want people to move forward so that they don't need to keep coming to you for every tiny step.

- Don't use your in-box as storage. Use it only for messages that still need to be dealt with. All others should be deleted (even in a "deleted items" folder that you never empty in case you need to retrieve the item later) or filed. Otherwise it's harder to quickly differentiate between what you've already processed and what you still have to address. We know some of you reading this keep items in your in-box and use flags to highlight items for further action, but we find that people can't resist developing such complicated color-coded systems for themselves that the system eventually breaks down.

- Use e-mail folders. For instance, if you're managing a project and are expecting feedback from six people, create a folder for the project, put all related e-mails in that folder, and then set a reminder on your calendar to deal with them. That reminder is crucial, since you shouldn't kid yourself that you'll spontaneously read through folders other than your in-box without a trigger.

- Admit defeat, and start over. If you have such an untamed mess in your in-box that you don't know where to start, try this. Recognize that anything in your in-box more than a week old is almost certainly forgotten. Create a folder that says, "Older stuff," and drag everything in your in-box older than a week into there. Use the items from the past week to practice the suggestions above, and then roll forward, enjoying your newly found sense of pride in your clean in-box.

Follow these rules and you'll typically have fewer than ten e-mails remaining in your in-box at the end of the day.

KEY POINTS

- How you manage yourself and your time and how you stay organized will have a serious impact on the results you get.

- At its core, time management is about maintaining and acting with clarity regarding what's most important for you to accomplish.

- The biggest time management mistake that most managers make is spending their time on what's immediately at hand or what's most comfortable to work on rather than what's most important. Figure out what one or two things are most important to accomplish on any given day, and make those your priorities. Whenever possible, do them before other things have the chance to intervene.

- Remember the principle of comparative advantage: you should be spending your time in the areas where you're much better positioned to add value because the payoff will be greater.

- As a manager, you should be spending your time managing, not squeezing managing in between the cracks.

- Scheduling work blocks into your calendar will ensure you have time to do your most important work each week, and can prompt you to handle interruptions differently.

- There are lots of different organizational systems that work well, but if nothing else, any good system should ensure that every piece of information has one designated home outside of your own head.

Additional Reading

David Allen, *Getting Things Done: The Art of Stress-Free Productivity* (New York: Penguin Books, 2001).

TOOL 11.1

SAMPLE DAILY LIST

Today's Big Rocks

1. Prep agenda for message training for regional directors in Ohio (see Joanne's e-mails to me on this)

2. Draft job description for Comms Assistant (work from Development Assistant doc; also Google to see if any good samples are online)

Take five minutes at the start or end of each day to update your daily list. Keep any necessary items from yesterday and cut and paste new items from your weekly and from your calendar.

Other Action Items

*   Delegate to Jennie: compile a short list of good PR firms that might work for our needs

*   Review draft agendas for summits in Houston/D.C./Baltimore

*   Meet with Jason, Dave re: guidelines for policy directors for principal meetings

*   Birthday card for Ann

*   Call Sue back; stress importance of deadline

At the top of your daily, write down the key things you need to accomplish in order for the day to have been successful.

Put personal to-do items on your daily as well, so everything is in one place.

Two-Minute Tasks

*   Forward newsletter to Walter

Waiting For

*   Data from Josh by COB

Your daily should be short and contain only the work you want or need to get done that day. Keep other projects on your weekly or midrange lists so they don't clutter your daily.

TOOL 11.2
SAMPLE WEEKLY-PLUS LIST

August 11–15

This month will be successful if: Plans for Ohio and San Francisco events are finalized; asks to five major funders are sent; summit materials are sent out.

> *To clarify for yourself what's most important, write at the top of your weekly what your "big rocks" for the month are.*

Development

- **Final revisions of plan for San Francisco Bay Area event (need final plan by Monday; event is 8/26)**
- Write memo about fundraising plan for 2013

> *Items in bold are "must do" this week.*

Recruitment and Selection

- Prep agenda for message training session with regional directors
- Get tickets, hotel for site visit to Ohio
- Latino marketing: meet with Lucy to measure progress against goals (basic materials available in Spanish by 8/30; look into focus groups and decide on plan by 9/20). Mention meeting James last week—possible partner/resource?

> *Regular font items should be done this week.*

Alumni

- Materials for summits in Houston/D.C./Baltimore—due 8/15
- Review draft agenda and talking points; edits to be incorporated by COB Wednesday
- Final read-through of binder

General Marketing

- Web site
  - Public site: identify contacts for recruitment, HR, development by 8/22
  - Train all contacts by 9/30
  - Maintain quality control of public and CMA Web site per system established—ongoing
- Print PSA distribution (ongoing as we get requests)
- Consider creating guidelines for policy directors for principal meetings—talk to policy directors, have recommendation for Thomas by 8/25
- Meet with Jason, Dave on this

PR

- Explore hiring firm to help on the PR front for short term. Convene meeting with Connie and Thomas by 8/29
- Delegate to Jennie: compile a short list of good PR firms that might work for our needs
- Full transition to Johanna of basic procedures/processes/responsibilities and basic media inquiries by 8/29
- Schedule two meetings w/Johanna this Friday to check in on transition so far and in one month to follow up

Team

- Jennie: delegate finding a PR firm, review preparations for Ohio site visit
- David, Jason: guidelines for policy directors for principal meetings—describe need, ask for input, get sample?
- Johanna: review last week's media inquiries
- Lucy: Spanish-language materials—step-back, timeline (James)
- Staff meeting: my Ohio trip, vacation schedules

Personal

- Submit dental reimbursement
- Mom birthday
- Call AF, JW, LT
- Buy *The Book of Hard Choices*

In a good system, there are as few homes as possible. Keep one list for both your professional and personal to-do items.

W/F

- Web site materials from Johanna
- Revised draft of letter from Julie
- Goals from Alan

Someday/Maybe

- Summer reading—*Bel Canto; End of Poverty*
- Holiday cards and/or party?
- Refresher course for Spanish
- Team hike
- Casa Oaxaca (restaurant recommendation from SK)

Use a w/f (waiting for) section to keep track of the tasks you've asked others to do, and a someday/maybe section to capture items for future consideration.

CHAPTER

12

MANAGING UP

Up to this point we've talked about how to manage people who report to you. But unless you're a rare exception, you have a boss too. Even executive directors typically report to a board. And just as you can get better results through effective management practices with those who report to you, so you can maximize your results by using the right practices with the person who manages you.

We want to be clear: managing up isn't about manipulating your boss or managing her perceptions. It's about working with your boss in the way that will produce the best possible results for the organization.

In this chapter, we start by discussing your sphere of control and the importance of focusing on what you can control rather than what you can't. We'll look at some specific approaches you can take, including getting explicitly aligned, making it easy for your boss to get you what you need, being emotionally intelligent, and having your own act together. We'll also address some concerns unique to managers who are in a second-in-command role.

YOUR SPHERE OF CONTROL

If you have frustrations about your boss, you're far from alone. Most people do, even when that boss is a good manager. Maybe your manager isn't responsive enough to e-mail, or she cancels meetings at the last minute, or she changes her mind after you thought a decision had been made—or you might be dealing with another grade of problems altogether, such as a boss who's the type of wimp or tyrant that we discussed in Chapter Ten.

Whatever your frustrations, one key to working effectively with any boss and to keeping your own sanity is to get clear in your own mind about what you can and can't control and to focus on making the pieces you can control go as smoothly as possible. Rather than stewing over an aspect of your boss that you can't change, it's far more productive to understand that her working style may not change dramatically and to find ways to work effectively within that context. (Of course, you can always hope—and maybe leave a copy of this book on her chair!)

For instance, if you have a busy manager who frequently cancels your weekly meeting, rather than being paralyzed by frustration and unable to move forward without your boss's input, you could say, "I know you're really busy, but can I talk to your assistant and get ten minutes on your calendar?" You also might anticipate that she's likely to cancel your meeting tomorrow because of an upcoming board meeting, and as a safety measure, grab her for two minutes after today's staff meeting to ask your most pressing question.

As you brainstorm about how you might respond to a less-than-ideal context, think creatively, and don't feel locked into how you've been doing things up until now (especially if those techniques haven't been getting you what you need). If your boss doesn't respond to your e-mails, print the e-mail out and leave it on her chair. Or leave her a voice mail telling her how you plan to move forward if you don't hear from her by the end of the week.

Again, the point here is to not get so focused on your boss's less-than-ideal behaviors that you miss the things that are in your control. So with your sphere of control in mind, let's turn to some specific strategies that can work.

Get Aligned

A lot of disagreements between managers and managees at their core stem from a lack of alignment about what the managee's priorities should be, how work should be conducted, and how the relationship should operate. This lack of alignment can be a significant root cause of dissatisfaction on both sides of the relationship, so it's essential to surface it and fix it.

Ideally you and your boss would agree about what you'll do, how you'll do it, and how the two of you will work together at the start of your relationship. But if you're struggling in an existing relationship, it's not too late to step back and get aligned now.

Priorities

Talk regularly throughout the year about your goals and priorities. Start by getting clear about what success would look like for you this year, as well as what you should not spend energy on at all. At least every quarter and often more, talk explicitly about what you'll be focused on in the next few months. These periodic alignment checks can be very simple, such as, "For the next two months, I'll be spending a lot of energy getting the membership department straightened out and I'm not going to worry about filling the gaps on the communications team until after that."

Managers and managees are often clear in their own minds on these questions but haven't connected with each other on them. An explicit discussion can bring conflicting assumptions to the surface and resolve them.

How to Approach Specific Issues

In order to ensure you're both in agreement when it comes to how you'll operate, it can be hugely helpful to raise potentially tricky situations and talk through how you plan to handle them. For instance, you might discuss how to handle a low-performing staff member who reports to you, or how to handle an adversarial coalition member. By getting in sync on these sorts of things up-front, you'll be able to act with more confidence, knowing that you won't be unpleasantly surprised to learn that your boss had an entirely different take on the topic than you did.

Scope of Your Authority

Proactively discuss what decisions of yours your boss wants to be kept informed about, what sorts of things she'd like to be consulted on, and what she wants final approval over. The MOCHA (manager-owner-consulted-helper-approver) model in Chapter Two is a helpful tool for talking this over. And in keeping with making your boss's job easy, as we discuss in the next section, you might propose what you think the right assignment of decision-making rights is.

Communication Systems

Make sure to establish a system for checking in and getting questions answered. For instance, you might have a regular weekly meeting, plus conversations throughout the rest of the week as the need arises. Whatever system you decide on, err on the side of investing a good amount of time talking at the beginning of your relationship (or when rebooting it); you can always reduce it over time.

Important: Once your system is established, put yourself in charge of making it work, meaning that if your boss cancels a meeting, you should take the lead on rescheduling it. We often see people in this situation leave the ball in their boss's court. Although this might be the way to handle a social situation where someone cancels plans, it's not the way to handle your boss, or you may rarely get to meet with her.

Make Your Boss's Job Easy

As a manager of others, you well know the demands that come with management. Almost by definition, your boss probably has an even broader role than you, with many competing demands. So once you've agreed on general expectations and how you'll work together, another way to get good results with your boss is to make things as easy as possible for her.

Apply the Principles of Delegation Upward

When you delegate a responsibility to a staffer, you articulate the desired outcome, constraints, and prioritization (because you read Chapter Two!). Do the same thing when your manager gives you a responsibility in order to make sure you're aligned. For instance, if your manager asks you to oversee the development of a new logo, you might say, "So we're looking for a logo that's professional and modern, and we want it to convey forward momentum. It sounds like the budget needs to be kept under two thousand dollars, and I'm thinking I shouldn't tackle this until after we're done with the spring conference. Does that sound right?" Once you're both aligned, take the two minutes to do a repeat-back e-mail, so that weeks later, you both remember what was decided on. And just as with when you're delegating to others, help your boss stay engaged by checking in on an ongoing basis, offering updates, and giving her chances for input as the project unfolds. For instance, you might suggest to your manager that once you have developed five good options for the logo, you'll run them by her to get her views.

Make It Easy for Her to Give Her Input

Ask yes/no questions, keep e-mails short, and suggest solutions so your boss can respond quickly with a yes or no. Just as you want to keep your staffers from handing you the monkey (see Chapter Two), keep your own monkeys off your boss's back. Saying, "What should I do about X?" puts the problem on her. You make it easier for both of you if you say, "I've been wrestling with what to do about X. I've thought about A, B, and C, and I think we should do C because . . . Does that sound okay to you?"

Remind Her of Context

When you've been tightly focused on a project, it's easy to forget that your manager's attention might have been on other things. Instead of expecting your manager to retain all the details you've talked about previously, a simple reminder of context or past decisions can be enormously helpful. For instance, if you're checking in with your boss about a project that you've discussed in the past, assume that she's probably not as focused on it as you are and say something like, "As a reminder, here's where we are on the schedule, and this is what we talked about last month."

As an example, the first e-mail that follows doesn't remind the manager of the context, doesn't suggest a solution, and doesn't facilitate a quick yes or no answer. Contrast it with the second e-mail. Which would you rather receive from one of your staff members?

> To: Maya
>
> From: Rick
>
> Subject: Spring conference
>
> Rafael Martin will be out of the country in April. Is there someone else we should give an award to instead?

> To: Maya
>
> From: Rick
>
> Subject: Spring conference awards
>
> We talked last week about giving an award at the spring conference to Rafael Martin, but it turns out he'll be out of the country then. I propose giving an award to Michelle

Swenson instead—we can highlight the great work she did in her district around the Senate vote, and this will also give us more geographical diversity in our awardees. Sound good to you?

Notice Her Themes and Address Them Proactively
If you pay attention to the kinds of questions your boss asks, you'll draw larger messages about the sorts of things that she'll care about in the future. You can then anticipate those things in advance and address them before she has to ask, which will make you both happier with the relationship. It's also useful to understand why she focuses where she does, so if you're ever unsure, ask. Asking "What's driving that?" or "Just so I understand, which part of this is worrying you?" can often lead to a conversation that gives you both more insight into each other.

Ask for Feedback After a Project Is Over
While ideally your boss would be offering feedback on her own, in reality she may be pulled in numerous other directions. Make it easy on her, and get what you need, by raising it yourself. Simply saying, "Can we debrief about how this went?" and then offering your own view and asking for hers can make it easier for her to tell you what she really thinks.

Be Emotionally Intelligent
We often work with clients who are emotionally intelligent in how they approach the people who work for them but fail to apply the same skill in working with their own manager. Rather than delving into the Freudian roots of these clients' struggles with authority, our advice is to keep it simple.

Don't Take It Personally
There will be times when you have a different point of view than your manager does on something where she is the ultimate decision maker. When this happens, you should advocate for what you believe, and if you think your boss is making a mistake, part of your job is to explain the reason. But if your boss ultimately picks a different route, it's helpful to have reasonably thick skin: don't take it personally, and keep your ego out of it. It's a bonus if you can find the humility to recognize that she might even be right!

Don't Forget Your Boss Is Human
Now that you're a manager yourself, you know the deep dark secret: bosses are human too. There may be times when your boss is grouchy, frustrated, or frazzled, or times when she would appreciate hearing that she handled something well. In addition, realize that in the same way you might have sensitivities about the relationship, she may too. For instance, if you're taking on responsibilities that used to be hers, she likely won't appreciate hearing that they used to be a disaster until you came along. All of this is to say, be thoughtful.

Don't Stew in Silence

The most effective managees tend to see the responsibility for making the relationship work smoothly as theirs. If you're frustrated about something, such as your manager undermined a decision you made, raise it, talk about the impact, and discuss how it could go differently in the future. Mistakes will happen, so use them as opportunities to strengthen your relationship. Of course, be smart about this: you'll get better results if you raise these issues at a moment when your boss has time to consider them, just as you would if you were speaking to a subordinate about a sensitive issue.

Have Your Act Together

We hear from a lot of people who think their managers are overly controlling or micromanaging. As you know from being a manager yourself, most managers don't like being control freaks, but they become that way when they don't have confidence that things will get done well otherwise. It follows that if your boss is controlling, the easiest way to solve the problem is to give her confidence that things are under control. In other words, stay on top of things, do what you say you're going to do, take good notes on the subtleties of what your boss asks you to do so you do it right, don't let things fall through the cracks, and generally be someone she can rely on. You might be surprised how much easier your boss becomes to work with when you have your act together.

If your boss is a control freak, the easiest way to solve the problem is to give her confidence that things are under control.

SPECIAL CONSIDERATIONS FOR SECOND IN COMMANDS

More and more organizations are moving to a structure with an executive director and a second in command. These number twos might have the title of managing director, chief operating officer, deputy director, or chief of staff. Although the specifics of the labor division vary, often a number two's role is to ensure that the organization hits its goals, with all that that entails, including managing people, checking in on progress, and overseeing organization-wide systems. The number one's job is to make sure the goals are right in the first place by overseeing strategy, to engage internally on high-priority tactical issues, and often to do significant amounts of external relations.

Regardless of the exact setup, being the second in command can produce a unique set of frustrations, such as a boss who reverses your decisions when staffers go around you to her, or needing to hold people accountable when they're working more closely with your boss than with you. Because of this, it's especially crucial that a number one and number two are aligned and on the same team.

Here are five keys to making a second-in-command position work smoothly:

1. *Get explicitly aligned.* Because a second in command is likely to be handling tricky or potentially controversial situations, the alignment conversations that we discussed

above are even more crucial here. Over time you'll likely find that you've developed basic understandings that will apply from one situation to the next, so you'll be able to act in more and more situations without needing to check in as often. You should still continue to get aligned on particularly sensitive situations, however.

2. *Do your aligning behind the scenes.* Just as effective parents show a united front to their kids, you and your boss should generally try to do your aligning in private—and in advance when possible. Of course, if you didn't talk something through beforehand and you discover while meeting with others that you disagree on an issue, it's fine to have divergent opinions. In this case, be sure you ultimately send a clear signal to the staff about which way to head, and you should ensure that the two of you are clear about which of you has the final decision-making authority.

3. *Expect a learning curve, and debrief regularly.* We can almost promise you that things won't go perfectly smoothly at the start. You might make a judgment call that your boss thinks was a mistake, or she might inadvertently step into your sphere of authority, particularly if a number two is a new position for the organization. This is normal. Don't get discouraged or upset by it; in fact, see these bumps as useful opportunities to help you clarify expectations and get more aligned. To make sure that you actually do this, agree on a time in advance (say, from 2:00 to 3:00 P.M. on the first Friday of every month) when you'll review some specific examples and talk about how things are working and what you both could do differently. Not only will this strengthen your operations overall, but these conversations will help you get more inside your boss's head so that you become more and more instinctively aligned with her over time.

4. *When you're in the middle, bring the ends together, particularly when one of them is your boss.* While you'll be able to resolve many situations on your own, it's important to differentiate between when your job is to solve something yourself and when it is to get the right people to talk to each other so that the problem gets solved. This often simply means ensuring that the right people get together and that the right questions get asked. For instance, if you notice that your boss frequently makes extensive edits to the op-eds written in her name by the communications director, don't get caught up in being a go-between, ferrying messages back and forth or trying to guess what's driving your boss's edits. Instead, facilitate a meeting between the two, and rather than focusing just on the most recent set of edits, ask questions to help your boss articulate the underlying principles driving her edits.

5. Your job is to streamline your boss's involvement, not remove her. As the second in command, you'll be intimately steeped in the day-to-day details of your organization in a way that your executive director won't (and shouldn't) be. It's key to avoid feeling as if you're the one who "really" knows what's going on; that's

a toxic path that will keep your executive director disengaged and eventually frustrated and can harm both of your effectiveness. Instead, use your detailed knowledge to spot and point out to her areas where she should engage, whether it's weighing in on how to frame a sensitive issue in a press release or congratulating an employee for an achievement.

Tool 12.1 offers a sample plan for establishing a division of labor between the executive director and the second in command.

KEY POINTS

- Managing up is about working with your boss in the way that will produce the best possible results for the organization.

- One key to working harmoniously with any boss is to get clear in your own mind about what you can and can't control and to focus on making the pieces you can control go as smoothly as possible.

- Talk explicitly with your manager about goals and priorities, how you'll approach tricky or sensitive issues, how she wants to be involved in decisions, and communication systems.

- Put yourself in charge of making the relationship and your communication systems work. Take the lead on rescheduling meetings, raising issues for discussion, and so forth.

- Make your boss's job easy by applying the principles of delegation upward, providing fast ways for her to provide input, reminding her of context, and asking for feedback after a project is over.

- Be emotionally intelligent by not taking things personally, remembering that your boss is human, and speaking up when you're frustrated.

- Have your own act together.

- If you're a second in command, it's particularly important for you and your boss to get aligned behind the scenes and to remember that your job is to streamline your boss's involvement, not to remove her.

Additional Reading

Nathan Bennett and Stephen A. Miles, "Second in Command: The Misunderstood Role of the Chief Operating Officer," *Harvard Business Review*, May 2006.

BoardSource: Articles, books, tools, and training for nonprofit boards. Some content is available to members only. www.boardsource.org

TOOL 12.1

SAMPLE DIVISION OF LABOR PLAN

Division of labor between:

Ruth Johnson, founder and executive director
Alan Alperowicz, chief operating officer

> *Functions should be all the areas where there is any role confusion or potential role confusion.*

Function	Ruth's Role	Alan's Role
Board	Manage board relations and serve as point person	Support Ruth as requested
Fundraising	Owns 2013 fundraising goal; lead strategist and pitch maker	Ensure Ruth has support she needs (help develop plan and manage execution effectively); be a resource to Ruth
External relations	Lead spokesperson for and face of organization	Serve as spokesperson on occasion and own key external meetings
Issue and campaign management	Consult on major decisions and (rarely) use veto power to stop a particular action; give input and suggest ideas on day-to-day issues	Responsible for making decisions on all day-to-day issues, figuring out process for decision making (including what meetings need to happen and how they should be run), and consulting Ruth as needed; get Ruth's input on all major decisions
Staff management	Manage Alan and back him up once decision has been made; use veto power sparingly over management decisions	Manage all day-to-day operations, including office of the CEO, Communications, Development, Research, Finance, and HR; determine appropriate staff roles and reporting lines; evaluate staff; make hiring and firing decisions, consulting Ruth as appropriate
Annual plan	Give up-front input on and have final sign-off on plan	Manage to annual plan and ensure goals are met; drive next year's goal-setting process
Strategic vision	Set strategic vision	Be a resource to Ruth in setting vision
Legal compliance	Consult on key matters	Manage legal team around relevant issues in order to ensure legal compliance
Budget	Provide upfront input and sign off on final budget	In consultation with Ruth (especially on relevant development issues), develop and manage budget
Special projects	Develop new ideas and consult on implementation	Ensure projects are executed well, with emphasis on building needed capacity (for example, hiring top talent to carry out special projects)

CONCLUSION
PERSONAL QUALITIES OF A GREAT MANAGER

In the preceding chapters, we've discussed the practices of great managers a great deal, but we haven't talked much about their personal qualities. That's because great managers come in many different packages, and we don't believe that you need to become someone you're not in order to excel as a manager.

That said, before closing, we'd like to take a look at what kind of person it takes to do well the sorts of practices this book examines. As you read this conclusion, keep in mind that in our experience, even managers who don't start out with all of these qualities end up bringing them out in themselves as they internalize the practices we have covered in this book.

So what personal qualities do great managers have or grow to have? If you've read this far, it won't surprise you to learn that we don't think that being a great manager is about having the most charisma or giving motivational speeches. Those things can be nice, but ultimately they're not essential. Fundamentally, a great manager is someone who cares passionately about getting results. And that can't be faked. If you are truly determined to get results, it becomes the fire that fuels everything you do— overriding ego, the discomfort of having hard conversations, and even the desire to be liked. It leads you to do the sorts of things we've discussed in these chapters:

- Rather than delegating and disappearing, staying involved to make sure there's no implementation gap

- Making sure that people are clear about their goals and that those goals represent significant progress

- Holding people accountable for meeting high performance standards

- Being assertive about moving out staff members who don't perform

- Treating people decently even when you're frustrated with them

A great manager is someone who cares passionately about getting results.

225

These are all parts of how you get significant, sustained results.

In our experience, no matter what the rest of the package looks like, this intense determination to get results leads great managers to display qualities like these:

- Great managers constantly worry about the real impact of their work rather than appearances. They have deep integrity about their missions, which leads them to pick goals and projects that will represent truly meaningful progress, not just an easy success to impress funders.

- When they run into roadblocks that might deter the average person, great managers persist until they find a way past the obstacle.

- Because great managers are determined to be successful, they make hard decisions that may be unpopular (such as abandoning a strategy that isn't producing results) or personally painful (such as letting go a loyal but lower-performing staff member).

- Although they may never be entirely comfortable having difficult conversations, great managers put aside their personal discomfort and have them anyway. They make themselves use words like, "I'd like you to do this differently," or "I'm concerned about something I've noticed recently," or even, "If this doesn't change, we will have to let you go."

- Great managers are almost ruthless when it comes to identifying ways the organization could perform better (beginning with themselves), and they tend to display a deep commitment to learning from experience and adapting their approach to make it as effective as possible.

- Because of this, they are willing and even eager to take feedback and genuinely want to hear dissent. They don't get defensive or shut out differing opinions; in fact, you may hear them thanking a staff member for sharing complaints or concerns, and they really mean it.

At their core, all of these qualities come down to one thing, which is the same place where we started: a relentless, even obsessive, determination to get results. It's a prerequisite for great management, and everything follows from there.

We hope this book has shown you how to best harness that determination to achieve significant, dramatic results—results that will help you change the world.

APPENDIX

GETTING STARTED

We hope you'll come back to this book regularly as you go about your work. But right now, here are ten immediate steps you can take to implement some of the most important concepts we've discussed in this book:

1. Take a big project that your team is working on, and use the MOCHA components of ownership—manager, owner, consulted, helper, and approver—to clarify responsibilities related to it.

2. If your staff doesn't have concrete, measurable goals for the year, pick one person to try this out with and schedule a meeting to start the process of creating them.

3. Make a daily list of the items you should accomplish today.

4. Put weekly check-in meetings with each of your direct reports on your calendar for the next month.

5. Schedule work blocks on your calendar for the next month.

6. Tell a staff member something she did well recently.

7. Think of one person who would be a great addition to your staff someday, and invite her to meet you for coffee to hear about where she sees her career heading.

8. Schedule a step-back meeting with your lowest performer, and draft your talking points.

9. Schedule a debriefing on a recently finished project.

10. Schedule an hour on your calendar to brainstorm a preliminary list of the core values you want your team's culture to reflect. Then schedule a meeting with your team to discuss them.

Don't put these off. By implementing them right away, they're more likely to stick.

ACKNOWLEDGMENTS

Many people assisted us in the creation of this book with their feedback and patience, and we owe them great thanks.

Many of Jerry's former colleagues at Teach For America were enormously helpful. Among others, Elissa Kim, Kriste Dragon, Steven Farr, Rebecca Helmer, and Maia H. M. Levner not only read and commented on portions of the original text; more important, they put up with Jerry while he was learning to be a decent manager. Teach For America's founder, Wendy Kopp, taught Jerry if not most of what she knows about management, at least most of what he knows about it.

At The Management Center, our clients and allies, who are far too numerous to name, served as test cases for early versions of this text. Julie Stewart and Mary Price at Families Against Mandatory Minimums deserve special thanks for their patience and support as our original clients, as does Jon Cowan at Third Way for his insightful comments on the previous edition of this book.

At the staff level, our past and current colleagues made critical contributions to developing the concepts and the content that we set out here. Ethan Fletcher gets much of the credit for the tools at the ends of most chapters, several of which former intern Lydia Poon helped create. Abigail Kim drafted significant portions of the original chapter on time and systems. Amy Huffman and Elizabeth Brown contributed by finding better ways to explain core concepts through our training program, and we incorporated many of their ideas here. And neither this book nor The Management Center would exist without our unofficial coauthor, Rebecca Epstein.

The Management Center also would not exist without its founder, benefactor, and spiritual guide, Peter B. Lewis.

Finally, Jerry's wife, Liza, not only edited parts of the original text but also put up with his ruining several weekend excursions by dragging the manuscript along with him. (Jerry has since adopted our own advice from the chapter on time and systems and is now a model and attentive husband when he is not at work.)

ABOUT THE AUTHORS

Alison Green has written extensively on management practices, including in a weekly column for *U.S. News & World Report* and also for her own blog, Ask a Manager (www.askamanager.org).

As chief of staff of the Marijuana Policy Project, she oversaw day-to-day staff management. Previously she worked as the communications director and publications director for two grassroots advocacy organizations and spent six years as a staff writer and campaign coordinator for People for the Ethical Treatment of Animals (PETA). At PETA, her accomplishments included making headlines for an effort that resulted in Procter & Gamble's placing a moratorium on animal testing; designing and launching a campaign to reach college students; teaching students how to work with the media and organize on campuses; authoring a guide to campus activism; and bringing the animal rights message to the pages of many conservative newspapers.

Jerry Hauser is the founding CEO of The Management Center in Washington, D.C., whose mission is to help nonprofit leaders turn their good intentions into great results. He brings to this work his dual passions for promoting social change and creating high-performing organizations. His previous roles include serving as the CEO of the Advocacy Institute and as the second-in-command at Teach For America, where he helped the national nonprofit grow from $8 million to $38 million in annual revenue and from three thousand to seventeen thousand applicants each year. Jerry also learned about creating strong organizations while he was an associate at the management consulting firm of McKinsey & Company.

Jerry began his career as a high school math and history teacher in Compton, California. He holds a B.A. from Duke University and a J.D. from Yale Law School, where he was a senior editor of the *Yale Law Journal.* Most important, he is the proud father of twin boys, Alex and Theo, to whom he hopes to impart his passion, if not his lack of talent, for playing soccer.

A NOTE TO READERS

We believe this book will get better as you put the concepts here into practice and let us know what works and what doesn't. Please send your comments—things you like and things we could improve—to alison@managementcenter.org.

ABOUT THE MANAGEMENT CENTER

Our mission at The Management Center in Washington, D.C., is to help nonprofit leaders turn their good intentions into great results. We do this by providing hands-on coaching in managing people and running organizations to executive directors and senior leaders of select high-impact nonprofits and by offering training and publications to the broader field. We have worked closely with over fifty national nonprofit organizations since our founding in 2006 and have reached thousands of others through our training programs and the previous edition of this book.

For more information and to sign up for our free monthly e-mail of management tips, go to www.managementcenter.org. If you would like to learn more about our trainings, e-mail us at info@managementcenter.org.